D1446778

Anthropology and Social Theory

A JOHN HOPE FRANKLIN CENTER BOOK

Anthropology and Social Theory CULTURE, POWER, AND THE ACTING SUBJECT

Sherry B. Ortner

DUKE UNIVERSITY PRESS DURHAM AND LONDON 2006

© 2006 Duke University Press

All rights reserved

Printed in the United States of America on acid-free paper ∞

Designed by Heather Hensley

Typeset in Minion by Keystone Typesetting, Inc.

Library of Congress Cataloging-in-Publication Data appear on the last printed page of this book.

Several of these pieces have been previously published. The original publication information is as follows:

"Reading America: Preliminary Notes on Class and Culture." Reprinted by permission from *Recapturing Anthropology: Working in the Present*, edited by Richard G. Fox. Copyright © 1991 by the School of American Research, Santa Fe.

"Resistance and the Problem of Ethnographic Refusal," *Comparative Studies in Society and History* 37:1 (1995): 173–93. © 1995 Society for Comparative Study of Society and History. Reprinted with the permission of Cambridge University Press.

"Identities: The Hidden Life of Class," *Journal of Anthropological Research* 54:1 (1998): 1–17. Reprinted with permission.

"Generation X: Anthropology in a Media-Saturated World," *Cultural Anthropology* 13:3 (1998): 414–40. Copyright © 1998 American Anthropological Association. Reprinted with permission.

"Subjectivity and Cultural Critique," *Anthropological Theory* 5:1 (2005). © 2005 Sage Publications. Reprinted by permission of Sage Publications Ltd.

FOR TIM AND GWEN
With love as always

CONTENTS

ACKNOWLEDGMENTS

The papers in this collection have specific histories, and each carries its own section of acknowledgments. In addition I wish to thank Ken Wissoker of Duke University Press for unfailing interest in my work, and for friendship that goes beyond that. I also wish to thank the readers of the manuscript, one of whom—Akhil Gupta—revealed his identity to me, and one of whom remains anonymous. Both provided extremely useful comments.

Updating Practice Theory

W hen practice theory came on the scene in the late 1970s, the theoretical landscape was dominated by three major paradigms: interpretive or "symbolic" anthropology, launched by the work of Clifford Geertz; Marxist political economy, whose leading practitioner was probably Eric Wolf; and some form or other of French structuralism, launched by Claude Lévi-Strauss, but by that time beginning to be replaced by various poststructuralisms.

All of these represented important moves beyond an earlier hegemonic functionalism. Where functionalists asked, how do things hang together?, Geertz asked, what do they mean? Where functionalists viewed social systems as largely benign and tending toward stability, Marxists emphasized the exploitative nature of capitalism and other social formations, which provokes ongoing movements for destabilization and change. And where functionalists asked about the practical function of institutions, Lévi-Strauss showed that both practical institutions, like kinship, and seemingly impractical ones, like myth, operated according to an underlying logic or "structure."

At one level these were very different enterprises, and to some degree were opposed to each other. But from another point of view they all had one thing in common: they were essentially theories of "constraint." Human behavior was shaped, molded, ordered, and defined by external social and cultural forces and formations: by culture, by mental structures, by capitalism. Of course, structural constraints of various kinds are real and are not being denied. Indeed I will argue later that some critiques of the culture concept have lost the important element of constraint in that concept. But a purely constraint-based theory, without attention to either human agency or to the processes that produce and reproduce those constraints— social practices—was coming to seem increasingly problematic.

In sociology (less in anthropology) an early challenge to this constraint perspective was mounted in the work of Erving Goffman (1959, 1967) and other practitioners of so-called interactionism. But interactionism in turn was too extreme, setting aside virtually all structural constraints and focusing on the microsociology of interpersonal interaction. Interactionism never achieved anything like the influence of the other schools, but it staked out and occupied the space of the opposition, and kept alive a version of the so-called structure/agency opposition.

Practice theory took up the challenge of overcoming this opposition. Three key works came out within a very short space of time in the late 1970s and early 1980s: Pierre Bourdieu's *Outline of a Theory of Practice* (1978), Anthony Giddens's *Central Problems in Social Theory: Action, Structure, and Contradiction in Social Analysis* (1979), and Marshall Sahlins's *Historical Metaphors and Mythical Realities: Structure in the Early History of the Sandwich Islands Kingdom* (1981). Each in its own way set out to conceptualize the *articulations* between the practices of social actors "on the ground" and the big "structures" and "systems" that both constrain those practices and yet are ultimately susceptible to being transformed by them. They accomplished this by arguing, in different ways, for the *dialectical*, rather than *oppositional* relationship between the structural constraints of society and culture on the one hand and the "practices"—the new term was important—of social actors on the other. They argued as well that "objectivist" perspectives (like Wolf's political economy) and "subjectivist" perspectives (like Geertz's interpretive anthropology) were not opposed ways of doing social science but represented "moments" (Bourdieu 1978:3) in a larger project of attempting to understand the dialectics of social life. These works were, in short, enormously important in at least beginning to lay out the mechanisms by which the seeming contradiction— that "history makes people, but people make history" (Ortner 2003:277)— is not only not a contradiction, but is perhaps the profoundest truth of social life.[1]

Put in other words, practice theory offered genuine resolutions of problems that had been plaguing the field, some dating back to functionalism, and some generated by the new schools of theory of the '60s and '70s. It restored the actor to the social process without losing sight of the larger structures that constrain (but also enable) social action. It "grounded" cultural processes— discourses, representations, what we used to call "symbol systems"—in the social relations of people "on the ground." Its conception of those grounded social relations in turn was (to varying degrees) Marxist and/or Weberian, rather than functionalist, opening up the space for questions of power and inequality with which I and many others had become increasingly concerned in the 1970s.

From that period on, practice theory became the general frame within which I would cast my work. Yet for all the invaluable ways in which it potentially liberated the field from the old oppositions, it in turn—how could things be otherwise?—had some significant limitations. Thus almost from the outset I found myself tinkering with the framework, drawing on other major changes inside and outside of anthropology. This essay is in many ways a history of that tinkering. It involves pulling in a great deal of work by others but emphasizes the ways in which I used both practice theory itself and those other bodies of work within my own writings, including both earlier writings and the essays in this book.

There were three major areas in which significant new work was going on, and which I saw as offering major correctives for and improvements to the basic practice theory framework. The first was what I will call "the power shift," associated with the work of James Scott, Michel Foucault, Raymond Williams, and others, and linked in various ways with work in critical studies of colonialism, gender, race, and ethnicity. Next was what Terrence McDonald (1996) called "the historic turn," a broad movement to historicize work in the social sciences and thus to move beyond the static frameworks that had carried over into practice theory from functionalism.

And finally there was what I will call the reinterpretation(s) of culture. It is this last that is the main focus of the present volume. As I have explored the implications of the power shift (especially in Ortner 1996) and have taken the historic turn (especially in Ortner 1989, 1999, 2003) in earlier works, I will only briefly review them here, although they remain vitally important to the works in this volume as well. But the critiques and retheorizations of culture in the past several decades remain to be examined, in relation to questions of practice (and power and history).

Early Expansions

THE POWER SHIFT

In more or less the same period in which practice theory came on the scene, there emerged an important body of work rethinking questions of "power." These included such diverse works as Raymond Williams's *Marxism and Literature* (1977), Michel Foucault's *History of Sexuality Part I* (1979), and James Scott's *Weapons of the Weak* (1985). These converged in various ways with the florescence of critical studies in gender, race, ethnicity, and colonialism. Since I had been actively working in the arena of feminist anthropology, and specifically in those years with questions of "male dominance," it was virtually inevitable that I would become aware of the relative weakness of practice theory on this issue. Practice theory did not ignore power, of course, but neither did it make it central to the theoretical framework in the ways that seemed called for by this type of critical work on inequality and domination.

In retrospect it seems to me that my work on gender inequality was pushing me toward some kind of practice theory approach in the first place. On the one hand I wanted to understand the cultural construction of gender relations in more or less the classic Geertzian way. In fact, in the introduction to *Sexual Meanings* (1981), Harriet Whitehead and I adapted Geertz's famous phrase and wrote that the book was concerned with "gender as a cultural system." But we went on to say that we were interested in more than the logic and workings of the gender system, that we wanted to understand, as it were, where it was coming from. Put in other words, we wanted to understand the ways in which such systems were "grounded" in various kinds of social relations, and, I would now say, social practices.

My own article in that volume, called "Gender and Sexuality in Hierarchical Societies" (1981), involved inventing a kind of practice theory approach without knowing exactly what I was doing. I had not yet read any practice theory,[2] but looking back at that paper, I realize I was groping toward a method that would help me solve some of the puzzles of unequal, and sometimes violently unequal, gender relations in a range of Polynesian societies. For example, I was interested in the treatment of daughters of chiefs, who were on the one hand elaborately beautified and on the other hand kept under very tight paternal control. I argued that these girls were pawns in an elaborate cultural game (as I would now call it) of male prestige. The idea was that, once one figured out the game—that is, the configuration of practices involving the players in question, its underlying logic, and its cultural goal—the puzzling elements would make sense. I will not spend time summarizing the interpretation. The point here is simply that my work in a particular arena of power relations—gender—was pushing me toward some kind of a practice theory framework, which involved an analytic device that I later (1996a) came to call "(serious) games."

The early practice theorists did not, as I said earlier, ignore issues of power. They dealt with it in various ways. At issue in part is the relative weight given to power as organized into the cultural or institutional order (which Giddens calls "domination"), and "power" as an actual social relation of real on-the-ground actors (which Giddens calls "power"). Both are important, but a strong emphasis on structural power tends ironically to move away from the question of real practices. We see this most clearly in *Outline of a Theory of Practice*. Social relations of power and inequality, especially patriarchal relations, are central to the book. But they are never explored as specific formations of power, involving specific ideologies and practices. Rather, Bourdieu devotes most of his intellectual efforts to the elaboration of the notion of *habitus*, a deeply buried structure that shapes people's dispositions to act in such ways that they wind up accepting the dominance of others, or of "the system," without being made to do so. Sahlins tends to follow a similar pattern. While he describes practices of interpersonal power in the Hawaiian case, he tends to give a much greater role to impersonal forms of constraint, built into the structures of asymmetry that ran through every relationship in that hierarchically organized society. Giddens appears somewhat different. He has a useful discussion of what he calls "the dialectic of control" (1979:145 ff), in which he argues that systems of control can never work perfectly, because those being controlled have both agency and understanding and thus can always find ways to evade or resist. His arguments fit well with those of James Scott, one of the power theorists to be discussed below. The difference is perhaps that for Giddens power is just one of many modalities of practice, while for Scott and the other power theorists it is absolutely central to the framework.

Let me turn to those power theorists and what they had to offer. My choice of theorists here—Foucault, Scott, and Williams—may appear somewhat puzzling. At the very least the reader might be wondering why I list no theorists of gender, racial, or colonial domination. I can only say that these three figures offer the most general tools for examining any form of domination and inequality, including those of gender, race, and colonialism. Thus Foucault has played a major role in the work of one of the most influential theorists of feminism, Judith Butler (e.g., 1997), and in the work of the towering figure in (post)colonial studies, Edward Said (e.g., 1978). Scott's work has generated a virtual industry of studies of "resistance" of all sorts, including especially slave and peasant resistance movements. Raymond Williams is the founding ancestor of that vast school of scholarship called "cultural studies," which has generated important work on the power relations of gender, race, class, and youth.

The three theorists can be placed along a spectrum that is defined by one of the central problematics of studies of power: the question of the pervasiveness or invasiveness of power. At one end we have Foucault, who has argued that power is socially ubiquitous, suffused through every aspect of the social system, and psychologically deeply invasive. There is no "outside" of power. At the other end we have James Scott, who takes the position that, while there is certainly a great deal of power in play in social life, it is much less mentally invasive than others have argued.[3] He proposes (1990) that dominated people understand very well what is going on, and even have explicit traditions— "hidden transcripts"—of critique and resistance. If they do not actively resist, it is only because they are held back by the sheer political and economic power of the dominating group. Finally, Williams (1977) takes a kind of intermediate position, seeing actors as to some degree in the grip of "hegemonies," but picking up Gramsci's argument to the effect that hegemonies are never total and absolute, in several senses. They are never total in a historical sense, because in the flow of history, while one may talk of hegemonic formation(s) in the present, there are always also remnants of past ("residual") hegemonies and the beginnings of future ("emergent") ones. And hegemonies are also never total in the psychological sense, because people always have at least some degree of "penetration" (if not virtually full awareness, as Scott would argue) into the conditions of their domination.

All of these perspectives are useful for particular purposes, and I have used all of them in one context or another. But I have found the Gramsci-derived notion of hegemonies as strongly controlling but never complete or total to be the most useful in my various attempts to inject more power into a practice approach. For example, in "Gender Hegemonies" (1996b) the notion of incomplete hegemonies allowed me to move beyond a simplistic notion of "universal male dominance," not so much by finding "cases" of non-male dominance but by recognizing that male dominance always coexists with other patterns of gender relations; what is important is the mix, and the relations between the elements.

Putting this all together in the introduction to *Making Gender* I began to sketch out what I called a "feminist, minority, subaltern, etc., theory of practice," which focused in part on questions of direct resistance, but more on ways in which domination itself was always riven with ambiguities, contradictions, and lacunae. This means in turn that social reproduction is never total, always imperfect, and vulnerable to the pressures and instabilities inherent in any situation of unequal power. I brought this view to bear on the relationship between Sherpas and Western mountaineers ("sahibs") in Himalayan mountaineering (*Life and Death on Mt. Everest*, 1999). In that study I was able to show "real" resistance: It is not well known in the outside world, for example, that the supposedly happy compliant Sherpas often went on strike on Himalayan expeditions. But I also explored a central contradiction in the Western mountaineers' views of, and treatment of, the Sherpas. On the one hand the Westerners were powerful (as white, as Western, as employers, and, in the early years, as quasi-military leaders). On the other hand they often developed a great deal of affection and admiration for the Sherpas with whom they worked. This contradiction was not lost upon the Sherpas, who were able to exploit it often quite successfully, to bring about significant transformations in the structure of the Sherpa-sahib relationship, and of Himalayan expeditions in general, over the course of the twentieth century.

In the end the two bodies of theory can be easily merged. The three founding practice theorists can be interestingly seen to parallel the three positions on the spectrum of the psychological "depth" of power. Bourdieu is most like Foucault, in that his notion of habitus is one of a deeply internalized structure, powerfully controlling and largely inaccessible to consciousness (see also de Certeau 1984). Giddens is more like Scott, emphasizing the ways in which actors are at least partially "knowing subjects" (see, e.g., 1979:5) who are able to reflect to some degree on their circumstances and by implication to develop a certain level of critique and possible resistance. And finally Sahlins is most like Williams. He subscribes to a notion of strong cultural hegemonies but also allows for certain, shall we say, cracks in the structure, as for example when he talks about how the gendered food taboos of eighteenth-century Hawaiians "did not sit upon Hawaiian women with the force [they] had for men" (1981:46), a small difference that would make a large difference in the long run.

Looking at the relationship from the point of view of the power theorists, we can see that their integration with practice theory was already (potentially) there. Thus, Foucault's interest in locating the production of power less in macro-institutions like the state and more in micro-interactions like the priest-penitent relationship, has obvious affinities with practice theory's interest in looking at ground-level sources of larger formations. Scott's interest in resistance is nothing other than a way of asking the question of how (certain kinds of) practices may transform structures. And Raymond Williams argued that "hegemonies" had to be understood not as "structures" external to individuals but as "the whole lived social process" (1977:109), which "has continually to be renewed, recreated, defended, and modified . . . [and] also continually resisted, limited, altered, challenged" (1977:112)—which has in short to be both practiced and resisted. In a way one could say that all these new power theories were themselves varieties of practice theory as well.

I said earlier that the emergence of various theories of power was more or less simultaneous with the emergence of early practice theory. The same is true, interestingly, of "the historic turn." One realizes in retrospect just how theoretically fertile that period during the late 1970s and early 1980s was. We turn then to the historic turn.

THE HISTORIC TURN

My sense of the necessity to historicize practice theory came primarily out of theoretical developments on this side of the Atlantic. Several varieties of historic turn had taken shape in anthropology, including Marxist-inspired historical "political economy," as in Eric Wolf's *Europe and the People without History* (1981); certain forms of cultural history (e.g., Geertz's *Negara* [1980]); and the early work on colonial history launched by Bernard Cohn (1980), which would later become a major enterprise across many academic disciplines. The historic turn(s) were enormously important both methodologically, in destabilizing the traditionally static modes of ethnographic inquiry, and substantively, in insisting that the traditional world of anthropological objects—"cultures"—were not timeless and pristine objects, but were themselves products of the restless operation of both internal dynamics (mostly local power relations) and external forces (such as capitalism and colonialism) over time.[4]

In the founding works of practice theory, Bourdieu had insisted on the importance of time, not only in the unfolding of interactive practices and their outcomes, but in giving meaning to those interactions. He gives (1978:6–7) the famous example of the meanings produced by the manipulation of temporality in gift giving: If the gift is reciprocated too quickly, this implies an eagerness "to close the books" and end the relationship. If it is reciprocated too slowly, it implies a low level of interest in the relationship, or even active disrespect. Yet Bourdieu never really tried to write historical practice theory (or perhaps better said, practice-theorized history), to look at the ways in which real histories, as both durations and events, are shaped by practices within and against existing "structures."

From my point of view, by contrast, practice theory was not only intrinsically temporalized in the relatively small-scale sense discussed by Bourdieu, but that in effect it did its best work in the context of full-blown historical analysis. Indeed in *High Religion* I said explicitly that "a theory of practice is a theory of history" (192). This is because the playing out of the effects of culturally organized practices is essentially processual and often very slow: the construction of social subjects, often from childhood; the practices of life of young people and adults; the articulation of those practices with larger events in the world, often moving to a very different rhythm. Although one can form hypotheses—guesses, more likely—about the long-term implications of present practices, their effects in terms of social reproduction and social transformation are often not visible, nor interpretable, until some time after the fact.

Of the three founding practice theorists, only Marshall Sahlins proposed an explicitly historical form of practice theory. He develops his theory within the framework of a historical case, that of the encounter between Europeans and native Hawaiians in the eighteenth century. He theorizes from this example a number of important ways in which practices operate to affect the course of history. The first is that acts and objects have different meanings in the "collective symbolic scheme" (1981:69) and in the plans and intentions—the "interests"—of acting subjects. Sahlins calls this the difference between conventional and intentional meanings (ibid.). The second is that, while people act in the world according to their own cultural conceptions, the world is under no compulsion to conform to those conceptions. In both cases it follows that every practice, every move, puts those cultural categories and conceptions "at risk," making them vulnerable to revision and revaluation. Thus, while most practices may be "conservative," operating within an existing framework of meaning and normally reproducing that framework, yet those meanings can be shifted in practice (especially by powerful people) and in any event all practices operate within "a balky world" (Sewell 2005:179) that threatens to undermine their intended meanings or effects.

Finally, Sahlins insists on seeing historical change as an outcome of the articulation between local and translocal power dynamics. All of my own recent monographs emphasize the importance of this kind of multilevel approach. Thus in *High Religion* (1989) I traced the (local) history of the founding of Buddhist temples and monasteries among the Sherpas, a history of sometimes violently competitive relations among religious leaders and other big men. But this history in turn was shown to be inextricably implicated in larger political histories—the variable effects of (at different times) the British Raj in India, the Nepal state, and the Sherpas' religious relations with Tibet. In *Life and Death on Mt. Everest* (1999), I traced the history of the changing relations between Sherpas and international climbers in the Himalayas, but again I anchored that history in turn in larger historical shifts. Thus for example I explored the impact of the global feminist movement on mountaineering in the seventies, bringing both Western and Sherpa women into the sport, and wreaking a certain amount of havoc in both social relations and cultural assumptions on both sides. And finally, in *New Jersey Dreaming* (2003), I traced the differential histories of social mobility of members of the Class of '58 of Weequahic High School in Newark, N.J., as embedded in differential relations of class, race, ethnicity, and gender. But I anchored that history in turn in larger cultural and political movements in the United States—the Beat movement of the 1950s and, in the 1960s and '70s, civil rights, the counterculture, the women's movement, and more.

In the present volume "the historic turn" is less visible than in the full-scale, and very obviously historical, monographs just discussed. But it is here in more subtle ways. For after all "history" is not just about the past, nor is it always about change. It may be about *duration*, about patterns persisting over long periods of time, which is the case with a pattern discussed in "Reading America" and "Identities" (both in this volume), namely the relative absence of a class discourse in hegemonic American culture. It may also be about *situating* an analysis or interpretation in a particular, historically understood *moment*, a move that will also be visible in several of the articles, but especially "Generation X." There I explore the emergence of the idea of Generation X, and the specific characteristics both attributed to its members (e.g., "slackers") and evinced by them (mainly anxieties over their financial futures). The article has a section of recognizable "history," tracing changes in the public representation of Generation X over time. But it is implicitly historical throughout, in that the phenomenon only emerges at a particular point in time, and it is the moment itself—the beginning of the polarization of the American class structure, still going on today—that is the key to the interpretation.

It is probably obvious from the foregoing that the historicization of practice theory was not wholly distinct from "the power shift." Questions of "history" were largely questions of the reproduction or transformation of relations of power and inequality. The same will be true of questions of "culture," to which we now turn.

Culture in Practice

Early practice theory, particularly as developed in Bourdieu and Giddens, lacked a recognizable concept of culture. Neither author evinced a sense of the ways in which practice itself was culturally organized, explicitly or implicitly, by things like charter myths (Sahlins 1981), "cultural schemas" (Ortner 1989, Sewell 2005), cultural scripts (Alexander 2004), "serious games" (Ortner 1996a, "Power and Projects" [this volume]), and the like. Both also lacked a sense of (or perhaps an interest in) the ways in which "cultural movements" (anything from the Beat movement, noted above, to the Reformation) reshaped both practices and subjectivities. While certain culture-like elements were present in both of their frameworks (habitus is certainly a kind of cultural formation, and Giddens has a chapter on "Ideology and Consciousness"), it seemed clear from the outset, to this anthropologist at least, that practice theory needed a much more fully developed conception of culture and its role in the social process. But what kind of culture does it need? To answer that question is to plunge into the recent culture debates, and to try to see the variety of ways in which this old and tenacious concept is being rethought and refashioned.

The critique of the culture concept in anthropology has, as virtually every anthropologist knows by now, centered primarily (though not exclusively) around the problem of essentialism. Classic anthropology tended to portray groups of people as having "a culture," as being in the grip of that culture, and as acting in ways that could be explained largely by reference to that culture. The (cultural) anthropologist's job, at least within the dominant tradition of the field almost from the beginning, was to unearth a people's culture, to work out its logic and coherence, and to show the ways in which it undergirded most of the formalized practices (e.g., rituals), patterns of practice (e.g., child rearing), and the ordinary and extraordinary behavior of members of the group. While the initial development of the anthropological concept of culture emerged from impeccable intentions—as an alternative to the concept of "race," as providing a sympathetic way of thinking about difference, and as providing a positive way of achieving cross-cultural understanding—it was hard to contain the concept within this basically liberal frame. Thus culture in the classic sense could, within a different political mind-set, easily turn into stereotype (ethnic, racial, class), and sometimes in fact dangerous stereotype —groups can be labeled (even "profiled") as intrinsically culturally prone to this or that (good or bad, model minorities or terrorists) pattern of behavior.

For this reason and others, over the past several decades many anthropologists have argued for dropping the culture concept altogether (for an overview of the issues, see Ortner, ed., 2000; see also Fox 1999). Ironically, however, scholars in other intellectual arenas sidestepped the whole anthropological quagmire and began both using and transforming the concept in exciting and powerful ways. One can identify at least three distinct but overlapping trends, which again have their roots primarily in the same period as all the other work discussed above—the late 1970s and early 1980s. The first is associated with the original Birmingham School of "cultural studies" which involved both ethnographic work (e.g., Willis 1977) and media studies (e.g., Hall et al. 1980). Second, media studies became a large-scale trend in its own right and has by now swept across virtually all social science fields, including anthropology (e.g., Ginsburg et al. 2002). And finally, as part of retheorizing the concept for anthropology itself, there was the founding of the journal *Public Culture* in

1988. The mission of the journal, as announced in the opening editorial comment, was to look at culture not as attached to and defining of particular groups of people, but as part of "global cultural flows" and "the global cultural ecumene" (1988: 1, 3; see also Appadurai 1996).

These novel approaches to culture have several things in common, differentiating them collectively from the classic view of culture in anthropology. The first is their very tight involvement with "the power shift." All of them view culture as highly politicized, or as elements of a political process. In addition all of them attempt, in various ways, to loosen up the relationship between culture and specific groups of people. Although there are perhaps "epicenters" of particular cultural formations (what we would have thought of as "cultures" in the past), nonetheless culture has at the same time become an at least partially mobile object. Not only does it move around (like media) across social, cultural, and political boundaries. It also, and perhaps because of that mobility, can be seen to be much more variably deployed or appropriated than had been assumed of culture in the classic sense. Phrases like "public culture" or James Clifford's "traveling cultures" (1997) capture this more mobile view of cultural forms and forces (see also Gupta and Ferguson 1992: 48–49).

To these important changes I would add one more, which I will illustrate, along with the others, through the articles in this collection. Let me return for a moment to the early Birmingham cultural studies school, which actually embodied two somewhat distinct tendencies. On the one hand there was the media studies work, which treated culture as a set of public texts, to be analyzed for the kinds of ideological work they did. In the present book both "Reading America: Preliminary Notes on Class and Culture" and "Identities: The Hidden Life of Class" essentially follow this strategy. They take a variety of cultural "texts," including novels (in "Reading America"), labels for groups (in "Identities"), and more and ask what kinds of ideological formations are being constructed in and through those texts—specifically, the near erasure of "class" from dominant American discourse.[5] "Identities" also goes further and asks—the practice theory move—what kinds of social dynamics have gone into making and sustaining a specific version of that discursive pattern, in which ethnic categories often stand in for class categories?

But the other trend in the early cultural studies work was to use something suspiciously like the classic concept of culture, yet to change it by embedding it in a different kind of story, a different kind of context. This is to say that the concept itself is not actually reworked. It still embodies the notion, which was part of the classic concept, that culture is both enabling (allowing people to see, feel, imagine, understand some things), and constraining (disabling people from seeing, feeling, imagining, and understanding other things).

But this relatively unreworked concept of culture takes on a very different cast when it is embedded in narratives of power and inequality. We see this for example in *Learning to Labor*. Willis's concept of culture is really no different from the classic American model—culture provides a set of frameworks and values through which "the lads" see and act upon the world. Willis does not even see it as "ideological" in and of itself, or at least he does not discuss it primarily in those terms. Rather he asks how it enables a certain pleasurable set of practices of everyday resistance for the lads in the school, while at the same time disabling them from seeing how they are acting contrary to their own interests in the long run. In other words Willis makes the old and relatively unreconstructed concept do new kinds of work, by embedding it in a narrative of capitalist reproduction: "how working class kids get working class jobs." (See also Ortner, ed., 1999.) I will call this the new-old concept of culture.

Several essays in this collection make use of this embedding move and this new-old concept of culture. I should note here that I am also very drawn to the idea of public culture in the more mobile, and perhaps global, sense discussed above, and will return to this issue at the end of this section. But in a number of these essays I try to hold onto the powerful elements of the old culture concept while getting past its limitations, by deploying it within different kinds of narratives—narratives of power and inequality. Let me start with the idea that culture is "constraining." This is very much part of the old concept of culture—the idea that people in a particular society are constrained by their cultural frameworks to be as they are and act as they do. When culture was seen through relativist lenses, and was seen as essentially benign, this idea of cultural constraint was itself a relatively benign idea. Yet the issue of "constraint" takes on a very different cast in a different kind of narrative. Thus in "Subjectivity and Cultural Critique" I pursue the idea of cultural constraint via the idea that culture shapes the subjectivities of people not so much as members of particular groups (although that is not totally irrelevant) but under specific historic regimes of power. The regime in question for that essay is that of late capitalism, and I draw upon the works of Fredric Jameson and Richard Sennett to explore the essentially unhappy forms of consciousness culturally produced under this regime.

It is worth noting in this case that culture is "loosened up" from its mooring within particular groups not so much by geographic mobility, which is what tends to be emphasized by the media studies perspective, or by the idea of "traveling cultures," but by temporal mobility. This suggests that we think of "the historic turn" as another form of making culture more of a mobile phenomenon, yet one that does not lose the possibility of exploring its—at times, and for some people—deeply constraining power.

Let me turn then to the idea of culture as "enabling." This too is part of the classic concept of culture. It was central to Geertz's discussion in "The Growth of Culture and the Evolution of Mind" (1973a), where he argued that without culture—external systems of symbols and meanings—people would not be able to think at all. It was also central to his discussion of functions of religion which, when it works, allows people to deal with suffering, meaninglessness, and chaos (1973b). But once again I insert questions of the enabling workings of culture into narratives of power and inequality. Thus in "Resistance and the Problem of Ethnographic Refusal," I draw on James Scott's (1990) notion of "hidden transcripts" as cultural resources that enable the very idea of resistance, as well as many of its specific forms. And in "Power and Projects: Reflections on Agency" I explore the cultural construction of agency as both a kind of empowerment and as the basis of pursuing "projects" within a world of domination and inequality.

Finally, there is one essay in this volume that ties together (or at least includes within the single frame of the essay) questions of "public culture" and questions of culture and subjectivity in the new-old sense discussed above: "Generation X: Anthropology in a Media-Saturated World." On the one hand I spend time on the public culture, the media representations of "Generation X," seen as a specific group with its own distinctive consciousness. I trace the ways in which the representations change over time and across social space, as they pass through different hands (novelists, demographers, advertisers and others in marketing, social commentators, and writers of popular journalism). On the other hand I explore, through published ethnographies and some interviews with Xers I conducted in the early '90s, the "culture" of Gen X itself. Here I use the approach discussed above, taking a fairly unreconstructed concept of culture as productive of certain subjectivities (specifically, certain anxieties), but inserting it into yet another narrative of late capitalism, that of the changing class structure of the United States.

That essay ends there, and the idea of "Generation X" has by now largely faded into the background of the public culture. One rarely sees references to it now. But in fact that generation is now coming into power in certain key culture industries, and specifically for my purposes, in media production. Young men and women of 35 or 40 years of age are now moving into important positions of creativity in Hollywood. One might ask: Even if nobody is writing about it any more, is there a distinctive GenX sensibility that is manifesting itself in at least a recognizable segment of Hollywood media productions? Preliminary interviews with GenX players in Hollywood suggest that some certainly think so. In any event, I take this as a launching point for a project in which I will continue to combine questions of culture (in the new-old sense), power, and history in examining the production of those most mobile of cultural artifacts, the media products of Hollywood.

Conclusions: Power, History, Culture

I noted earlier that all the theoretical developments discussed in this essay were virtually contemporary with one another, with key publications in each of the major areas—practice theory, "the power shift," "the historic turn," and "cultural studies"—virtually all appearing in the late 1970s and early 1980s. All were important, and one could really start with any one of them and pull in the others.

For me practice theory seemed the most compelling. It was a general theory of the production of social subjects through practice in the world, and of the production of the world itself through practice. The first part did not seem new to me. My Weberian-Geertzian training was in large part about the production of subject(ivitie)s, and in ways that seemed to me more rich and interesting than, say, Bourdieu's conception of habitus (although the term is certainly handy). But the second part—the production of the world through human practice—seemed new and very powerful, providing a dialectical synthesis of the opposition between "structure" (or the social world as constituted) and "agency" (or the interested practices of real people) that had not previously been achieved. Moreover, the idea that the world is "made"—in a very extended and complex sense, of course—through the actions of ordinary people also meant that it could be unmade and remade. That is, practice theory had immediate political implications that connected with my feminist concerns. And finally practice theory was attractive because it was (is) a very broad and capacious theoretical framework. It was missing a lot, but everything that was missing—a better theory of culture, a more central role for power, any history at all (in Bourdieu and Giddens)—was also at the same time implied by the terms of the theory.

Meanwhile, exciting work in all those "missing" areas was going on in other parts of the intellectual landscape. The "power shift" was generated by the enormous politicization of the real world which began in the late sixties, and which included both social movements and academic studies concerned with various forms of domination and inequality, particularly gender and race. The historic turn was similarly linked to the social movements and real-world events of the '60s and '70s. The most obvious link was between the growing academic interest in colonialism and the contemporary struggles (or worse) in the many postcolonial nations in which anthropologists had traditionally worked. But in the introduction to *The Historic Turn in the Human Sciences*, Terrence McDonald links the historic turn to domestic social movements as well:

> The rise of the civil rights movement, the "rediscovery" of poverty, and the pros-
> ecution of the war in Vietnam revealed . . . the inability of theories of consensus and
> status attainment, abundance, and modernization to explain current events. The
> domestic social movements arising in response to those events—for example, civil
> rights, antiwar, welfare rights, and parallel movements for the rights of women and
> others—placed both agency and history back on the agenda (1996:5).

I have argued, then, that practice theory in its early European versions (hegemonically, those of Bourdieu and Giddens) desperately needed both history and a more elaborated sense of the play of power in social life. In its ahistoricity, and its relatively low level of interest in questions of power—and despite a radically different theoretical agenda—it could appear as a throwback to the static and apolitical frameworks of functionalism. This impression is strengthened by the emphasis on social reproduction rather than social transformation in the works of both authors.[6] While again the intent and meaning of this emphasis is very different, nonetheless it seems to echo functionalism's concern with social stability, coherence, and continuity. Sahlins was a strong exception on both dimensions—power and history—and thus gives us a story of radical social transformation, as Hawaiian chiefly power, religious tabus, and gender inequalities were all unmade and/or remade over the course of a protracted historical encounter between unequally powerful parties.

And what about culture? Why does practice theory need culture, as the essays in this collection illustrate in many different ways? This question can be answered by harking back to the issues of power, history, and social transformation with which I began. For what social transformation in a deep sense means is not only the rearrangement of institutions. It involves the transformation of "culture," in both its new-old and its newer senses. Taking culture in the new-old sense, as the (politically inflected) schemas through which people see and act upon the world and the (politically inflected) subjectivities through which people feel—emotionally, viscerally, sometimes violently— about themselves and the world, social transformation involves the rupturing of those schemas and subjectivities. And taking culture in the newer—public, mobile, traveling—sense, social transformation works in part through the constant production, contestation, and transformation of public culture, of media and other representations of all kinds, embodying and seeking to shape old and new thoughts, feelings, and ideologies. In both senses, then, to adapt an old adage, social transformation must also be cultural transformation or it will be nothing.

A note on the contents and organization of what follows: My more purely theoretical work on the subjects discussed in this introduction was done over a period in which I was also developing an ethnographic and historical project on class in American culture, using my own high school graduating class as the ethnographic subjects. The ethnography was eventually published as *New Jersey Dreaming: Capital, Culture, and the Class of '58* (2003). As part of the New Jersey Dreaming project, I also published a series of interpretive papers on the cultural construction of class in America. The present volume thus includes both straight theory papers and interpretive papers related to the American case, as they all illustrate, in different ways, the issues discussed in this introduction. After some experimentation with organization, I have settled on a chronological ordering.

CHAPTER 1

Reading America: Preliminary Notes on Class and Culture

Anthropologists are turning in increasing numbers to the study of modern American society. When I was in graduate school in the sixties it was virtually unheard of to get the blessings of the department (not to mention a grant) to do American fieldwork. The only project in my era to get such backing was a study of American drag queens (Newton 1972), and one could argue that this was only because drag queens were seen as very exotic and "other."

This essay is part of a larger project on the cultural construction and social experience of class in the United States. Its point of departure is the relative absence of a discourse of class in hegemonic American culture. This does not mean that class is never mentioned or addressed, for of course it is. But it means that other categories of social difference are much more prominent, including especially race and ethnicity, and these are taken to be much more significant in defining who one is and what one's life possibilities will be. Obviously I need to define what is meant by class; I will survey a range of approaches and definitions in a later section of the chapter.

In terms of theoretical inspiration, this essay is most closely tied to the Birmingham school of cultural studies, with its emphasis on interpreting representations, discourses, and ordinary language as elements of the hegemonic processes that sustain systematic inequalities. I begin with an overview of the place of "class" in anthropological studies of the United

States, showing how, until the late 1980s, class was largely (though not entirely) absent from that literature. In the following section, I survey a range of theoretical positions on class, as well as some of the realities of class in the United States (e.g., high rates of social mobility) and of American ideology (e.g., the cult of the individual) that combine to mute class discourse as such.

I then turn to the central argument which is that, although class goes largely unspoken in American social life, it is not actually discursively absent. Rather it is displaced into culturally more salient discourses, and specifically for purposes of this essay, discourses of gender and sexuality. I proceed to develop this argument through a critical interpretation of such discourses, as found in three arenas: ethnographies of working class communities; ethnographies of high schools; and some of the fiction of Phillip Roth. In all three cases I show that representations of gender and sexuality are heavily, if cryptically, "classed." The implications of this go in two directions. On the one hand we come to see one of the places where class is, in a sense, discursively hiding. On the other hand, we come to see that, if discourses and practices of gender and sexuality are carrying a secret burden of class meanings, this lends a degree of what I will call "surplus antagonism" to such relations.

Finally in the conclusion I will return to reflect upon the cultural and ideological processes we will have seen at work in these interpretations.

Point of Entry: Class and Culture in America

I begin with a consideration of the ways in which class as a problem has and has not appeared in social science discourse in the United States. Specifically, I focus on the presence of class in ethnographies (rather than in survey studies), because—for me, still—the ethnography provides the "thickest" form of information. The first thing that strikes an anthropologist reading the ethnographic literature on America, written by both sociologists and anthropologists, is the centrality of "class" in sociological research and its marginality in anthropological studies. Sociologists may argue intensely over the meanings and implications of class, but there is no doubt that it is a meaningful category of discussion for them. Given that until recently the sociologists virtually "owned" America as a research domain, even for ethnographic research, most of the ethnographic work by sociologists was in one form or another concerned with class.[1] The sociologists' concern with class also extended into the work of the one anthropologist to conduct a major ethnographic study in the

United States before World War Two, W. Lloyd Warner. In the monumental Yankee City project (beginning with Warner and Lunt 1941) Warner both accepted the sociological emphasis on class and transformed it with his "emic," anthropological perspective. I will say a bit more about Warner below; he merits a paper himself but cannot be discussed in any detail here.

Other than the Yankee City project there were scattered anthropological forays into American community studies before the seventies, but anthropologists did not come into the ethnography of America in a major way until that decade. The difference of focus between the sociologists and the anthropologists is breathtaking. The anthropologists studied the marginal areas of society: street gangs (Keiser 1969), retirement communities (Jacobs 1974), and ethnic groups (mostly Jews [e.g., Myerhoff 1978; Kugelmass 1987]). They sought out "classic" anthropological topics like kinship (Schneider 1980; Neville 1987), ritual (Errington 1987), and "coming of age" (Moffatt 1989). They did general community studies focusing on "friendship" and "individualism" (Varenne 1977). All of the abovementioned works are excellent studies, and we learn a great deal from them about the workings of many parts of American society. But with a few exceptions before the eighties—*Rockdale* (Wallace 1972) is really the only one that comes to mind—they did not bring class into analytic focus at all.[2] The entire section on "social structure" in a 1975 reader on the anthropology of American culture—*The Nacirema* (Spradley and Rynkiewich 1975)—consists of entries concerning "totemism," "caste," "social race," ethnic relations, social identity formation in high schools, and urban networks. A second reader (Arens and Montague 1976) similarly has a section called "Social Strategies and Institutional Arrangements"; it includes entries on coffee drinking, friendship, moonshining, poker, astrology, volunteer firemen, and healthcare-seeking behavior. I do not mean to ridicule these concerns; the ethnography of the minutiae of everyday life can be very revealing. Nonetheless there is a tendency to avoid almost any kind of macrosociological analysis, let alone to make class a central category of research.

Besides for the most part ignoring class, anthropological studies of the United States have had a chronic tendency to "ethnicize" the groups under study, to treat them as so many isolated and exotic tribes. This is true even for studies of what are clearly class-defined groups—longshoremen (Pilcher 1972) or construction workers (Applebaum 1981). The major exception to this tendency before the eighties is found in ethnographies of African American communities (e.g., Hannerz 1969, Stack 1974). These studies attempt to work out various compromises between, on the one hand, the classic anthropological desire to see the cultures of these communities as having a certain authenticity in their own terms (i.e., the "ethnicizing" move) and, on the other, the recognition that African Americans are not simply another interesting ethnic group, but rather operate within a larger structure of racial inequality and a larger cultural hegemony.[3]

Yet studies of black communities implicitly continue the tradition of working around the (class-)edges of American society. Only since the late 1980s have we seen anthropologists—who are, after all, overwhelmingly white and middle class—take the bull by the horns and tackle both the American white middle class as such and the complex dynamics that reproduce the American class structure. I would mention only two such studies here. One is Katherine Newman's study of the experience of middle-class families whose primary wage earners lose their jobs (1988). Newman explores the sudden and novel experience of powerlessness undergone by middle-class people in these circumstances, and the ways in which they are forced to deal with themselves and the social universe under these conditions. Another study is Penelope Eckert's ethnography of a suburban high school near Detroit (1989). Eckert studied the social groups of high school—"jocks" and "burnouts." She is particularly conscious of the class factors underlying these social categories and groups. Her book most closely resembles Paul Willis's landmark work, *Learning to Labor* (1977), and although it is not as powerfully written, it nonetheless has the real advantage of looking at both the (largely middle-class) jocks and the (largely working-class) burnouts as mutually constituting one another within a single social universe.

So what is class? There is, to say the least, no single answer. The debates among sociologists (joined as well by some economists, political scientists, historians, and others) take place along several major axes. There is first of all a split between the so-called bourgeois theorists and the Marxists. Broadly speaking, bourgeois theorists in one form or another treat class as "stratification"—as a set of differential positions on a scale of social advantage—rather than as a set of fundamentally conflictual relations. Marxists, by contrast, work from a theoretical model in which classes are not merely sets of differentially successful people but are derived from the specifically exploitative form of production that is capitalism, and are inherently antagonistic.

Further cleavages are visible within each camp. The bourgeois theorists tend to split among themselves between those who think class should be defined by objective indicators (such as income, occupation, and education), and those who think class should be defined in terms of how the natives themselves create social rankings, that is, in terms of something like "status." A good example of the first is Lipset's and Bendix's classic study, *Social Mobility in Industrial Society* (1957), which treats class as almost entirely equivalent to occupation. A good example of the second is Coleman's and Rainwater's *Social Standing in America* (1978), which is entirely concerned with how people define and rank "status."[4] There are further divisions within these ranks, and also certain mixings and matchings: the objectivists tend to ask in their last chapter how their objective indicators line up with native categories; those who emphasize native categories or "statuses" tend to ask in their last chapter how these line up with objective indicators like income or education.

The Marxists have their own splits. As Erik Olin Wright puts it, there are scholars who are interested in "class structure," as against the scholars who are interested in "class formation" (1985:9–10). Wright himself falls largely on the "class structure" side, concerned with the ways in which capitalism is or is not functioning the way Marx thought it did or should, and the implications thereof. Some of the major issues here include the implications for capitalism (as well as for Marxist theory and social transformation) of the growth of the salaried middle class, of different forms of the state, and of different modes of relationship between state and economy. The "class formation" thinkers, for their part, are primarily concerned with the problem of how and why classes (normally, the working class) do or do not come to be self-conscious political actors. This camp in turn seems to be undergoing further splits: On the one hand, we have a kind of austere structural approach to the question of class formation, as seen in Anthony Giddens's *The Class Structure of the Advanced Societies* (1973). Giddens is concerned with the "variables," in a sociological sense, that do or do not facilitate such coming to awareness. On the other hand there is the historical sociology camp, deriving much of its inspiration from E. P. Thompson's *The Making of the English Working Class* (1966). Here the argument is that we should stop looking at what the working class has only infrequently done, which is become conscious of itself as the vehicle for revolutionary social change. Instead we should look at the extraordinary range of ways in which it has formulated and expressed a distinct identity and a distinct relationship to the rest of society (Katznelson and Zolberg 1986, Somers 1989).

Let me approach this range of theoretical and methodological perspectives obliquely, by restating the problem for the present chapter. It is well known that American natives almost never speak of themselves or their society in class terms. In other words class is not a central category of cultural discourse in America, and the anthropological literature that ignores class in favor of almost any other set of social idioms—ethnicity, race, kinship—is in some ways merely reflecting this fact. Paul Fussell speaks of the discourse of class in America as being under a "taboo" (1983). And in an ethnographic study of a chemical plant in Elizabeth, New Jersey, the British sociologist David Halle found that the plant workers defined themselves as "working men" and "working women," but did not see themselves as members of a "working class" (1984: chapter 10). In those rare instances in which they used class terms at all, they described themselves—as the vast majority of Americans do—as "middle class."[5]

At the same time it is clear that class is a "real" structure in American society, whether it is recognized in folk discourse or not. Part of this reality is what is described in the classic Marxist account of differential relations to the means of production: some people own most of the major systems of the production of wealth in America, while others produce that wealth yet garner for themselves only a small part of its value. Another part of the reality of class is one that is increasingly talked about in neo-Marxist discussions about the salaried middle class: power (administrative, regulatory, etc.) over other people's lives, whether one owns a piece of the means of production or not (Poulantzas 1974; Vanneman and Cannon 1987). And part of it, discussed most directly in studies of African Americans and other poor minorities, has to do with discrimination, prejudice, stigmatization, and pain. Indeed, if one asks which aspects of the reality of class are displaced into the discourses of ethnicity, race, and gender, they are really largely the second two dimensions just noted. That is, if Americans can be said to have a discourse of class at all, it is, like that of both Marx and the bourgeois theorists, an economistic one: Americans have a discourse of money. What are not represented by the folk, and only fragmentarily represented by the class theorists, are both the power and the pain of class relations.

It is important to note here that I take the position that class is not the only such "objective" structure of domination, that it is no more or less real than a number of others, and that it should not be construed as more fundamental.[6] Further it is not distinguished from other such structures as being somehow more "material"; all structures of domination are simultaneously material and cultural. Nonetheless it is real in the sense that one can speak of its existence and its constraints even when it is not directly articulated in folk discourse. In fact, as I shall argue in this essay, it does appear in folk discourse (no "reality" could fail to do so), but not in terms that we would immediately recognize as a discourse "about class."

But if the constraints of class are real, so too, apparently, are the high rates of social mobility in the American system. There are literally hundreds of studies of mobility, done at different times and with different assumptions over the course of the twentieth century, but the statistical findings seem to be relatively consistent with one another, and I will begin with the ones provided in Lipset's and Bendix's classic *Social Mobility in Industrial Society* (1957). The authors conducted an exhaustive survey of mobility studies and came up with the following figures: The average for upward mobility (narrowly defined as a shift from manual to nonmanual labor) runs around 33 percent, with a range from 20 percent to 40 percent. The average for downward mobility runs around 26 percent, with a range from 15 percent to 35 percent (p. 25, and chapter 2 passim). These rates are quite high. They mean that, on average, one out of three male Americans (only males were studied) will personally experience upward mobility in his lifetime; on average, one out of four will personally experience downward mobility. And, although this is an old study, it was revisited in the mid-1980s by Robert Erikson and John Goldthorpe, with both newer data and more advanced methods. Their figures remain in the ranges found by Lipset and Bendix (1985:12).

According to Lipset and Bendix the United States is not unique in having these high rates of mobility. The central point of their book is that such rates are characteristic of all the class societies, including Europe as well as the United States. What is unique about the American system is its ideology. Where European cultures have tended to emphasize traditional ranks and statuses, and to portray themselves as more rigid in class terms than they really are, the United States has glorified opportunity and mobility, and has portrayed itself as more open to individual achievement than it really is. There is nothing terribly new about this point, but it is, I think, one of many strands feeding into what is probably a massively overdetermined phenomenon: the relative absence of class discourse in American culture. The deeply individualistic grounding of American social thought no doubt also plays a role in generating this absence, in that classes are social categories that cannot be understood in terms of individual motives and desires. Anyone who has taught an introductory social science course to American undergraduates knows the extent to which society is culturally conceived by them as the sum of empirical, skin-bound individuals, and social institutions are conceived as the products of individual motives, desires, and wills. These two points in turn may be combined to suggest a reason for the patterns of displacement (and not just absence) that we see. Because hegemonic American culture takes both the ideology of mobility and the ideology of individualism seriously, explanations for nonmobility not only focus on the failure of individuals (because they are said to be inherently lazy or stupid or whatever), but shift the domain of discourse to arenas that are taken to be "locked into" individuals—gender, race, and ethnic origin.

Whatever the explanation (and again, this is a highly overdetermined phenomenon), one of the effects of jamming the cultural airwaves with respect to class is to be seen in what Richard Sennett and Jonathan Cobb have called "the hidden injuries of class" (1972). Poorer and less successful Americans tend to blame themselves for their failures and not to recognize the ways in which their chances for success were circumscribed from the outset. Another of the effects, I suggest, is the one to be documented in this chapter: a displacement of class strain and friction into other arenas of life, a displacement not without its costs for experience in those other arenas.

Class and the Social Geography of Gender and Sexual Practices

The particular pattern I want to focus on here is the displacement of class frictions into the discourse and practices of gender and sexual relations. The basic point, which emerged for me more or less accidentally as I read a set of American community studies with, initially, no particular agenda, is this: gender relations for both middle-class and working-class Americans (I did not look at elites) carry an enormous burden of quite antagonistic class meaning. To turn the point around, class discourse is submerged within, and spoken through, sexual discourse, taking "sex" here in the double English sense of pertaining to both gender and the erotic (see Ortner and Whitehead 1981). And while the general point of displacement holds for both middle-class and working-class discourse, it works differently in each case. I start with the working class.

(I should note here that I will use the present tense throughout the rest of this chapter, though the examples to be discussed run from the early fifties through the early eighties. The patterns in question seem to have been, with only minor variations, impressively durable.)

WORKING CLASS DISCOURSES OF SEX AND CLASS

I begin with the assumption that the classes are relationally constituted, that they define themselves always in implicit reference to the other(s). Thus, while we normally think of class relations as taking place between classes, in fact each class contains the other(s) within itself, though in distorted and ambivalent forms. This is particularly visible in the working class, where the class structure of the society is introjected into the culture of the working class itself, appearing as a problematic choice of "lifestyles" for working-class men and women— a choice between a lifestyle modeled essentially on middle-class values and practices and one modeled on more distinctively working- or lower-class values and practices.[7] This split, which is given different names by different ethnographers and different groups, shows up in virtually every study of both white and black working-class communities. One example may be seen in Herbert Gans's classic study (1962) of an urban working-class community in Boston. Gans sees two major styles of working-class life, which he labels the styles of the "routine seekers" and the "action seekers" (1962:28). To this basic split he adds two more extreme types: the "maladapteds" at the very bottom of the working class and the "middle-class mobiles" at the top of the class. The general pattern of these styles will be intuitively comprehensible to any American native. Routine seekers follow a relatively settled lifestyle centered on family and work. Action seekers, by contrast, live the "fast" life, centered importantly on relations with "the boys," the male peer group; family and work are avoided or minimized as much as possible. Of the two more extreme versions of this basic split, middle-class mobiles are similar to routine seekers except that they are more oriented, as the label suggests, toward actual upward mobility. Maladaptives are similar to action seekers but generally have a problem such as alcoholism or drug abuse that renders them more irredeemable.

To characterize the split within working-class culture in terms of activity (as in "action seekers") and passivity (as in "routine seekers") is reminiscent of Paul Willis's account of the culture of British working-class high school students (1977). Willis focused on the "lads," or the nonconformists, who divided the school between themselves and what they called the "ear'oles": "The term ear'ole itself connotes the passivity and absurdity of the school conformists for 'the lads.' It seems that they are always listening, never doing, never animated with their own internal life, but formless in rigid reception" (1977:14, see also Sennett and Cobb 1972:82).

The same pattern of lifestyle split, between a "middle-class" lifestyle (whether oriented toward actual upward mobility or not) and a working- or lower-class lifestyle, shows up in the black ghetto neighborhood studied by the Swedish anthropologist Ulf Hannerz:

> The people of Winston Street often describe themselves and their neighbors in the community as comprising two categories distinguished according to way of life. . . . Some refer to one category—in which they usually include themselves—as "respectable," "good people," or, more rarely and somewhat facetiously, as "model citizens." More seldom do they refer to this category as "middle class." . . . They use these labels to distinguish themselves from what they conceive of as their opposites, people they describe as "undesirables," "no good," "the rowdy bunch," "bums," or "trash." (1969:34–35)

In sum, there is a general tendency for working- or lower-class culture to embody within itself the split in society between the working and the middle class. This split appears as a subcultural typology of "styles": the action seekers versus the routine seekers, the lads versus the ear'oles, the respectables versus the undesirables.

From the actor's point of view the split in turn appears as a set of choices, a set of life possibilities between which a young man growing up within the working class will consciously or unconsciously choose. Here is where class, now translated as "lifestyle," intersects with the discourses and practices of gender and sexuality. For it appears overwhelmingly the case in working-class culture that women are symbolically aligned, from both the male point of view and, apparently, their own, with the "respectable," "middle-class" side of those oppositions and choices. Thus every sexual choice is symbolically also a class choice, for better or worse.

This pattern is again seen in virtually every ethnography of working-class culture. Gans describes it for the neighborhood he studied in Boston: "Marriage is a crucial turning point in the life of the West End boy. It is then that he must decide whether he is going to give up the boys on the corner for the new peer group of related siblings and in-laws—a decision related to and reflected in his choice of a mate" (1962:70). In the extreme instance, which is to say the instance of (would-be) mobility, the couple will move to the suburbs. Such a move is generally blamed (by "the boys") on the wife's ambitions (Gans 1962:53), and this may indeed be the case. Gans goes on to say that these kinds of pulls create a great deal of strain between husband and wife (1962:70).

David Halle, in his ethnography of chemical workers in Elizabeth, New Jersey (1984), reports many of the same patterns and explores them with great insight. His fine-grained ethnography shows that the perception of women as more "middle class" than men, and as aligned with middle-class values and practices, extends into (or emerges from) the workplace as well as the domestic situation. Within the single plant studied the men normally work in the production areas, while the women normally work in the office. The men's jobs are dirty and physical, while the women's jobs both allow and require them to be more dressed up and to remain clean throughout the day. Further, women in the office work more closely and directly with management. For all these reasons they are apparently symbolically associated with management (Halle 1984:61).

As Halle explored with male workers their own cultural category of "working man," he found that the term contained several meanings: it meant quite literally working, as opposed to not working (the very rich and the "welfare bums" are similar in not working at all); it meant hard, physical labor as opposed to soft, easy work; and it meant productive labor as opposed to purposeless paper pushing. To the male workers, even women with paid employment, including the clerical and office workers in the men's own plant, were not seen as "working" (1984:206):

RESEARCHER: How about secretaries? [i.e., are they "working persons"?]
WORKER: No! They often spend half the afternoon reading magazines. I've seen them through the window.

And in another interview (Halle 1984:207):

RESEARCHER: How about secretaries?
WORKER: No, they work in an office. . . . They just answer the phone and type letters.

Let me return to the issue of women as not merely displaying middle-class patterns (as in the cleanly dressed secretary) but of actually seeming to enforce such patterns on men. While it is the perception of "the boys" that it is women, as wives, who exert a middle-class pull on their husbands, this perception may have some basis in women's actual practice. Although Halle's information comes mostly from male informants, their claims are specific enough to have the ring of true reporting. Thus, many men say that their wives complain about their social status being too low and exert pressure on them to change their kinds of work, or at least their behavioral styles, in a more "middle-class" direction (Halle 1984:59). Husbands found this irritating, to say the least. Issues of behavioral style—how a man eats or speaks, for example—connect to (or are perceived as being connected to) lack of education, and are "particularly explosive since the overwhelming majority of workers are very sensitive about their lack of formal education" (60).

The pattern is essentially identical in the black neighborhood studied by Ulf Hannerz, who did talk to women as well as men. He found that while women recognized variation among men in terms of lifestyle, there was a general tendency to lump all men in the "nonrespectable" pool, and themselves implicitly in the respectable group (Hannerz 1969:97, 99). Nor are these symbolic alignments simply matters of "discourse" abstracted from lived experience. Both Halle and Hannerz discuss at some length the ways in which men's and women's perceptions of each other articulate with a pattern of often highly conflictful and unhappy gender relations. Although some of Halle's male informants (one suspects that Gans would have classified them as "routine seekers") felt that their wives' (real or imagined) middle-class inclinations "rescued them from the wild life-style of the male culture, a lifestyle they believe would in the end have been their downfall" (Halle 1984:64), this feeling was less common than its opposite—that women's real or supposed identification with middle-class ideals placed their husbands under a great deal of strain.

At this point class no longer appears as a choice of lifestyle but as an imposed pressure and constraint. Yet the imposition appears to come not from class "enemies"—the rich, the politicians, the pampered sons of the middle class—but from the men's own girlfriends and wives. I will return to this point below.

Given both the high rates of social mobility in America and the strong cultural emphasis on its possibility and desirability, each class has a characteristic stance on its implications. Moreover each class views the others not only, or even primarily, as antagonistic groups but as images of their hopes and fears for their own lives and futures. For the white working class it is the black working class (which is poorer and less secure than the white) that represents their worst fears for themselves; this, as much as any putative threat of economic competition, underlies much of white working-class racism where it appears. The middle class, in contrast, is a source of tremendous ambivalence from a working-class perspective. Middle-class status is highly desirable for its greater material affluence and security, but undesirable for all the ways in which its patterns are culturally "other," and for the ways in which upward mobility would pull one away from kin, friends, or neighborhood.

For the middle class the pattern of fears and desires is different. There is much less ambivalence about upward social mobility, since much of it would not involve significant changes of "culture." The "fear of falling," however (to borrow a phrase from Barbara Ehrenreich's excellent study of middle-class culture [1989]), is intense. This may be true particularly at the lower edge of the class, and particularly for new arrivals, but it seems to be a general and pervasive substrate of middle-class thought. If much of working-class culture can be understood as a set of discourses and practices embodying the ambivalence of upward mobility, much of middle-class culture can be seen as a set of discourses and practices embodying the terror of downward mobility.

In both cases the complex attitudes held about adjacent classes derive from the classes functioning as mirrors of these possibilities. Although the middle class and the working class may be inherently antagonistic as a result of their positioning within the capitalist productive order, in the phenomenology of class cultures the frictions between them seem largely to derive from this mirroring function. And for each class, the frictions are introjected into, and endlessly replayed through, social relations internal to the class itself.

My sense is that it is parent-child relations in the middle class that carry much of the burden of introjected "class struggle" and even class "war," comparable to the ways in which gender carries this burden in the working class. There is no doubt that gender carries a lot of this for the middle class as well, and I will come back to that in a moment. But it seems to me—and at this point I speak more from my experience as a native than from anything I have seen yet in ethnographies—that there is the kind of both chronic friction and explosive potential in middle-class parent-child relations that one sees in working-class gender relations (see especially Ehrenreich 1989: chapter 2).

At a practical level there is always the question of whether middle-class children will successfully retain the class standing the parents have provided them. As a result of this practical question, which revolves around issues of education, occupation, and (here is the intersection with gender) marriage choice, there are tremendous parental attempts to control their children's behavior, over a much longer span of time and to a much later age than in the working class. (Both Willis [1977:21–22] and Gans [1962:56–57] indicate that working-class parents do not attempt to impose, and especially to extend, these kinds of controls.) But if middle-class parents see their children as embodying the threat of a working-class future (for the children if not for themselves), and attempt to control them accordingly, adolescent children respond in kind. They criticize their parents' values, which is to say essentially class values, and they resist their parents' controls precisely through represen-tations of lower-class affiliation—language, hairstyle, clothing, music, and sometimes cross-class friendships and cross-class dating or sexual relation-ships. It is hardly a novel observation that much of middle-class adolescent culture is drawn both from "real" working-class culture (e.g., by way of the working-class origins of many rock groups) and from marketing fantasies of what working- or lower-class culture looks like. In any event, it is clear that the discourse of parent-child relations (specifically parent-child conflict) in the middle class, like the discourse of gender in the working class, is simulta-neously a class discourse. It draws on and feeds the fears and anxieties that make sense if we assume that the classes view each other as their own pasts and possible futures.

But, although parent-child relations carry a good bit of the burden of class antagonism or fear in the middle class, discourses on gender and sexuality are not without their own significant freight of class meanings. Here, however, the pattern is quite different from that seen in the working class. Where for the working class, class is, in effect, pulled into the subculture and mapped onto internal relations of gender and sexuality, for the middle class, gender and sexuality are projected out onto the world of class relations.[8] Specifically, the working class is cast as the bearer of an exaggerated sexuality, against which middle-class respectability is defined.

One of the best places to see these patterns is in predominantly middle-class high schools. They almost always contain at least some kids from working-class backgrounds, and the high-school ethnosociology tends to build distinctions around these differences, reproducing the split between respectable and nonrespectable that is so central to working-class culture. This split is called by endlessly different names in different schools. In my high school in the fifties, the terminology was inconsistent—the respectables were largely merged with the dominant ethnic category (Jews), while the non-respectables were usually called "hoods," a term that was apparently of near-national scope at that time. In the school studied by Gary Schwartz and Don Merten in the early seventies the terms were "socies" and hoods (1975). In the school studied by Penelope Eckert in the early eighties the terms were "jocks" and "burnouts" (1989). Whatever the labels the social category split marked by these terms is almost never recognized by the students as a class split, and the terms used for it almost never refer to class or even money differences—a good example of the taboo on class discourse in America. Nonetheless the split tends to map rather accurately onto differences that adults or parents or social scientists would recognize as class differences.

The distinctions between the two groups are marked in a whole range of ways, including clothing, language, haircuts, and attitudes toward teachers, schoolwork, and school citizenship. But for the middle-class adolescents one of the key dimensions of difference is a supposed difference in attitudes toward and practices of sex. Middle-class kids, both male and female, define working-class kids as promiscuous, highly experienced, and sexually uncon-strained. I give one ethnographic example; the pattern is so well known that it does not require extensive illustration. Schwartz and Merten studied sorority initiation rites in a middle-class American high school (1975). The high-school social system was divided by the sorority girls (who were at the top of it) into "socialites," or "socies," and "hoods" or "greasers." (The authors also identify an unnamed middle category that is neither really "hoody" nor cool enough to be among the "socies," but which is said generally to approve of "socie" values.)[9]

While the bulk of Schwartz's and Merten's article focuses on interpreting the sorority hazings as initiation rites that facilitate identity transformations of various kinds (which is doubtlessly true), the authors move into a discussion of the class dimensions of the categories toward the end. Here we see the ways in which class differences are largely represented as sexual differences:

> For socie girls, those who subscribe to the adolescent version of a middle-class way of life are morally acceptable; girls who follow the adolescent variant of a working-class way of life are morally contemptible. All of our socie informants felt that hoody girls tended to be promiscuous, sloppy, stupid, and unfriendly (Schwartz and Merten 1975:207).

Clothing and cosmetic differences are taken to be indexes of the differences in sexual morals between the girls of the two classes:

> The act of smearing [socie sorority] pledges with lipsticks on hell night [of the initiation rites] is a veiled reference to what socies believe is a most salient feature of the hoody cosmetic style, the use of makeup in ways that resemble the appearance of a slut. . . . Socies interpret hoody hairstyles, in which the hair is worn massed on top of the head and is held together by a liberal application of hair spray, as a sign of a lack of sexual restraint (Schwartz and Merten 1975:210).[10]

It is painfully ironic that the same girls who are taken to be "sluts" by middle-class sorority girls will be taken by their own men to be agents of middle-class values and resented as such. Here truly is a "hidden injury of class."[11]

As in the case of the working class this kind of sexual mapping of classes will also appear, at least to some middle-class actors, as a set of choices or possibilities for their own lives. There is both a similarity with and a difference from working-class patterns. For both groups, there is a sense that different women will pull men in different directions in class terms. For the working class the pattern, or at least the threat, tends to be generalized to all women, and men do not represent themselves as having a great deal of agency in the matter. For middle-class men, however, there seems to be more of a notion of choice. Women of various class positions appear as a kind of smorgasbord of sexual-cum-class possibilities, most of which are not likely to be realized, but all of which are apparently "good to think."[12] Although there might be some ethnographic work on this that I have not yet come across, the pattern is most clearly seen in certain American novels. This brings me to the final section of my discussion.

Fiction as Ethnography

Is ethnography fiction? If by that we mean that ethnography is always partial, always inadequate to the fullness of its object, and always colored by the author's interests in the broadest sense, then the answer is certainly yes. But if the question is meant to imply that in most ethnographies any resemblance to people living or dead is purely coincidental, then the answer, as even James Clifford would agree (1986:7), is certainly no, and the question is simply mischievous. Interestingly, while anthropologists increasingly ponder the fictionality of ethnography, a number of major American novelists (and some minor ones as well) seek to cast their fictions as ethnographies.[13] Saul Bellow sprinkles his novels with references to cultural and physical anthropology. The paragraph on Bellow at the front of *Humboldt's Gift* (1975) informs us— out of all the myriad personal and professional details it might have mentioned—that Bellow was an anthropology major as an undergraduate. And in Philip Roth's novel, *The Counterlife*, he essentially accuses himself of being an ethnographer.

In *The Counterlife*, Nathan Zuckerman, the character who stands in for Roth in many of his novels, sort of dies (I say "sort of dies" because it is something more complex than that, but I do not want to give away the plot), and his editor delivers a eulogy for him. Zuckerman had written a novel called *Carnovsky*, a fairly clear stand-in for Roth's famous (or infamous) novel, *Portnoy's Complaint*. The editor says of Zuckerman,

> On the evidence of *Carnovsky*, he would have made a good anthropologist; perhaps that's what he was. He lets the experience of the little tribe [the Jews of the Weequahic section of Newark], the suffering, isolated, primitive but warmhearted savages that he is studying, emerge in the description of their rituals and their artifacts and their conversations, and he manages, at the same time, to put his own "civilization," his own bias as a reporter—and his readers'—into relief against them (Roth 1988a:239).

In fact, Zuckerman/Roth has precisely the inverse problem of today's ethnographers (as represented in Clifford and Marcus 1986): Pretending to write fiction, he is accused of telling the truth. As the editor continues in the eulogy, "Why, reading *Carnovsky*, did so many people keep wanting to know, 'Is it fiction?' "—implying that Roth was simply writing the most thinly disguised autobiography. In his autobiography, wonderfully called *The Facts* (1988b), Roth feels compelled to deny this.

Philip Roth grew up in a self-described "lower middle-class" family, in my neighborhood of Newark, New Jersey. He graduated from my high school, Weequahic High School, in 1951. He is clearly a figure of great interest for my New Jersey project, at a whole range of levels. I do think he is a brilliant ethnographer (indeed, I think a good part of the great ethnography of America is in novels), but he is also, for purposes of the present essay, a great informant. In order to conclude my discussion of the ways in which class is spoken through images of gender and sexuality, I will look at Roth's two major Newark novels, *Goodbye, Columbus* and *Portnoy's Complaint*.

Roth's first book, *Goodbye, Columbus and Five Short Stories*, won the 1960 National Book Award for fiction. In the title story the narrator is a young Jewish man named Neil Klugman who works in the Newark public library and lives with his aunt and uncle in Newark. The aunt and uncle are clearly working class: among other indicators, they are described as going to Workman's Circle meetings.[14] Neil falls in love with Brenda Patimkin who, though also Jewish, has clearly moved far up the ladder of money and status in the middle class. Both the money and the status are signalled by the fact that her family lives in Short Hills (an expensive suburb to which Jews from Newark aspired to move if they could afford to do so). Brenda's parents disapprove of Neil, whose lower status is signalled largely through disparaging references to Newark. As the story progresses, Brenda worries about whether Neil will turn into the kind of person of whom her parents will approve, while Neil is ambivalent about whether he can or wants to do so. Nonetheless Neil and Brenda begin sleeping together, and Neil insists that she get a diaphragm. When Brenda goes back to Radcliffe in the fall, she leaves the diaphragm in her drawer and her mother finds it. Her parents are very upset, and Brenda feels she can no longer bring Neil into her house. The relationship is over.

The main story line is paralleled by the story of a little black boy who comes to the library where Neil works, to look again and again at a book of Gauguin paintings. For the boy these paintings are paradisiacal, and he looks at them with great longing: "These people, man, they sure does look cool. They ain't no yelling or shouting here, you could just see it . . . that's the fuckin life" (Roth 1960:37). Neil finds that he cares about the boy's interest in the pictures, and when another borrower tries to check out the book, Neil lies in order to keep it available in the stacks for the boy. But then Neil takes a vacation from the library to spend a week at the Patimkins' before Brenda goes back to school. When he returns, the book is checked out and the little boy never comes back. He assumes that the boy was disappointed about the book's being checked out, but he tries to tell himself that it is all for the best: "He was better off, I thought. No sense carrying dreams of Tahiti in your head, if you can't afford the fare" (1960:120).

That the story is explicitly about dreams and fears of mobility could not be much clearer. Yet it is a peculiarity of the narrative that Neil has, quite late in the story, what can only be described as a revelation, in which it comes to him as a great shock that he might have been engaged in social climbing. While waiting in New York City for Brenda to come back from her diaphragm fitting, Neil goes into St. Patrick's Cathedral and has a conversation with God about what he's been doing (Roth 1960:100).

> What is it I love, Lord? Why have I chosen? Who is Brenda? The race is to the swift. Should I have stopped to think?

> I was getting no answers but I went on. . . . Where do we meet [Lord]? Which prize is you?

> . . . I got up and walked outside, and the noise of Fifth Avenue met me with an answer:

> Which prize do you think, *schmuck*? Gold dinnerware, sporting-goods trees, nectarines, garbage disposals, bumpless noses, Patimkin Sink, Bonwit Teller—

The revelation is necessary, I would argue, because Roth has done what our cultural discourse always does—displaced the class meanings of his story, conscious though they are at one level, into domains of gender, race, and sex.

Roth's other major Newark novel, *Portnoy's Complaint*, was published in 1967. Although it was a huge best seller and made Roth a great deal of money, it did not win any awards. On the contrary it was actually banned from some libraries in the United States (and apparently in some places still is) for obscenity. The story takes the form of the narrator, Alexander Portnoy, talking to his psychiatrist about his psychological and sexual problems. There is little in the way of plot. At the time of the novel Portnoy is the assistant commissioner for the New York City "Commission on Human Opportunities" and, as he signals throughout the book, a kind of generalized liberal working on various poverty programs and the like. In speaking to his psychiatrist Portnoy rambles over his life till then—his relationships with his parents and with women.

A class framework is invoked at the beginning, through a language of ethnicity. Portnoy's father works for a large insurance company, which he holds in a certain awe but which he also loathes for its anti-Semitism. These feelings come together around the image of the president, an upper-class WASP named N. Everett Lindabury: "'Mr. Lindabury,' 'The Home Office' . . . my father made it sound to me like Roosevelt in the White House in Washington . . . and all the while how he hated their guts, Lindabury's particularly, with his corn-silk hair and his crisp New England speech, the sons in Harvard College and the daughters in finishing school, oh the whole pack of them up there in Massachusetts" (Roth 1967:8). Moreover, although his father is very good at selling insurance, it is clear that the company will never promote him because he is Jewish. Both the WASPness of N. Everett Lindabury and the Jewishness of Portnoy's father (and himself) have, in the context, clear class meanings. Whereas in *Goodbye, Columbus*, class signals were set up in part between Jews, in terms of where they lived and how much money they had, here the class structure is projected entirely onto other groups, and entirely in terms of ethnicity. The upper class is represented by WASPs, the middle class by Jews, and the lower class by other ethnics—Italians, Poles, Irish, African Americans.

The various classes/ethnicities in turn are, for Portnoy, personified most directly in terms of the women with whom he has sex. He is fascinated with non-Jewish women, at first with the working-class girls who live around his neighborhood and who are, not surprisingly, assumed to be—and sometimes are—sexually available. Later, when he leaves Newark and goes to college, and later still when he works in Washington on behalf of various good social causes, he becomes involved with upper-class WASP women, but he also continues to be involved with lower-class/non-Jewish women. At the actual time of the story he is just ending an affair with a woman whose father was, we are told in the first lines of her introduction, an illiterate coal miner in West Virginia.

Portnoy never has sex with a Jewish woman, or in the code of the story, with a woman of his own class. Since class appears as a matter of either discrimination, from above to below, or climbing, from below to above, but never as a matter of simply being where one is, and since sex for Roth is the idiom of these forms of class orientations, there can be no sex with Jewish—which is to say middle-class—women. This point may provide some insight into what is perhaps the most foregrounded aspect of Portnoy's sexuality in the book: his luxuriant masturbation. The masturbation that threads its way through the story, and that more than anything else generated the obscenity charges when the book first came out, seems to occupy the space created by the missing sex with women of Portnoy's own class.

Returning to women we can see that they form a kind of landscape of class/ethnic sexual possibilities. But there is more. Not only are the classes displaced onto different ethnicities, the classes/ethnicities in turn are projected through a geography of sexual practices: working-class girls are willing to do anything sexually, while WASPs apparently have problems with all but the most conventional forms of sex. In Portnoy's high school there was Bubbles Girardi, whose brother was a boxer and whose father drove a cab by day and a car for the mob by night. Bubbles performed various sex acts for Portnoy and his friends when no other girl they knew was available for sex at all. And now there is the Monkey, the daughter of the illiterate West Virginia coal miner. The Monkey, we are told several times, will do absolutely anything at all, including at one point hiring a prostitute to join them for a three-way sexual engagement.[15] The Monkey, though now a highly paid fashion model, is herself barely literate, bearing the scars of her own class origins. Alex finds himself falling in love with her but cannot imagine marrying this lower-class person. This is one of the things that has driven him to the psychiatrist.

The class/ethnicity of the WASP women, by contrast, is represented through repressed and conventional sexuality. Portnoy acquires his first WASP girlfriend, Kay ("Pumpkin") Campbell, in college. At first they do not have sexual intercourse at all: she is "the girl who has let me undo her brassiere and dry-hump her at the dormitory door" (Roth 1967:220). Later they evidently have sex and there is a pregnancy scare, but eventually the relationship breaks up because Kay will not convert to Judaism. With the other WASP woman in the book, Sarah Abbot Maulsby, nicknamed "the Pilgrim," sex is again completely conventional: "In bed? Nothing fancy, no acrobatics or feats of daring and skill" (1967:234). In particular Sarah Abbot Maulsby is unable or unwilling to practice oral sex on Alex, which upsets him in a way that is more than simple sexual rejection, as we shall see in a moment (1967:238).

Class is thus spoken through a language of sexual practices, as well as through languages of gender and ethnicity. As in the case of *Goodbye, Columbus*, an initial awareness of class as a major source of Portnoy's pain is systematically displaced and dispersed over several hundred pages of characters and activities that embody class but do not articulate it. But again, as in *Goodbye, Columbus*, there is a kind of waking up at the end, a kind of revelation about the underlying politics of his sexuality. It begins as Portnoy is talking to his psychiatrist about Sarah Abbott Maulsby: "What I'm saying, Doctor, is that I don't seem to stick my dick up these girls, as much as I stick it up their backgrounds" (Roth 1967:235). And then the story closes back onto his father's class/ethnic oppressions: "She could have been a Lindabury, don't you see? A daughter of my father's boss!" (1967:237). Moreover he decides that her resistance to oral sex with him was an act of class prejudice: "My father couldn't rise at Boston & Northeastern for the very same reason that Sally Maulsby wouldn't deign to go down on me! Where was the justice in this world?" (1967:238). And finally, explaining why he left her: "No, Sally Maulsby was just something nice a son once did for his dad. A little vengeance on Mr. Lindabury for all those nights and Sundays Jack Portnoy spent collecting down in the colored district. A little bonus extracted from Boston and Northeastern, for all those years of service, and exploitation" (1967:241).

Roth's female characters—from Portnoy's overcontrolling mother to a whole range of mostly characterless sex objects—leave a lot to be desired. Yet I think that a narrow analysis of Roth's works as texts on the bottomless sexism of a certain kind of male would miss precisely the point I have sought to make: there is sexism, to be sure, but it is all bound up with the narrator's experiences of (class) discrimination (or rather his pain over his father's experiences thereof), as well as with his own (rather feeble) efforts to do good in the world. This is not to reduce sexism to a kind of eroticized classism. But it is to say that, if Freud and Foucault have taught us that there is a sexual underside to all social difference, we must also recognize that there is at least potentially a social-power underside to all sexual difference. Without denying the possibilities of a systematic feminist critique of Roth and the more general patterns of masculinity that he may represent, this is what I have sought to show.

At the same time, as I said earlier, such displacements are not without their costs. If class is displaced into other arenas of social life, then to that extent these other arenas must be carrying a burden of what might be called "surplus antagonism," over and above whatever historical and structural frictions they embody in their own terms. We saw this clearly in the case of working-class gender relations, both black and white. Frictions between men and women had as much to do with their symbolic (and perhaps subjectively embraced) class alignments as with anything related to their gender roles as such. Women were seen as middle-class agents within the working class, a perception that emerged on the light side in jokes, but on the dark side in a kind of bitterness heard in many informants' comments about their marriages. A similar kind of surplus antagonism may be discovered, I think, in race and ethnic frictions, but these questions must be reserved for another paper.

A Short Conclusion

This essay has been an exercise in the critical interpretation of cultural formations. We have seen how class, as a major form of inequality in the United States, is systematically rendered unrecognizable through processes of discursive translation, displacement, and introjection. The Freudian language was originally accidental, seeming to me simply a handy vocabulary for talking about symbolic processes. But in the end it struck me that such language was more appropriate than I thought, for it points to the fact that such displacements do not simply affect cognitive processes, hampering the recognition and awareness of class. They also have an emotional impact, eliciting pain and stress in selves and in relationships.

Class warfare may be dead, or certainly quiescent, at the moment. But it seems to live on in the cruel language and the cruel acts among gendered and classed actors that I have examined in this essay. Working-class men feel belittled by their wives' lack of respect, with wives implicitly or explicitly viewing their husbands as inferior in class terms. Elite sorority girls are cruelly hazed, partly through having to perform acts of gendered and classed lowness. (The representations involved in the hazing, involving caricatures of style seen among working-class young women, would be very hurtful to those young women as well, but they do not have access to the elite precincts of sororities. Rather they get the secondary signals of being looked down on in the everyday life of school.) And finally Alexander Portnoy conducts his sex life through a screen of class markers, abandoning women for being both too high and too low in class terms, and calling his most recent lover, a daughter of an illiterate coal miner, "the Monkey." The displacement of class meanings into languages of gender and sexuality may take place at the level of discourse but discourse, as Foucault has insisted, is never divorced from real practices and real feelings.

CHAPTER 2

Resistance and the Problem of Ethnographic Refusal

This essay traces the effects of what I call ethnographic refusal on a series of studies surrounding the subject of resistance.[1] I argue that many of the most influential studies of resistance are severely limited by the lack of an ethnographic perspective. Resistance studies in turn are meant to stand in for a great deal of interdisciplinary work being done these days within and across the social sciences, history, literature, and cultural studies.

Ethnography of course means many things. Minimally, however, it has always meant the attempt to understand another life world using the self—as much of it as possible—as the instrument of knowing. As is by now widely known, ethnography has come under a great deal of internal criticism within anthropology (see especially Gupta and Feruson 1992, 1997), but this minimal definition has not for the most part been challenged.

Classically, this kind of understanding has been closely linked with fieldwork, in which the whole self physically and in every other way enters the space of the world the researcher seeks to understand. Yet implicit in much of the recent discussions of ethnography is something I wish to make explicit here: that the ethnographic stance (as we may call it) is as much an intellectual (and moral) positionality—a constructive and interpretive mode—as it is a bodily process in space and time. Thus, in a recent useful discussion of "ethnography and the historical imagination," John and Jean

Comaroff (1992) spend relatively little time on ethnography in the sense of fieldwork but a great deal of time on ways of reading historical sources ethnographically, that is, partly as if they had been produced through fieldwork.

What, then, is the ethnographic stance, whether based in fieldwork or not? It is first and foremost a commitment to what Geertz has called "thickness," to producing understanding through richness, texture, and detail, rather than parsimony, refinement, and (in the sense used by mathematicians) elegance. The forms that ethnographic thickness have taken have of course changed over time. There was a time when thickness was perhaps synonymous with exhaustiveness, producing the almost unreadably detailed descriptive ethnography, often followed by the famous "Another Pot from Old Oraibi" kind of journal article. Later, thickness came to be synonymous with holism, the idea that the object under study was "a" highly integrated "culture" and that it was possible to describe the entire system or at least fully grasp the principles underlying it.

Holism in this sense has also been under attack for some time, and most anthropologists today recognize both the hubris of the holistic vision and the innumerable gaps and fissures in all societies, including the so-called premodern societies that were imagined to be more integrated and whole than fragmented modern societies. Yet I would argue that thickness (with traces of both exhaustiveness and holism) remains at the heart of the ethnographic stance. Nowadays, issues of thickness focus primarily on issues of (relatively exhaustive) contextualization. George Marcus (1986), for example, examines the ways in which ethnography in the local and usually bodily sense must be contextualized within the global processes of the world system. And the Comaroffs emphasize the need always to contextualize the data produced through fieldwork and archival research within the forms of practice within which they took shape: "If texts are to be more than literary topoi, scattered shards from which we presume worlds, they have to be anchored in the processes of their production, in the orbits of connection and influence that give them life and force" (1992:34). Martha Kaplan and John Kelly (1994) also insist on a kind of density of contextualization, in their case by articulating the characteristics of the dialogic space within which a political history must be seen as unfolding.

If the ethnographic stance is founded centrally on (among other things, of course) a commitment to thickness, and if thickness has taken and still takes many forms, what I am calling ethnographic refusal involves a refusal of thickness, a failure of holism or density which itself may take various forms. This study, then, is about some of the forms of ethnographic refusal, some of its consequences, and some of its reasons, organized around the topic of resistance. A few words first about resistance.

Resistance and Domination

Once upon a time, resistance was a relatively unambiguous category, half of the seemingly simple binary, domination versus resistance. Domination was a relatively fixed and institutionalized form of power; resistance was essentially organized opposition to power institutionalized in this way. This binary began to be refined (but not abolished) by questioning both terms. On the one hand Foucault (for example, 1978) drew attention to less institutionalized, more pervasive, and more everyday forms of power. On the other hand James Scott (1985) drew attention to less organized, more pervasive, and more everyday forms of resistance. With Scott's delineation of the notion of "everyday forms of resistance" (1985), in turn, the question of what is or is not resistance became much more complicated.[2] When a poor man steals from a rich man, is this resistance or simply a survival strategy? The question runs through an entire collection of essays devoted to everyday forms of resistance (Scott and Kerkvliet 1986), and different authors attempt to answer it in different ways. Michael Adas (1986), for example, constructs a typology of forms of everyday resistance, the better to help us place what we are seeing. Brian Fegan (1986) concentrates on the question of intention: If a relatively conscious intention to resist is not present, the act is not one of resistance. Still others (e.g., Stoler 1986; Cooper 1992) suggest that the category itself is not very helpful and that the important thing is to attend to a variety of transformative processes, in which things do get changed, regardless of the intentions of the actors or of the presence of very mixed intentions.

In the long run I might agree with Stoler and Cooper, but for the moment I think resistance, even at its most ambiguous, is a reasonably useful category, if only because it highlights the presence and play of power in most forms of relationship and activity. Moreover we are not required to decide once and for all whether any given act fits into a fixed box called resistance. As Marx well knew, the intentionalities of actors evolve through praxis, and the meanings of the acts change, both for the actor and for the analyst. In fact the ambiguity of resistance and the subjective ambivalence of the acts for those who engage in them are among the things I wish to emphasize in this essay. In a relationship of power the dominant often has something to offer, and sometimes a great deal (though always of course at the price of continuing in power). The subordinate thus has many grounds for ambivalence about resisting the relationship. Moreover there is never a single, unitary subordinate, if only in the simple senses that subaltern groups are internally divided by age, gender, status, and other forms of difference and that occupants of differing subject positions will have different—even opposed, but still legitimate—perspectives on the situation. (The question of whether even a single person is "unitary" is addressed later in this essay.)

Both the psychological ambivalence and the social complexity of resistance have been noted by several, but not enough, observers.[3] Brian Fegan talks about being "constantly baffled by the contradictory ways peasants talked about the tenancy system in general, or about their own relations with particular landlords" (1986:92). Moreover, the peasants of Central Luzon whom Fegan studied were psychologically uncomfortable with both acts of resistance and acts of collaboration: "Many men talking to me privately about the stratagems they use to survive, broke off to say they found theft from the landlord, working for the landlord as guards, arms dealing, etc., distasteful. But what else could a person with children do?" (1986:93).

In a different vein, Christine Pelzer White says that "we must add an inventory of 'everyday forms of peasant *collaboration*' to balance our list of 'everyday forms of peasant resistance': both exist, both are important" (1986: 56). She goes on to present examples from postrevolutionary Vietnam of varying alliances between sectors with different interests, including "the state and peasantry against the local elite[,] . . . the peasants and the local elite against the state[, and] . . . the state and individuals [mostly women] against [male] household heads" (1986:60).

Closely related to questions of the psychological and sociopolitical complexity of resistance and nonresistance (and to the need for thick ethnography) is the question of authenticity. Authenticity is another highly problematic term, insofar as it seems to presume a naive belief in cultural purity, in untouched cultures whose histories are uncontaminated by those of their neighbors or of the West. I make no such presumptions; nonetheless, there must be a way to talk about what the Comaroffs call "the endogenous historicity of local worlds" (1992:27), in which the pieces of reality, however much borrowed from or imposed by others, are woven together through the logic of a group's own locally and historically evolved bricolage. This is what I mean by authenticity in the discussions that follow, as I turn to a consideration of some of the recent literature on resistance.

I should note here that the works to be discussed constitute a very selected and partial set, and I make no claim to cover the entire literature. In this era of interdisciplinarity scholarly exhaustiveness is more unattainable than ever, but, more important, the works are selected here either because they have been very influential or because they illustrate a fairly common problem or both. In any event, the point of the discussion is to examine a number of problems in the resistance literature arising from the stance of ethnographic refusal. The discussion will be organized in terms of three forms of such refusal, which I will call sanitizing politics, thinning culture, and dissolving actors.

Sanitizing Politics

It may seem odd to start off by criticizing studies of resistance for not containing enough politics. If there is one thing these studies examine, it is politics, front and center. Yet the discussion is usually limited to the politics of resistance, that is, to the relationship between the dominant and the subordinate (see also Cooper 1992:4). If we are to recognize that resistors are doing more than simply opposing domination, more than simply producing a virtually mechanical reaction, then we must go the whole way. They have their *own* politics—not just between chiefs and commoners or landlords and peasants—but within all the local categories of friction and tension: men and women, parents and children, and seniors and juniors; inheritance conflicts among brothers; struggles of succession and wars of conquest between chiefs; struggles for primacy between religious sects; and on and on.

It is the absence of analysis of these forms of internal conflict in many resistance studies that gives them an air of romanticism, which Lila Abu-Lughod (1990) has correctly charged. Let me take one example, from a fine book that I admire on many other counts: Inga Clendinnen's *Ambivalent Conquests: Maya and Spaniard in Yucatan, 1517–1570* (1987). Clendinnen recognizes that there were Maya chiefs who had significant advantages of material resources, political power, and social precedence. She also recognizes that, in this sort of polity, chiefs had many obligations in turn to their subjects, including the redistribution of (some) wealth through feasts and hospitality and the staging of rituals for the collective well-being. Yet the degree to which she emphasizes the reciprocity over the asymmetry of the relationship systematically excludes from the reader's view a picture of some of the serious exploitation and violence of the Mayan political economy. Chiefs engaged in "extravagant and casual taking" (143), "were allocated the most favoured land for the making of *milpa*" (144), and "were given the lords' share of the game taken in a communal hunt [and] levied from the professional hunters" (144); their land was worked by war captives, and their domestic system was maintained by "female slaves and concubines" (144). Yet Clendinnen balances the mention of each of those instances of systematic exploitation with some mention of how much the chiefs gave in return, culminating in an account of a ritual to protect the villagers from threatened calamity: "In those experiences, when the life of the whole village was absorbed in the ritual process, men learnt that the differences between priest, lord and commoner were less important than their shared dependence on the gods, and the fragility of the human order" (147).

Clendinnen goes on to say (1987:47) that "the cost of all this (although it is far from clear that the Maya regarded it as a cost) was war," which was waged between chiefs of neighboring groups. In war "noble captives were killed for the gods; the rest, men, women and children, were enslaved, and the men sold out of the country" (148). What is wrong with this picture? In the first place one presumes that some Maya—the captives who were to be executed, and the men, women, and children who were enslaved, not to mention everyone else in the society who had to live with the permanent possibility of such violence —"regarded it as a cost." In the second place Clendinnen never puts together the pieces of her account to show that the sense of "shared dependence" of chiefs and commoners, insofar as it was successfully established at all, was in large part a product of the displacement of exploitation and violence from the chief's own subjects to those of his neighbors.

There seems a virtual taboo on putting these pieces together, as if to give a full account of the Mayan political order, good and bad, would be to give some observers the ammunition for saying that the Maya deserved what they got from the Spanish. But this concern is ungrounded. Nothing about Mayan politics, however bloody and exploitative, would condone the looting, killing, and cultural destruction wrought by the Spanish. But a more thorough and critical account of precolonial Mayan politics would presumably generate a different picture of the subsequent shape of the colonial history of the region, including the subsequent patterns of resistance and nonresistance. At the very least it would respect the ambivalent complexity of the Maya world as it existed both at that time and in the present.[4]

The most glaring arena of internal political complexity glossed over by most of these studies is the arena of gender politics.[5] This is a particularly vexed question. Members of subordinate groups who want to call attention to gender inequities in their own groups are subject to the accusation that they are undermining their own class or subaltern solidarity, not supporting their men, and playing into the hands of the dominants. "First-world" feminist scholars who do the same are subject to sharp attacks from "third-world" feminist scholars on the same grounds (see C. Mohanty 1988). It seems elitist to call attention to the oppression of women within their own class or racial group or culture when that class or racial group or culture is being oppressed by another group.

These issues have come into sharp focus in the debates surrounding *sati*, or widow burning, in colonial India (Spivak 1988; Jain, Misra, and Srivastava 1987; Mani 1987). One of the ways in which the British justified their own dominance was to point to what they considered barbaric practices, such as sati, and to claim that they were engaged in a civilizing mission that would save Indian women from these practices. Gayatri Chakravorty Spivak has ironically characterized this situation as one in which "white men are saving brown women from brown men" (1988:296). Thus analysts who might want to investigate the ways in which sati was part of a larger configuration of male dominance in nineteenth-century Indian society cannot do so without seeming to subscribe to the discourse of the colonial administrators. The attempts to deal with this particular set of contradictions have only multiplied the contradictions.

Overall, the lack of an adequate sense of prior and ongoing politics *among* subalterns must inevitably contribute to an inadequate analysis of resistance itself. Many people do not get caught up in resistance movements, and this is not simply an effect of fear (as James Scott generally argues [1985, 1990]), naive enthrallment to the priests (as Friedrich [1985] argues about many of the nonresisting Mexican peasants), or narrow self-interest. Nor does it make collaborators of all the nonparticipants. Finally, individual acts of resistance, as well as large-scale resistance movements, are often themselves conflicted, internally contradictory, and affectively ambivalent, in large part due to these internal political complexities.

The impulse to sanitize the internal politics of the dominated must be understood as fundamentally romantic. As a partial antidote to this widespread tendency it might be well to reintroduce the work of the so-called structural Marxists in anthropology and their descendants. Structural Marxism (the Bloch 1975 reader is a good place to start; see also Meillassoux 1981 and Terray 1972) took shape as a response to this romanticizing tendency within the field of anthropology and as an attempt to understand non-Western and precapitalist forms of inequality on the analogy with Marx's analysis of class within capitalism. Tackling societies that would have been categorized as egalitarian precisely because they lacked class or caste, structural Marxists were able to tease out the ways in which such things as the apparent benevolent authority of elders or the apparent altruism and solidarity of kin are often grounded in systematic patterns of exploitation and power.

The structural Marxist project took shape at roughly the same time as did feminist anthropology.[6] The two together made it difficult for many anthropologists, myself included, to look at even the simplest society ever again without seeing a politics every bit as complex, and sometimes every bit as oppressive, as those of capitalism and colonialism.[7] As anthropologists of this persuasion began taking the historic turn, it seemed impossible to understand the histories of these societies, including (but not limited to) their histories under colonialism or capitalist penetration, without understanding how those external forces interacted with these internal politics. Sahlins's account (1981) of the patterns of accommodation and resistance in play between Hawaiians and Europeans in the eighteenth and nineteenth centuries; some of Wolf's discussions in *Europe and the People without History* (1982); my own history (1989) of Sherpa religious transformations, linking indigenous politics and culture with larger regional (Nepal state and British Raj) dynamics; Richard Fox's study (1985) of the evolution of Sikh identity under colonialism —all of these show that an understanding of political authenticity, of the people's own forms of inequality and asymmetry, is not only not incompatible with an understanding of resistance but is in fact indispensable to such an understanding.

Thinning Culture

Just as subalterns must be seen as having an authentic, and not merely reactive, politics, so they must be seen as having an authentic, and not merely reactive, culture. The culture concept in anthropology has, like ethnography, come under heavy attack in recent years, partly for assumptions of timelessness, homogeneity, uncontested sharedness, and the like that were historically embedded in it and in anthropological practice more generally. Yet those assumptions are not by any means intrinsic to the concept, which can be (re)mobilized in powerful ways without them. Indeed a radical reconceptualization of culture, including both the historicization and politicization of the concept, has been going on at least since the mid-1980s in anthropology, and the attacks upon its traditional form are by now simply overkill (see Dirks, Eley, and Ortner 1994). In any event like James Clifford (1988:10), one of the major figures in the attack on the concept of culture, I do not see how we can do without it. The only alternative to recognizing that subalterns have a certain prior and ongoing cultural authenticity is to view subaltern responses to domination as ad hoc and incoherent, springing not from their own senses of order, justice, and meaning, but only from some set of ideas called into being by the situation of domination itself.

Cultural thinning is characteristic of some of the most influential studies of resistance currently on the scene.[8] Some of the problems with this tendency may be brought into focus through a consideration of the way in which religion is (or is not) handled in some of these studies. I do not mean to suggest by this that religion is equivalent to all of culture. Nonetheless, religion is always a rich repository of cultural beliefs and values and often has close affinities with resistance movements as well. Let us then look at the treatment of religion in a number of resistance studies before turning to the question of culture more generally.

In one of the founding texts of the Subaltern Studies school of history, for example, Ranajit Guha (1988) emphasizes the importance of recognizing and not disparaging the religious bases of tribal and peasant rebellions. Indeed this is one of the central threads of Subaltern Studies writings, a major part of its effort to recognize the authentic cultural universe of subalterns, from which their acts of resistance grew. Yet the degree to which the treatment of religion in these studies is actually cultural, that is, is actually an effort to illuminate the conceptual and affective configurations within which the peasants are operating, is generally minimal.[9] Rather, the peasant is endowed with something called "religiosity," a kind of diffuse consciousness that is never further explored as a set of ideas, practices, and feelings built into the religious universe the peasant inhabits.

Guha and others in his group are jousting with some Marxist Indian historians who share with bourgeois modernization theorists a view of religion as backward. The Subaltern Studies writers, in contrast, want to respect and validate peasant religiosity as an authentic dimension of subaltern culture, out of which an authentically oppositional politics could be and was constructed. Yet Guha's own notion of peasant religiosity still bears the traces of Marx's hostility toward religion, defining "religious consciousness . . . as a massive demonstration of self-estrangement" (1988:78). In addition, instead of exploring and interpreting this religiosity of the rebels in any substantive way, he makes a particular textual move to avoid this, relegating to an appendix extracts of the peasants' own accounts of the religious visions that inspired their rebellion.

A similar casualness about religion, while paying it lip service, is evident in James Scott's *Weapons of the Weak* (1985). The point can be seen again not only in what Scott says and does not say but in the very shape of his text. There is no general discussion of the religious landscape of the villagers, and the discussion of religious movements in his area, many of which had significant political dimensions, is confined to a few pages toward the end of the book (332–35). During Scott's fieldwork a number of rumors of religio-political prophecies circulated in his area, as well as a "flying letter" containing similar prophecies. Like the testimonies of Guha's rebels, this letter is reproduced, unanalyzed, in an appendix. The fact that "rarely a month goes by without a newspaper account of the prosecution of a religious teacher accused of propagating false doctrines . . ." is also relegated to a footnote (335).

But cultural thinning, as noted above, need not be confined to marginalizing religious factors, nor is it practiced only by nonanthropologists (like Guha and Scott). In his landmark work, *Europe and the People without History* (1982), Eric Wolf devotes a scant five pages at the end of the book to the question of culture, largely in order to dismiss it. And in his superb study of the Sikh wars against the British (1985), Richard Fox similarly, and much more extensively, argues against the idea that culture informs, shapes, and underpins resistance at least as much as it emerges situationally from it.

There are a number of different things going on here. In part Wolf and Fox (and perhaps some of the others) are writing from a sixties-style materialist position. Sixties-style materialism (in anthropology at least) was opposed to giving culture any sort of active role in the social and historical process, other than mystifying the real (that is, material) causes of formations and events. At the same time, however, Wolf's and Fox's positions converge with later, and not necessarily materialist, criticisms of the culture concept (for example, Clifford and Marcus 1986) as homogenizing, dehistoricizing, and reifying the boundaries of specific groups or communities.

Coming from a different direction, Raymond Williams (1977) and other Birmingham cultural studies scholars (for example, Hall and Jefferson 1976) were actually revitalizing the culture concept. Williams specifically wanted to overcome the split between materialism and idealism and to focus on the ways in which structures of exploitation and domination are simultaneously material and cultural. He approached this through Gramsci's notion of hegemony, which Williams defined as something very close to the classic anthropological concept of culture but more politicized, more saturated with the relations of power, domination, and inequality within which it takes shape. This was healthy for the culture concept and for an anthropology that had moved significantly beyond the oppositions of the sixties. But it raised the old specter of "mystification" and "false consciousness." If domination operates in part culturally, through ideas and—in Williams's phrase—"structures of feeling," then people may accept and buy into their own domination, and the possibility of resistance may be undermined. Further, as James Scott argued, analysts who emphasize hegemony in this relatively deep, culturally internalized, sense are likely to fail to uncover those "hidden transcripts" of resistance and those non-obvious acts and moments of resistance that do take place (Scott 1990).

In fact, of course, in any situation of power there is a mixture of cultural dynamics. To some extent, and for a variety of good and bad reasons, people often do accept the representations that underwrite their own domination. At the same time they also preserve alternative "authentic" traditions of belief and value that allow them to see through those representations. Paul Willis's now classic book, *Learning to Labour* (1977), is particularly valuable in addressing this mixture of hegemony and authenticity involved in relationships of power. Willis's discussion of the ways in which the subculture of the working-class lads embodies both "penetrations" of the dominant culture and limitations on those penetrations—limitations deriving from the lads' own subcultural perspectives on gender—is highly illuminating. Martha Kaplan and John D. Kelly (1994) similarly underscore the cultural complexity of power and resistance. Drawing on Mikhail Bakhtin and, less explicitly, on Marshall Sahlins, Kaplan and Kelly frame their study of colonial Fiji as a study of contending discourses within a dialogic space. Setting aside, for the most part, the category of resistance, they insist on the thickness of the cultural process in play in colonial "zones of transcourse" (129), where "multiple grammars operate through contingently categorized people" (127). The result is a complex but illuminating picture of shifting loyalties, shifting alliances, and above all shifting categories, as British, native Fijians, and Fiji Indians contended for power, resources, and legitimacy (see also Kaplan 1990; Kelly and Kaplan 1992; Orlove 1991; Turner 1991 and n.d.).

Indeed a strong alternative tradition of resistance studies shows clearly that cultural richness does not undermine the possibility of seeing and understanding resistance. Quite the contrary: This tradition allows us to understand better both resistance and its limits. Many of the great classics of social history —for example, E. P. Thompson's *The Making of the English Working Class* (1966) and Eugene Genovese's *Roll, Jordan, Roll* (1976)—are great precisely because they are culturally rich, providing deep insight not only into the fact of resistance but into its forms, moments, and absences. Other outstanding examples of the genre include Clendinnen's *Ambivalent Conquest* (despite its weakness on Maya politics discussed above), William H. Sewell Jr.'s *Work and Revolution in France* (1980), and Jean Comaroff's *Body of Power, Spirit of Resistance* (1985).

Dissolving Subjects

The question of the relationship of the individual person or subject to domination carries the resistance problematic to the level of consciousness, subjectivity, intentionality, and identity. This question has taken a particular form in debates surrounding, once again, the Subaltern Studies school of historians. I should say here that I do not launch so much criticism against the Subaltern Studies historians because they are, in Guha's term, "terrible." On the contrary I find myself returning to their work because much of it is insightful and provocative and also because it is situated at that intersection of anthropology, history, and literary studies that so many anthropologists (and others) find themselves occupying, often awkwardly, in contemporary scholarly work.[10]

In any event Gayatri Chakravorty Spivak (1988a, 1988b) has taken the

Subaltern Studies school to task for creating a monolithic category of sub-altern who is presumed to have a unitary identity and consciousness. Given my arguments about the internal complexity of subaltern politics and culture made above, I would certainly agree with this point. Yet Spivak and others who deploy a certain brand of poststructuralist (primarily Derridean) anal-ysis go to the opposite extreme, dissolving the subject entirely into a set of "subject effects" that have virtually no coherence. Since these writers are still concerned with subalternity in some sense, they themselves wind up in in-coherent positions with respect to resistance.

Let me say again that in some ways I sympathize with what they are trying to do, which is to introduce complexity, ambiguity, and contradiction into our view of the subject in ways that I have argued above must be done with politics and culture (and indeed resistance). Yet the particular poststructural-ist move they make toward accomplishing this goal paradoxically destroys the object (the subject) who should be enriched, rather than impoverished, by this act of introducing complexity.

This final form of ethnographic refusal may be illustrated by examining an article entitled " 'Shahbano,' " on a famous Indian court case (Pathak and Rajan 1989). The authors, who acknowledge their debt to Spivak's work, address the case of a Muslim Indian woman called Shahbano, who went to civil court to sue for support from her husband after a divorce. Although the court awarded her the support she sought, the decision set off a national controversy of major proportions because the court's award (and indeed Shahbano's decision to bring the case to a civil court in the first place) contro-verted local Islamic divorce law. In the wake of the controversy Shahbano wrote an open letter to the court rejecting the award and expressing her solidarity with her Muslim coreligionists.

The authors' argument about the case runs as follows. The court's award, as well as the larger legal framework within which it was made, operated through a discourse of protection for persons who are seen to be weak. But "to be framed by a certain kind of discourse is to be objectified as the 'other,' represented without the characteristic features of the 'subject,' sensibility and/or volition" (Pathak and Rajan 1989:563). Within the context of such discursive subjectification, the appropriate notion of resistance is simply the "refusal of subjectification" (571), the refusal to occupy the category being foisted upon oneself. Shahbano's shifting position on her own case—first seeking, then rejecting, the award—represented such a refusal of subjectification, the only one open to her, given her situation. "To live with what she cannot control, the female subaltern subject here responds with a discontinuous and apparently contradictory subjectivity" (572). But "her apparent inconstancy or changeability must be interpreted as her refusal to occupy the subject position [of being protected] offered to her" (572).

Basically I agree with the authors' argument that every moment in the developing situation shifted to the foreground a different aspect of Shahbano's multiplex identity as a woman, as poor, as a Muslim. Indeed it does not require sophisticated theorizing to recognize that every social being has a life of such multiplicity and that every social context creates such shifting between foreground and background. I also agree (although the authors never quite put it this way) that, for certain kinds of compounded powerlessness (female *and* poor *and* of minority status), "the refusal of subjectification" may be the only strategy available to the subject. Yet there are several problems with the interpretation that need to be teased out.

First, returning to an earlier discussion in this essay, there is an inadequate analysis of the internal politics of the subaltern group—in this case, of the gender and ethnic politics of the Muslim community surrounding Shahbano. The authors make it clear that this is disallowed, for it would align anyone who made such an argument with the general discourse of protection and with the specific politics of the Hindu court vis-à-vis the minority Muslims: Transforming Spivak's aphorism cited earlier, the situation is one in which "Hindu men are saving Muslim women from Muslim men" (Pathak and Rajan 1989:566), and any author who addresses Muslim gender politics moves into the same position.

Yet one cannot help but feel a nagging suspicion about the on-the-ground politics surrounding Shahbano's open letter rejecting the court's award in the name of Muslim solidarity. Is the "refusal to occupy the subject position offered to her" (1989:572) an adequate account of what happened here, or might we imagine some rather more immediately lived experience of intense personal pressures from significant social others—kin, friends, neighbors, male and female—who put pressure on Shahbano in the name of their own agendas to renounce a monetary award that she desperately needed and had been seeking for ten years? Might one not say that "her refusal to occupy the subject position offered to her"—the only kind of agency or form of resistance accorded her by the authors—is the real effect in view here, that is, the (analytic) by-product, rather than the form, of her agency? In my reading, Shahbano was attempting to be an agent, to pursue a coherent agenda, and rather creatively at that. The shifting quality of her case is not to be found in her shifting identity (whether essentialized as subaltern consciousness or seen as strategic) but in the fact that she is at the low end of every form of power in the system and is being quite actively pushed around by other, more powerful, agents.

This reading brings us to the second problem with the discussion, and here again we must turn textual analysis against the authors' own text. The whole point of the poststructuralist move is to de-essentialize the subject, to get away from the ideological construct of "that unified and freely choosing individual who is the normative male subject of Western bourgeois liberalism" (Pathak and Rajan 1989:572). And indeed the freely choosing individual is an ideological construct, in multiple senses—because the person is culturally (and socially, historically, politically) constructed; because few people have the power to freely choose very much; and so forth. The question here, however, is how to get around this ideological construct and yet retain some sense of human agency, the capacity of social beings to interpret and morally evaluate their situation and to formulate projects and try to enact them.

The authors of " 'Shahbano' " realize that this is a problem: "Where, in all these discursive displacements, is Shahbano the woman?" (Pathak and Rajan 1989:565). But they specifically refuse to attend to her as a person, subject, agent, or any other form of intentionalized being with her own hopes, fears, desires, projects. They have only two models for such attending—psychological perspectives that attempt to tap her " 'inner' being" or a perspective that assumes "individualized and individualistic" heroic resistors—and they reject both (570). Instead their strategy is to focus on the mechanical interaction of a variety of disembodied forces: "multiple intersections of power, discursive displacements, discontinuous identities refusing subjectification, the split legal subject" (577). Thus, despite certain disclaimers at the end of the article, Shahbano as subject (or agent? or person?) quite literally disappears. The irrelevance of her understandings and intentions (not to mention her social universe and her history) to this analytic project is starkly brought home by the authors' own textual strategy of refusing to reproduce and interpret two press interviews that Shahbano gave, one to a newspaper and another on national television. The authors say, "We have not privileged these as sources of her subjectivity" (570). In fact they have not even presented them.

The de(con)struction of the subject in this way cannot be the only answer to the reified and romanticized subject of many resistance studies. On the contrary the answer to the reified and romanticized subject must be an actor understood as more fully socially and culturally constructed from top to bottom. The breaks and splits and incoherencies of consciousness, no less than the integrations and coherencies, are equally products of cultural and historical formation. Indeed, one could question whether the splits and so forth should be viewed as incoherencies or simply as alternative forms of coherence; not to do so implies that they are a form of damage. Of course oppression is damaging, yet the ability of social beings to weave alternative, and sometimes brilliantly creative, forms of coherence across the damages is one of the heartening aspects of human subjectivity (see also Cooper's [1992] critique of Fanon).

A similar point may be made with respect to agency. Agency is not an entity that exists apart from cultural construction (nor is it a quality one has only when one is whole or when one is an individual). Every culture, every subculture, every historical moment, constructs its own forms of agency, its own modes of enacting the process of reflecting on the self and the world and of acting simultaneously within and upon what one finds there. To understand where Shahbano or any other figure in a resistance drama is coming from, one must explore the particularities of all these constructions, as both cultural and historical products, and as personal creations building on those precipitates of culture and history.

A brilliant example of this alternative perspective may be seen in Ashis Nandy's *The Intimate Enemy: Loss and Recovery of the Self under Colonialism* (1983). Nandy begins by exploring the homology between sexual and political dominance as this took shape in the context of British colonialism in India. He then goes on to consider Indian literary efforts to react against colonialism that were in fact highly hegemonized, works that were "grounded in reinterpreted sacred texts but in reality dependent on core values [particularly of hypermasculinity] borrowed from the colonial world view and then legitimized according to existing concepts of sacredness" (22). But the book primarily examines individual literary, religious, and political figures who sought "to create a new political awareness which would combine a critical awareness of Hinduism and colonialism with cultural and individual authenticity" (27). Nandy is particularly interested in the ways in which Gandhi and other major voices of anticolonialism mobilized (and partly reordered) Indian categories of masculinity, femininity, and androgyny in formulating both resistance to colonialism and an alternative vision of society. Again and again he views these oppositional figures, even when severely victimized in their personal lives (see especially the discussion of Sri Aurobindo), as drawing upon cultural resources to transform their own victimhood and articulate new models of self and society.[11]

Nandy then comes back to the ordinary person who does not write novels, launch new religious systems, or lead movements of national resistance. In this context he seems to come close to the position of the authors of " 'Shahbano'" for he argues (in a more psychological language) that cultural and psychological survival may require the kind of fragmented and shifting self that Shahbano seemed to display (1983:107). Yet Nandy's discussion has a different tone. Partly this comes from his earlier exploration of broad cultural patterns, showing that the boundaries between such things as self and other, masculine and feminine, and myth and history, are both differently configured and differently valued in various strands of Indian thought. The shifting subject in turn is both drawing on and protecting these alternative cultural frames, as opposed to making a seemingly ad hoc response to an immediate situation of domination. Nandy's subjects also paradoxically retain a kind of coherent agency in their very inconstancy: "these 'personality failures' of the Indian could be another form of developed vigilance, or sharpened instinct or faster reaction to man-made suffering. They come . . . from a certain talent for and faith in life" (110). Thus Nandy's subjects, whether prominent public figures or common men and women, retain powerful voices throughout his book, while Shahbano representationally disappears.

Finally, however, it must be emphasized that the question of adequate representation of subjects in the attempt to understand resistance is not purely a matter of providing better portraits of subjects in and of themselves. The importance of subjects (whether individual actors or social entities) lies not so much in who they are and how they are put together as in the projects that they construct and enact. For it is in the formulation and enactment of those projects that they both become and transform who they are, and that they sustain or transform their social and cultural universe.

Textual Resistance

Running through all these works, despite in some cases deep theoretical differences between them, is a kind of bizarre refusal to know and speak and write of the lived worlds inhabited by those who resist (or do not, as the case may be). Of the works discussed at length in this essay, Clendinnen's goes to greater lengths than the others to portray the precolonial Maya world in some depth and complexity, yet in the end she chooses to pull her punches and smooth over what the material has told her. But Scott, Guha, and Pathak and Rajan quite literally refuse to deal with the material that would allow entry into the political and cultural worlds of those they discuss. The "flying letters" of Scott's peasants, the testimonies of Guha's peasants' visions, the press interviews of Shahbano are texts that can be read in the richest sense to yield an understanding of both the meanings and the mystifications on which people are operating. What might emerge is something like what we see in Carlo Ginzburg's *Night Battles* (1985): an extraordinarily rich and complicated world of beliefs, practices, and petty politics whose stance toward the encroachment of Christianity and the Inquisition in the Middle Ages is confused and unheroic yet also poignantly stubborn and "authentic"—a very Nandy-esque story.

There are no doubt many reasons for this interpretive refusal. But one is surely to be found in the so-called crisis of representation in the human sciences. When Edward Said (1979) says in effect that the discourse of Orientalism renders it virtually impossible to know anything real about the Orient; when Gayatri Spivak tells us that "the subaltern cannot speak" (1988a); when James Clifford informs us that all ethnographies are "fictions" (1986:7); and when of course in some sense all of these things are true—then the effect is a powerful inhibition on the practice of ethnography broadly defined: the effortful practice, despite all that, of seeking to understand other peoples in other times and places, especially those people who are not in dominant positions.

The ethnographic stance holds that ethnography is never impossible. This is the case because people not only resist political domination; they resist, or anyway evade, textual domination as well. The notion that colonial or academic texts are able completely to distort or exclude the voices and perspectives of those being written about seems to me to endow these texts with far greater power than they have. Many things shape these texts, including—dare one say it?—the point of view of those being written about. Nor does one need to resort to various forms of textual experimentation to allow this to happen —it is happening all the time. Of course there is variation in the degree to which different authors and different forms of writing allow this process to show, and it is certainly worthwhile to reflect, as Clifford and others have done, on the ways in which this process can be enhanced. But it seems to me grotesque to insist on the notion that the text is shaped by everything but the lived reality of the people whom the text claims to represent.

Take the case of a female suicide discussed in Spivak's famous essay, the one that concludes with the statement that "the subaltern cannot speak" (1988a: 308). It is perhaps more difficult for any voice to break through Spivak's theorizing than through the most typifying ethnography; yet even this dead young woman, who spoke to no one about her intentions and left no note before her death, forces Spivak to at least try to articulate, in quite a "realist" and "objectivist" fashion, the truth of the suicide from the woman's point of view:

> The suicide was a puzzle since, as Bhuvaneswari was menstruating at the time, it was clearly not a case of illicit pregnancy. Nearly a decade later, it was discovered that she was a member of one of the many groups involved in the armed struggle for Indian independence. She had finally been entrusted with a political assassination. Unable to confront the task and yet aware of the practical need for trust, she killed herself.
>
> Bhuvaneswari had known that her death would be diagnosed as the outcome of illegitimate passion. She had therefore waited for the onset of menstruation . . . Bhuvaneswari Bhaduri's suicide is an unemphatic, ad hoc, subaltern rewriting of the social text of *sati*-suicide (1988a:307–8).

With this discussion, it seems to me, Spivak undermines her own position (see also Coronil 1992). Combining a bit of homely interpretation of the text of the woman's body (the fact that she was menstruating) with a bit of objective history (the woman's participation in a radical political group), Spivak arrives at what any good ethnography provides: an understanding both of the meaning and the politics of the meaning of an event.

Another angle on the problem of ethnographic refusal may be gained from considering the implications of the fiction metaphor. Reverberating with ordinary language the fiction metaphor implies (though this is not exactly what Clifford meant) that ethnographies are false, made up, and more generally are products of a literary imagination that has no obligation to engage with reality. Yet the obligation to engage with reality seems to me precisely the difference between the novelist's task and the ethnographer's (or the historian's). The anthropologist and the historian are charged with representing the lives of people who are living or once lived, and as we attempt to push these people into the molds of our texts, they push back. The final text is a product of our pushing and their pushing back, and no text, however dominant, lacks the traces of this counterforce.

Indeed, if the line between fiction and ethnography is being blurred, the blurring has had at least as much impact on fiction as on ethnography. The novelist's standard disclaimer—"any resemblance to persons living or dead is coincidental"—is less and less invoked,[12] or less and less accepted. The response to Salman Rushdie's *Satanic Verses* (1989) shows in particularly dramatic form that the novelist can no longer pretend that, in contrast to ethnography or history, there is nobody on the other side of his or her text or that fiction can escape resistance.[13]

Finally, absolute fictionality and absolute silencing are impossible not only because those being written about force themselves into the author's account but also because there is always a multiplicity of accounts. The point seems simple, yet it seems to get lost in the discussions just considered. It is strange in this era of the theoretical "death of the author" to find theorists like Spivak and Clifford acting as if texts were wholly self-contained, as if every text one wrote had to embody (or could conceivably embody) in itself all the voices out there, or as if every text one read had boundaries beyond which one were not allowed to look. On the contrary in both writing and reading one enters a corpus of texts in which, in reality, a single representation or misrepresentation or omission never goes unchallenged. Our job, in both reading and writing, is precisely to refuse to be limited by a single text or by any existing definition of what should count as the corpus, and to play the texts (which may include, but never be limited to, our own field notes) off against one another in an endless process of coaxing up images of the real.

Conclusions

The point of this essay can be stated very simply. Resistance studies are thin because they are ethnographically thin: thin on the internal politics of dominated groups, thin on the cultural richness of those groups, thin on the subjectivity—the intentions, desires, fears, projects—of the actors engaged in these dramas. Ethnographic thinness in turn derives from several sources (other than sheer bad ethnography, of course, which is always a possibility). The first is the failure of nerve surrounding questions of the internal politics of dominated groups and of the cultural authenticity of those groups, which I have raised periodically throughout this essay. The second is the set of issues surrounding the crisis of representation—the possibility of truthful portrayals of others (or Others) and the capacity of the subaltern to be heard—which has just been addressed. Taken together the two sets of issues converge to produce a kind of ethnographic black hole.

Filling in the black hole would certainly deepen and enrich resistance studies, but there is more to it than that. It would, or should, reveal the ambivalences and ambiguities of resistance itself. These ambivalences and ambiguities, in turn, emerge from the intricate webs of articulations and disarticulations that always exist between dominant and dominated. For, the politics of external domination and the politics within a subordinated group may link up with, as well as repel, one another; the cultures of dominant groups and of subalterns may speak to, even while speaking against, one another;[14] and, as Nandy so eloquently argues, subordinated selves may retain oppositional authenticity and agency by drawing on aspects of the dominant culture to criticize their own world as well as the situation of domination. In short, one can only appreciate the ways in which resistance can be more than opposition, can be truly creative and transformative, if one appreciates the multiplicity of projects in which social beings are always engaged, and the multiplicity of ways in which those projects feed on, as well as collide with, one another.

CHAPTER 3

Identities: The Hidden Life of Class

In the mid-1990s Kwame Anthony Appiah and Henry Louis Gates published a rich and impressive reader called, simply, *Identities* (1995). The book consists of some twenty articles covering identities of every sort—racial and ethnic, gender and sexual preference, national and religious, and more. The word "class" appears on page 1 of the introduction, where we are told that the 1980s were a "period when race, class, and gender became the holy trinity of literary criticism." The writers then note that "In the 1990s, however, 'race,' 'class,' and 'gender' threaten to become the regnant clichés of our critical discourse." The book is concerned to "help disrupt this cliché-ridden discourse." Yet, although race and gender receive a good deal of attention, the reader is hard put to discover either the clichéd status of "class" or its disruption. The word never appears again in the book. Consulting the index one finds a single listing: "class, as cliché, page 1."[1]

The Appiah and Gates reader presents us with a paradox: the idea of identities based on "natural" characteristics is at once the most conservative and the most radical of notions on the contemporary political scene. Conservative, because the idea that identities are largely derived from natural characteristics fits all too easily with American cultural assumptions (see especially Segal 1998); radical, because the idea of embracing stigma and turning it into the basis of political agency has in fact been truly "disruptive" over the past two decades or so.

Some Theoretical Perspectives

Since at least the late nineteenth century race and ethnicity have been the dominant discourses of social difference in the United States. For reasons I have discussed in chapter 1 the discourse of class has tended to be relatively muted, though it becomes more audible from time to time under specific historical conditions. The immediate problem for this chapter, and for the larger project of which it is a part, is an old one: what is the relationship between race and ethnicity on the one hand and class on the other?

The approaches to answering this question have traditionally fallen into two broad categories. The strategy of the first is to ignore class: A good deal of the literature on race and ethnicity, going back a long way but also including much recent work, does this. Racial and ethnic categories are treated as primary social categories, giving or denying people access to resources, but the resources themselves are not arranged in any structurally constraining way. The Appiah and Gates reader, despite its in many ways very contemporary tone, nonetheless operates largely in this mode.

The second traditional approach to the relationship between class and race/ethnicity derives from a certain economistic perspective in which class factors have primacy in determining people's life chances. Race and ethnicity are important insofar as they provoke prejudice and discrimination in others, but they themselves do not constitute cultural formations that affect the ways in which their members operate in the world. Thus, for example, Stephen Steinberg (1989: chapter 3) has argued that there is nothing in "Jewish culture" that has given Jews an advantage in social mobility; rather, the important factor is that, compared to other immigrant groups, Jews came to the United States with certain sorts of urban and industrial skills (see also Sacks 1994). Similarly, with respect to African Americans, William Julius Wilson (1978, 1987) has emphasized a variety of material factors affecting African American poverty rates—rates of immigration to the north, age structure of the population, changes in the national economy—as against both contemporary prejudice against the group and social patterns within the group. And in an ethnographic mode Micaela di Leonardo (1984) has argued against cultural interpretations of the Italian-American experience in the United States. Instead, she sets out to show, first, that this experience has been very diverse and, second, that its patterns can be accounted for largely by economic and historical factors rather than by anything "typically" or culturally Italian (see also Gans 1962).

Before continuing it is important to clarify what is meant by class. By "class" Marx (1967 [1867]) meant positions created by the mode of production of capitalism; in the classic Marxist perspective, there were fundamentally two classes: the owners of the means of production and the workers. A good deal of the post-Marx debate has concerned what to do with the middle class, who are neither "owners," broadly speaking, nor workers. Yet the middle class has been the most dynamic part of the structure of capitalism, growing in size, wealth, and political importance over the course of the past century (for an overview, see Scase 1992). In any event, however, class in this framework is an objectively and/or structurally defined set of locations, regardless of how people themselves see and understand their social positions. The political (specifically, revolutionary) question in the classic Marxist framework has been precisely that of getting working-class actors to see their "objective" positionality and to act upon it.

The two views just outlined—one in which structurally defined classes have primacy, the other in which race/ethnic identities have primacy—must be seen as in some ways operating *within* the basic Marxist framework. Although they appear opposed to one another, both accept a world in which class, as an economically generated category, is distinct from and opposed to social categories defined by noneconomic criteria (whether seen as "cultural" or "natural"). But there have been a number of later theoretical departures on the idea of class that may move us away from this somewhat exhausted set of options.

Starting in the early '80s, many Marxist-inspired historians took "the discursive turn." Beginning with Gareth Stedman Jones's pathbreaking *Languages of Class* (1983) and developed further, and more radically, in Joan Scott's article "On Language, Gender, and Working-Class History" (1988a), some historians began exploring the idea that "class" was not an objectively defined object in the world, but a culturally and historically constructed identity. Stedman Jones looked at the political rhetoric of the Chartist movement in early nineteenth century England and argued that the rhetoric itself was constitutive of, and not merely representative of, the political collectivity in question, a collectivity that defined itself in terms of "class." As this position was summarized: "Linguistically, 'class' defined a constituency for the Chartist movement, and helped its parts to see themselves in a common project which the class-political form of address itself thereby constructed, rather than sec-ondarily reflecting a unity of interest that was already given in the economy and its social relations" (Dirks, Eley, and Ortner 1994:30).

Joan Scott, in turn, both extended and criticized Stedman Jones's position. Agreeing with Stedman Jones about the constitutive nature of language in society and politics, and about the constructed nature of class as a category, she nonetheless pointed out that Stedman Jones never really deconstructed the category of class itself. Scott argued that one needs to examine not only what is constituted by a category like class but also what is excluded in that constituting process. She argued as well that a category like class must be examined within a discursive field of related terms of social identity and social difference. Scott thus went on to discuss how the particular notion of the working class that took shape in the context of Chartism and related move-ments was in fact a gendered notion, defining the working class as basically male and positioning women in certain excluded and/or devalued ways vis-à-vis the social and political entity thereby constituted.

Two things are happening in these debates. One is a move that is familiar to cultural anthropologists: an argument for the importance of looking at some supposedly hard and objective social phenomenon as culturally constructed. But, although cultural anthropologists have made this move with respect to many other areas of social and cultural life, they have not for the most part made it with respect to "class." The second is the specifically critical (both poststructuralist and feminist) version of this move: the sense that cultural constructions are always "ideological," always situated with respect to the forms and modes of power operating in a given time and place.

The poststructuralist move with respect to class holds out the prospect of moving us beyond the alternatives about the "real" relative dominance of class or race/ethnicity noted earlier, and I will adopt this approach more or less wholesale in this essay. And since the dominant social categories in American discourse are race and ethnicity, the point here will be to deconstruct those categories to show the ways in which they embody a class referent, the ways they are in fact deeply "classed," just as Scott showed how "class" itself is deeply "gendered."[2]

The Dominance of Ethnic and Racial Categories

Race and ethnicity have enormous cultural salience in the discourses of social difference in the United States. This means, among other things, that when they are introduced into the discussion, they tend to swamp everything else. They seem to have a self-evident or natural quality that makes it hard to get past them. For example when I interviewed people for the New Jersey Dreaming project (more on this below) and introduced the term "class," informants immediately asked what I meant by that. But when I mentioned race or ethnicity, "everybody knew" what those things mean or refer to in the "real world." These self-explanatory categories, moreover, seem to carry with them a whole social theory: to know that someone is, say, Jewish or African American is to imagine that one has an explanation for their behavior or for their group's history and status in American society. In other words these categories are always already part of an ethno-anthropology, and when they are invoked in fieldwork, they make it almost impossible to bring other dimensions of social difference into focus.

A striking example of the dominant power of ethnic categories in American discourse may be found in Lloyd Warner's classic study of "Yankee City" (1961). One part of the Yankee City project was the study of the Tercentenary celebration put on by the Yankee City community. The celebration included an elaborate parade, and different floats for the parade were assigned by the organizing committee to different civic and religious groups of the town. One float was based on an important battle in the American Revolution led by Colonel Benedict Arnold, in whose regiment several sons of the town had served. The fact that Arnold eventually became a traitor to the American cause was not salient for the local upper-class Yankees, some of whose families evidently had ties to the Arnold family. For some reason—and the details of how it came about are unclear—the Jewish community of Yankee City either chose or was assigned this particular float as its contribution to the festivities. At that point everything erupted, as the juxtaposition of these two categories —Jews and Benedict Arnold—brought the most negative meanings of both to the fore. The committee, eager to smooth things over, announced that a mistake had been made. The Jewish community was reassigned to the float on Captain John Smith, and the crisis was resolved (Warner 1961:144–55).[3]

Given this tendency in popular culture for ethnic and racial categories to take over and reframe the discussion, the anthropologist is faced with a dilemma. One can attack the premise that ethnic culture "really" matters, as do some of the authors noted above. Or one can simply decide, if one thinks that the categories are irrelevant, to leave them out of the discussion. I cannot actually imagine any ethnography being written in the United States in which the ethnographic subjects are racially marked, but in which the author does not tell us that this is the case. No doubt this is because race carries an additional cultural freight over and above its "ethnic" aspects. There are, however, several examples in the literature in which the ethnographic subjects have an ethnic identity—specifically, in the cases most relevant for my project, Jewish identity—but the author does not tell.

One is Hortense Powdermaker's 1950 ethnography, *Hollywood the Dream Factory*. One knows from other sources (e.g., Gabler 1988) that an enormous part of the population of the movie industry and virtually the whole of its power structure (studio owners and producers) at the time of Powdermaker's study were Jewish. Moreover, much of Powdermaker's discussion of Hollywood culture is easily open to a Jewish reading. For example she discusses Hollywood producers' "constant fear of failure and the need for excessive profits on every picture" in terms of the "very high personal insecurity of most executives and producers" (Powdermaker 1951:95). Because Powdermaker never states that there is a Jewish subtext to her discussion, everything is open to multiple interpretations, but this and many other parts of the ethnography make a great deal of sense when read as reflections on Hollywood culture as the culture of insecure Jewish immigrants who were good at making money but who felt they could never gain social respect.

Similarly, in some of his earlier articles on Texas millionaires George Marcus does not reveal that one of the two major dynasties he studied was Jewish. In the monograph that later came out, *Lives in Trust* (1992), the Jewishness of the Kempner dynasty goes through a series of interesting transformations. First, the founder, Harris Kempner, is described as "a Polish immigrant" (Marcus 1992:23). Later he is described as "a Jewish immigrant," but the Jewishness is immediately set aside as not relevant to the study (99). Finally, a relatively full description of the Kempner family is given, in which their Jewishness is fairly prominent, but this is part of a discussion of ethnographic methodology, rather than of the central arguments of the book about wealth and family (150–60).

In the cases of both Powdermaker and Marcus I suspect the reasoning behind these omissions and/or ambiguities of representation was the same, and perfectly understandable in light of the point I am making here. That is, to tell the reader that these groups are Jewish, or to foreground their Jewishness in the text, is to risk tracking the discussion off in directions that the ethnographer wishes to avoid: given the cultural dominance of ethnic categories, the Jewishness of the group becomes the dominant fact and the explanatory principle of the study, whether the author wishes it or not.

My interest in all this derives from the fact that the focus of the New Jersey Dreaming project (Ortner 2003) was on the cultural construction of class in the United States. The ethnographic population for the project was my own high school graduating class, the Class of '58 of Weequahic High School in Newark, New Jersey. This group was 83 percent Jewish; the neighborhood—as I later learned—was more or less planned as a Jewish community. The remainder of the graduating class included about 11 percent non-Jewish whites and about 6 percent African Americans.

Since I defined the project precisely in terms of issues of class—the whole point was to try to bring class more strongly, and in new ways, into ethnographic and anthropological focus—I began with the position that the ethnic and racial composition of the group was largely irrelevant. In fact, being aware of the cultural dominance of ethnic and racial categories, I was planning to use some version of Powdermaker's and Marcus's "don't tell" (or don't tell much) strategy myself, in order to get around an ethnic or racial reading of the material. Rather, I planned to emphasize the class composition of the group—the mixture of "middle-class" and "lower-middle-class" kids, the significant but nearly invisible fault line within the supposedly seamless middle class, the ways in which the ethnic and even racial categories were in fact crosscut by the class divide. The more my social science friends insisted, in some shock, that I could not leave the heavy Jewish weighting of the Class of '58 out of the story, the more I was determined to press the issue.

Yet finally it was the fieldwork that changed my mind. I conducted about 150 interviews,[4] of which roughly 120 were with Jewish people. I never directly asked about Jewishness. I tried to ask about class. But the centrality of Jewishness to these people's lives and talk was overwhelming. It is all over my transcripts; I was chided for not asking about it; I simply could not leave it out.[5] If I were going to ignore this much native discourse, this much native passion, I might as well not have bothered doing the fieldwork.

Notes on Terminology

Before going on, I present a few notes on the terminology I will be using and the assumptions about class that lie behind it. I begin by assuming that something we call "capitalism" has a massive reality, as a set of discourses, practices, and institutions in the world. Capitalism, in turn, is indeed central to (but not exhaustive of) the genesis of social positions of wealth and power on the one hand and poverty and social weakness on the other. When talking about class in an objectivist sense we may usefully cluster the social positions generated by the organization and logic of capitalism and gloss them as "classes." Thus within such a perspective it is possible, and it makes sense, to talk about something like "the changing structure of class" in the United States, or globally, under "late capitalism." It was highly relevant to my project, for example, that a number of social and economic theorists have argued that "the middle class" has been coming apart in the middle since the 1970s, that the rich are getting richer and the poor poorer, and that there is a certain "caste-ification" of the upper middle class going on (Lind 1995).

Quite apart from all this is the question of class as an identity. Here we are back in the realm of discourse, that is, of how people talk about themselves and others, and of the larger shape of the discursive field from which people draw their categories. This is, for the most part, the level at which I will operate in this essay, the level of culture, ideology, discourse, *habitus*. In this context I will both use and deconstruct the native categories rather than those derived from objectivist (either Marxist or "bourgeois" social science) discourses. There is in fact a fair amount of slippage between the folk categories and the objectivist categories, an interesting and difficult problem in and of itself that I must set aside because of constraints of space.[6]

We may start at the lower end of the social scale. The choice of terms is immediately loaded. The phrase "working class" is rarely used and, indeed, usually rejected by people we might think of "objectively" as members of the working class. The chemical workers in Elizabeth, New Jersey, so brilliantly studied by David Halle (1984), for example, think and speak of themselves as "working men" but reject the phrase "working class." In class language in fact they think of themselves as "middle class," in contrast to people below them on the social scale, whom they designate as "lower class." The structure of the discourse, moreover, is heavily racially loaded: the "working class" (in social science and Marxist discourse) who call themselves "middle class" (in American cultural terms) are coded white; the "lower class" (in American cultural language, more or less coterminous with certain objectivist usages) are coded as racial and ethnic minorities.

In the terminology I will be using the largely-white-working-class-that-thinks-of-itself-as-middle-class will normally be labeled "lower middle class," for reasons discussed in the next chapter. I will use "lower class" in an extended version of the folk sense, to refer to the segment of the working class that is usually poorer and usually non-white, compared to the "lower middle class." I hope it goes without saying—but I will say it anyway—that this does not mean that there are no white "lower-class" people; indeed, they have recently begun to come into focus, in both popular and academic discourse (e.g., Talbot 1997; Wray and Newitz 1997). Nor does it mean that there are no persons of color further up the class ladder. I am simply trying to get a fix on the cultural referential range of these categories, on the one hand, and the relationship between that and (varying) academic uses, on the other.

Turning to the middle class we know that the vast majority of Americans think of themselves as "middle class." There is also a folk lexicon of subdivisions for this category—"upper middle," "lower middle," and just plain "middle"—and American natives will occasionally use these terms, though in general they do not like to subdivide the middle-class category.[7] Further, the term "lower-middle class" is very much disliked by those who might be so categorized, apparently because of the presence of the word "lower"; we may say that "lower-middle class" is to "(upper) middle class" as "lower class" is to "working class."

The plain "middle class" is the most slippery category. It is either used as the modest self-label for the upper middle class, which quickly gives way to an acknowledgement that one is probably "upper" middle class after all; or it is the covering label for the lower-middle class as just discussed. Either way there is almost no "there" there; to be plain middle class is almost always to be "really" something else, or on the way to somewhere else. At the same time the "middle class" is the most inclusive social category; indeed, it is almost a national category. In many usages it means simply all those Americans who have signed up for the American dream, who believe in a kind of decent life of work and family, in the worth of the "individual" and the importance of "freedom," and who strive for a moderate amount of material success. It is everybody except the very rich and the very poor.

I will have relatively little to say in this essay about the upper class, as they were not represented in Weequahic High School and played no role in the project. Should the subject come up I will use the phrase "upper class" in its standard folk usage, meaning, for the most part, people who are ethnically WASP and possessed (once or still) of "old money."

Finally, there is the term "class" itself. In general I follow Bourdieu (1984) in thinking about this. At one level the term "class" points to certain economic-cum-cultural locations defined within an objectivist perspective. Classes are not objects "out there," but there is something out there in the way of inequality, privilege, and social difference which the idea of "class" is meant to capture specifically in its economic dimension. At the same time class is, as already noted, an identity term and is in fact the only American identity term that is organized primarily around an economic axis. I will use it in both (objectivist and identity) senses throughout this essay, with clarification provided by context.

Models of Interrelationship

In chapter 1 I argued that class exists in America but cannot be talked about, that it is "hidden," that there is no language for it, but that it is "displaced" or "spoken through" other languages of social difference—race, ethnicity, and gender. I showed, for example, that the ethnosociology of most American high schools, in which kids are classified as "hoods," "jocks," "socies," "burn-outs," and so forth, is essentially an ethnosociology of class, though class—and even money—are virtually never referred to. There is a related language of class difference for high school girls, a language of sexual virtue. Thus girls classified as " sluts" and "whores" are almost always working-class girls; the language of sexuality is also a language of class. Finally, in that chapter I looked at some of the early novels of Philip Roth, probably the most famous graduate of Weequahic High School, and showed the ways in which virtually his whole sexual geography—who did what to whom in high school and beyond—was essentially a class geography; as Alexander Portnoy told his psychiatrist in Portnoy's Complaint (1967), "What I'm saying, Doctor, is that I don't seem to stick my dick up these girls, as much as I stick it up their backgrounds" (Roth 1967:235).

What I was drawing from this at the time was the idea that, once one recognized the ways in which class was "hiding" within other discourses, one could strip away the other discourses and get down to "class itself." I still think this can be right in some abstract sense—that one can construct a model in which class exists in pure form apart from these categories and "interacts" with them; for certain purposes this would be a useful way of looking at the question. Thus one could think of ethnic and racial identities as in a sense tickets to the various games of class in America and could play out the implications of this idea, which is actually the way in which I started to write this chapter. Or one could think of ethnic "cultures" as standing apart from class, yet providing better or worse skills for success in the games. This in fact is closest to the folk view of how ethnic cultures work in America, and it has been much contested—as noted above—by authors like Steinberg, di Leonardo, Sacks, and others.

Pushing further on the question of separation and difference between class on the one hand and race/ethnicity on the other, it seems clear that the two operate at least in part on different logics (see, e.g., Ringer and Lawless 1989). That is, to grossly simplify the opposition, class differences emerge from a logic of capitalist economic rationality, a logic of profit and loss, while racial and ethnic differences emerge from a logic of internally shared identity and externally projected pollution and stigma. Moreover, many would insist upon a further distinction between the logic of *racial* identity/prejudice and the logic of *ethnic* identity/prejudice (e.g., Sanjek 1994; Rogin 1996); this distinction will not play a role in this essay, and, as it has widely ramifying (and highly contested) implications, I will not try to address it here.

All of these relatively hard distinctions between race/ethnicity and class may be useful for certain analytic purposes and for certain dimensions of community and/or political practice. Here, however, I want to argue that *at the level of discourse* class, race, and ethnicity are so deeply mutually implicated in American culture that it makes little sense to pull them apart. That is, while I think there is important mileage to be gained from thinking of "class" and "ethnicity" or "race" as separate, but interacting, dimensions of American social geography, at the cultural level the idea of "interaction" or "intersection" in fact does little to illuminate what is going on. Taking the discussions in chapter 1 in slightly different directions, then, and thinking as well of my informants' almost irresistible tendency to translate class into ethnicity, I want to suggest a stronger proposition about the relation between class and race/ethnicity at the level of American cultural thought: that there is no class in America that is not always already racialized and ethnicized, or to turn the point around, racial and ethnic categories are always already class categories.

Connecting back to the earlier theoretical discussion, this is an argument about the shape of American discourse, about the semantic and ideological organization of a field of cultural categories about social difference. Yet discourse is never just "language"; it is both the basis and the object of real social practice, and I will move back and forth between the two levels in the following discussion. My primary example will be the discourse about Jewish ethnicity, as spoken both by the Jews themselves and by others; I will also draw in some examples, where relevant, concerning African Americans. The argument pertains mostly to the post–World War Two period, although in some ways it can be pushed back much further, as we shall see.

The Jews in/and/as the Middle Class

As a kind of thought experiment let us start with the idea that Jewishness is not only an ethnic and/or religious category but is, in fact, basically a class category as well, that one of the things that Jewishness means as a category is "middle class." This is not a statement about whether most Jewish people are middle class or not but rather something about Jewishness as a discursive object: that it is conceptually inseparable from middle classness. What are the implications of thinking about this point in this way?

The first is that it captures something central about Jewish identity (again, mostly since the Second World War), about the ways in which Jews represent themselves to themselves and others. Published studies and my own data show that Jews think of themselves as middle class regardless of "objective" class position. In a book on *The American Perception of Class*, Vanneman and Cannon (1987:218) tell us that "Jewish factory workers who dropped out of high school more often assume a middle-class placement than their Gentile counterparts." It is of course the case that most Americans think of themselves as middle class, but the authors' point is that the Jews are even more likely than most Americans to ignore objective indicators and place themselves relatively high on the social ladder.

The second implication of thinking about Jewishness as conceptually inseparable from middle classness is that it helps illuminate certain Jewish cultural practices. Jewish culture is famous for a strong aversion to, almost amounting to a prohibition against, marriage between Jews and non-Jews. I found the degree to which Jewish parents are upset about intermarriage, even today, striking in my study of the Class of '58; more striking to me was the degree to which this prohibition has a good bit of force even among their grown children. The reasons for, and the effects of, this prohibition are multiple, and I cannot pursue all of them within the confines of this essay. But one of the effects is to maintain a relatively homogeneous group in terms of class. My own experience growing up was that, since most of the non-Jews in the Weequahic section were at least occupationally working class (albeit often upwardly mobile in orientation), the prohibition worked primarily against down-class relationships.

There is nonetheless an increasing amount of Jewish intermarriage in the United States, something that is a matter of great concern within the Jewish community (see Horowitz 1997 for an overview). It is my impression—though I do not have enough data to say more than that—that most out-marriage in fact takes place at both edges of the social scale, among the high-education, high-income upper middles and among the low-education, low-income people at the other end. It is also my impression that when upper-middle-class Jews marry out, they retain ties with the community and strong Jewish identities, often bringing the non-Jewish spouse and the children into the fold. But when lower-class Jews marry out, they tend to drop out of the group and the category. If this is true—and again the data are largely anecdotal—these practices would tend to maintain the isomorphism of "Jewishness" and "middle classness" on the ground as well as conceptually.

And finally, there is the question of "culture." There has been extensive debate in the literature over whether Jewish culture is particularly well matched to American middle-class values and whether this accounts for the Jews' undeniable success in terms of social mobility.[8] A number of Marxist social scientists have opposed a cultural explanation. Stephen Steinberg (1989: chapter 3) has argued that the Jewish embrace of middle-class values, especially the value placed on education, followed rather than preceded their early economic success as immigrants and that the success was due to specific material and historical rather than cultural factors. In a very valuable article that both summarized and extended the critique Karen Sacks (1994) pointed out that the Jews who went into higher education in the earlier part of the century were the children of families that had already achieved some sort of economic success; she also emphasized the degree to which the Jews collectively benefited in the postwar era from the GI Bill and other federal programs designed to support "the middle class." On both points, then, their "culture" was not a leading factor.

All of this assumes, however, that there has been some single unchanging "middle-class" culture to which groups did or did not adjust and for which different groups had better or worse entry credentials. Yet "middle-class culture" or "dominant American culture" is something that is made and remade by real historical actors. We may begin to get past both the chicken-and-egg (cultural or material factors?) debate and the "cultural ticket" model if we ask about the making of middle-class culture itself. We may begin to do this by reversing the question about the Jews: If Jewishness is crypto–middle class, is the middle class crypto-Jewish?

At first glance of course, the answer is no. Most Americans think of themselves as "middle class"—actually Americanness itself may be inseparable from middle classness, but that's a different part of the argument—yet most Americans are not Jewish, do not think of themselves as Jewish, and would be rather startled at the idea that their class positioning might carry a kind of hidden Jewishness.

Here I am on thin ice, because what I am about to say is precisely the kind of thing that feeds certain anti-Semitic stereotypes, even in this era in which anti-Semitism is arguably waning (see Weiss 1996).[9] But I do think a case could plausibly be made that middle-class culture is not entirely separable from Jewish culture in America. I would point in particular to the role of the media—especially film and television, but also journalism—in the making of what we think of as American culture and especially in the making of the middle class as a cultural entity since World War Two (see especially Lipsitz 1990). And then I would point to the enormous role of the Jews in the making of film and television (see, again, Gabler 1988; Rogin 1996).[10] The Jews not only made films, they invented and dominated the entire industry. Until recently, however—and we can probably mark the change with Woody Allen —they did not make "Jewish" films; they made "American" films, premised on the centrality of generic "middle-class" values.[11]

As it turns out, a version of this argument has been made before, in Marx's essay, "On the Jewish Question" (1975 [1843]). I had read that essay long ago but had forgotten about the argument, perhaps because I disliked the tone and language of the essay. Marx says that the mainstream values of Western culture (which he identifies with "Christianity") are actually infused with a kind of cultural Jewishness. His argument is that there is no point in discriminating against Jews since the Jewish values and practices that "everyone" despises—greed, money-mania, what he calls "haggling"—are simply the values of the broader culture: "the practical Jewish spirit has become the practical spirit of the Christian peoples. The Jews have emancipated themselves in so far as the Christians have become Jews" (237).[12]

The idea that dominant Western culture, since the advent of capitalism, is heavily inflected with Jewish values and styles pushes the idea that the Jews "made" the culture much further back than the Hollywood movie industry. In fact Marx's arguments launched a debate over whom to blame for (or, in other perspectives, give credit for) the advent of capitalism itself. Max Weber later argued that it was the Protestants, while Werner Sombart responded to Weber that it was really the Jews after all (see Davis 1997 for an overview). I have no intention of entering into that debate here. My point is simply that cultural "fusions" (in this case of Jewishness and middle class–ness) come into being through a dialectical process in which both the dominant culture and subordinate categories shape one another over time.

To summarize briefly, I have been arguing here that American class discourse is in certain important respects fused with ethnicity and race. The nature of this fusion has no doubt changed over time, but there seems always to have been some sort of tendency to merge race/ethnic and class categories in American cultural thought. The fusion in turn has worked to the benefit of certain groups—in this case the Jews and, perhaps more recently, certain Asian groups. But the same fact, that class comes in racialized and ethnicized packages in America and that race and ethnicity are actually crypto–class positions, is obviously quite pernicious at the lower end of the structure. If to be Jewish is to be, in essence, middle class (whether one is "in reality" or not), then to be (to take the most obvious case) African American is to be seen or felt to be, in essence—and whether one is in reality or not—lower class. African Americanness carries a more or less automatic lower-class identity in the eyes of others; this much we know. But it also apparently carries a lower-class identity in terms of self-image: the same study that shows that Jews think of themselves as middle class even when they are factory workers also shows that African Americans tend to think of themselves as lower class, even when they are in high-status occupations: "Black managers with college degrees more often assert a working-class identity than equivalent white managers" (Vanneman and Cannon 1987:218).[13]

Conclusion: The Hidden Life of Class

What is the significance of arguing for a "fusion" between class and race/ethnicity in American cultural thought? I begin by returning to the point that, even if there is a fusion, race and ethnicity are in fact the dominant and more visible categories. That is, we may think of the fusion as a "structure," in the Lévi-Straussian sense of a particular relationship between categories. Thus, to say that the categories are fused is to say that we can never find either in pure form and that each is always hidden within the other. But the dominance of race and ethnicity within the fusion means that class is still more "hidden" and requires—at this point, at least—more intellectual archaeology.

The relative hiddenness of class in American cultural thought has a number of consequences. The first is that class tends to be the last factor introduced as an explanation of privilege and power on the one hand, poverty and social impotence on the other. Either we get explanations in terms of race and ethnicity (whether in the mode of credit or blame), or we get explanations in terms of personal initiative, pulling oneself up by one's bootstraps (or the failure to do so), or some combination of the two.[14]

Again, I follow Bourdieu (1984) fairly closely here in taking class in both its objective and subjective senses. Objectively "classes" are positions in social space defined by economic and cultural capital. People are born into those spaces and being born there has consequences—an idea that Americans probably dislike more than any other proposition about social opportunity in America. At the same time, class positionalities engender certain representations of the privileges and limits of those positions, a *habitus* of both external practices and internal senses of boundaries and/or possibilities.

The idea of "habitus" has certain similarities to the idea of "culture"—it is an internalized sense of the world, constantly renewed through practice in that world—but Bourdieu's emphasis is not on the ways in which different "habitus" produce different sets of "qualifications" for success. Rather, it is on the ways in which, within a given location and its habitus, there is a constant process of cultural "fixing," in which the objective conditions of life are made to seem natural, immutable, "just the way things are."

The idea of class habitus is potentially risky. Treated as just another word for "culture" it quickly re-creates some of the problems I have tried to avoid in this chapter. But understood as the internalized (and constantly renewed) set of representations of class-defined social location, and as the constant processes that naturalize them, it is a very powerful idea. What I would add, and what Bourdieu does not adequately explore, is the processes that constantly denaturalize them as well, the little cracks and openings that constantly appear as a result of the complex and constantly changing dynamics of practice.

The idea of habitus in turn directs us to the doubleness of class representations: part of the "public culture," on the one hand, and part of the subjectness, the "identities," of actors, on the other. The "hiddenness" of class operates in different ways on these two levels. At the level of public culture or discourse the hiddenness of class means that the discourse is muted and often unavailable, subordinated to virtually every other kind of claim about social success and social failure. At the level of actors-in-identities it means that the dialectic of the making and unmaking of habitus, of the internalization and externalization of limits and of their naturalization, is not open to reflection and self-reflection. Yet it is precisely in the internalization and naturalization of public discourses about "identities" that the fusion of class with race and ethnicity happens in American cultural practice.

The methodological implications thus are twofold. We must deconstruct the public discourse, and this deconstruction must itself always work in two directions: to find the hidden racializations and other naturalizations that operate within seemingly neutral social categories (e.g., "the middle class"), but also to reveal the hidden class underpinnings of naturally based identities (take your pick), as I have tried to do in this article. At the same time we must always go beyond the deconstruction of public discourse and attend ethnographically to the ways in which discourses enter into people's lives, both invading them in a Bourdieuian, even Foucauldian, sense and being implicitly or explicitly challenged by them in the course of practices that always go beyond discursive constraints.

CHAPTER 4

Generation X: Anthropology in a Media-Saturated World

> The cultural ubiquity of the professional middle class may seem to make it an easy subject for a writer. There is no need to travel to off-beat settings or conduct extensive interviews to find out what is on its mind. One does not need to consult specialists—sociologists or anthropologists—to discover how people in this class order the details of their daily lives. Their lifestyles, habits, tastes, and attitudes are everywhere, and inescapably before us. . . . Who can presume to step "outside" of it? Its ideas and assumptions are everywhere, and not least in our own minds.—Barbara Ehrenreich, *Fear of Falling: The Inner Life of the Middle Class*

My problem for this chapter concerns the relationship between "public culture" and ethnographic inquiry in the contemporary United States. By "public culture" I mean all the bodies of images, claims, and representations created to speak to and about the actual people who live in the United States: all of the products of art and entertainment (film, television, books, and so on), as well as all of the texts of information and analysis (all forms of journalism and academic production). "Public culture" includes all the products of what is commonly called the "media," but much more as well.

Public culture in this sense stands in a very complex relationship to "ethnography." First, public culture is both subject and object vis-à-vis the ethnographer. It claims, and the ethnographer must grant, that it stands as a competing subject, a competing authority: many journalists, as well as academics in many other fields, are jostling with ethnographers to tell "the truth" about U.S. culture. As we shall see when we turn to the public representations concerning Generation X, journalists and academics are constantly trying to subsume one another, to claim the position of subject and to turn one another into objects, data. Journalists quote both native informants and academic experts to weave a story about the here and now; academics do the same with journalists, as I will do in this essay. Ethnographers' "data" are part of the journalists' stories; journalists' reporting is part of the public culture and thus part of the ethnographic data.

In trying to think through this relationship several temptations need to be avoided. The first is the unmodified "cultural studies" or "media studies" temptation—the fantasy that one can understand the workings of public cultural representations solely by interpreting or deconstructing the representations. The second is the reciprocal of the first—the ethnographic fantasy that doing fieldwork in and of itself provides the kinds of "data" necessary to correct for the cultural studies illusion. As already noted ethnography and public culture—at least in the United States—are deeply intertwined and therefore cannot be set against one another in any clear-cut way.

It will be useful here to reintroduce the distinction between anthropology and ethnography. "Ethnography," or anyway a variety of "qualitative research" practices operating under that sign, is now being used in many disciplines and in many interdisciplinary arenas (including some arenas of cultural studies and media studies). But anthropology has always been more than ethnography. For one thing anthropologists themselves work extensively on "public culture"; that was in part what the Geertzian revolution of the 1960s (and since) was all about (Ortner 1984). For another both interpretive cultural work and on-the-ground ethnographic work (and more) have always been carried on in relation to larger theoretical frames that both shape such work and are revised by it.

In recent years there has been a tendency to parcel out these components— cultural studies scholars are seen as the specialists on public culture; literary critics and philosophers have claimed the zone of "theory"; and anthropology is increasingly identified simply with "ethnography." Complex academic and intellectual politics are in play here, and this is not the place to try to address them. Perhaps the most contested of the terms is "theory"—what counts as "theory"? Which disciplines are producing theory and which are merely consuming? My own sense of what counts as theory is very broad, as I will discuss in a bit more detail below. But in any event I resist the idea that anthropology's contribution to the current intellectual division of labor is simply ethnographic; in this essay I seek to reappropriate a larger anthropology in which ethnography, theory, and public culture are held in productive tension.

Throughout the 1990s I was engaged in a project on class and culture in the United States in the second half of the twentieth century. The ethnographic population for the study was my own high school graduating class (the Class of '58 of Weequahic High School in Newark, New Jersey) and their grown children.[1] The children of the Class of '58 in turn were born in the 1960s and early 1970s, and thus qualify at least demographically as authentic members of what has come to be called Generation X. Generation X has been the subject of extensive media coverage as well as films, novels, and television series. At first I did not think of the children of the class of 1958 as Generation Xers, even though technically they were. My natives were, for the most part, hardworking and success-oriented, while Xers—I had already picked up the stereotypes—were "slackers" and "whiners." But then I realized that my category failure raised some interesting questions about doing anthropology in contemporary media-saturated societies, and this realization opened the subject of this essay.

Generation X: The Public Culture

I will begin by drawing a picture of Generation X as an ideal type. It should be noted at the outset that virtually every statement in the following description has been contested at one point or another, by one writer or group or another. Moreover the characterization of Generation X (Gen X) has shifted over time, as different groups temporarily gained control over the image. Although it would be interesting to try to interpret the shifting imagery in relation to shifts of various kinds in the real world, unfortunately this will be impossible within the scope of the present essay. Here I simply provide a somewhat simplified overview of Gen X imagery as it has appeared since the mid-1980s.

The idea of the emergence of a distinctive generation in the mid-1980s began in the hands of demographers and marketing interests, and the initial journalism was mostly in demographic and economic journals like *American*

Demographics (*American Demographics* 1987; Edmondson 1987a) and *Fortune* (e.g., Deutschman 1990, 1992). In a second stage the idea moved into the site of popular magazine journalism (including *Newsweek, Business Week* [1991, 1992], *The New Republic,* and *The Atlantic Monthly*) and began addressing a more general public across the political spectrum. By now it is probably fair to say that it is the Xers themselves who control the representation (e.g., Holtz 1995; Nelson and Cowan 1994; Rushkoff 1994), although it has already been shaped by all the hands it has passed through.

One can see the play of various positionalities, interests, political claims, and marketing intentions at work in the competing representations. One can see as well that Generation X has quite literally been brought into being in the play of these representations. Finally one may come to feel—as the images never stabilize—that there is a kind of Baudrillardian process at work—a free play of signifiers with no referent, really, at all. In a way the discussions that follow are an attempt to move away from that vertiginous position, and to articulate an alternative standpoint.

We begin precisely with the question of the referent: who or what, out there, has been designated as "Generation X" and loaded up with (varying) meanings and attributes? The early referent was narrowly defined by demographics: the generation in question was born between 1965 and 1976 (*American Demographics* 1987). Nineteen sixty-five was the first year the birth rate started dropping after the baby boom (which began in 1946, right after World War Two); 1977 was the first year the birth rate began to rise again (*American Demographics* 1993). The earliest label for this group was drawn from the boom/bust opposition in economics: they were the baby busters who followed the baby boomers.

The narrow demographic parameters for the cohort have now been replaced, however, with much wider ones. It is now generally accepted, for reasons that are not entirely clear, that the generation in question begins with those born in about 1961 and ends with those born in about 1981 (Howe and Strauss 1993:12–13). The difference makes a difference. When the cohort was defined demographically (i.e., 1965–76), its most prominent feature was that it was much smaller than the preceding boomer generation. Its small size seemed to mean that things would be easier for the busters in almost every way: there would be less competition for jobs and for promotions (Williams 1985:122); colleges would be competing for busters' enrollments (Edmondson

1987b); and when they hit the home-buying market there would be a glut of starter homes at depressed prices, as the larger boomer population traded upward in housing (*American Demographics* 1992:27). "Demographers and economists forecast golden opportunities for this [1985 graduating] class and for those that follow . . ." (Williams 1985:122).

When the parameters were redrawn to include everyone born between 1961 and 1981, however, the picture of the generation changed. And here we come to the supposed characteristics of the cohort. The most prominent characteristics are economic: there are not enough jobs, there are certainly not enough well-paying jobs, and there are particularly not enough quality jobs available for the level of education and qualification many members of the cohort have achieved. People are basically overeducated (or anyway overcertified)[2] and underemployed.[3]

Further, the wages of the U.S. male had been dropping for some time. A *Business Week* article in 1991 reported that "the median income of families headed by someone under 30 is now 13% lower than such families earned in 1973" (1991:80). The article concludes that some socially undifferentiated group called "America's young people" are going to "mature in a less affluent world. And that spells trouble for all Americans, young and old alike" (1991: 85). A careful reading of the *Business Week* article shows that these predictions will not really apply to everyone equally. It turns out that families of this age group headed by college graduates actually show a 16 percent gain in income and not a 13 percent loss, but this is dismissed because it is only the effect of "working wives." The real impact is on families headed by people with only high school degrees (16 percent decline) and families headed by dropouts (33 percent). There are large racial differentials as well.

The significance of these differences will be clear later. The point for now, however, is that according to these accounts, "the middle class" has been very hard-hit by falling male wages, which force both spouses to work just to stay even. Even then, a couple has great difficulty keeping up economically. In particular they are going to have great difficulty buying that hallmark of middle-class status, a house, and certainly not one comparable to that in which they were brought up. The consequence of all this is the doomsaying prediction that has by now become one of the hallmarks of Generation X: "The baby busters may never match their parents' living standards. And that . . . would make them the first U.S. generation ever not to do so" (*Business Week* 1991:80; see also Newman 1993).

It is not at all clear what, if any, of this is objectively true. Take the one issue of whether or not Generation X will be able to afford a house. In both 1992 and 1993 *American Demographics* insisted that there was no problem. Not only was there said to be "a glut of starter houses" (1992:27), but mortgage rates were falling to "their lowest levels in 20 years" (1993:35) and have remained very low since then. But objective reality is not precisely what is at issue.

In addition to generating a bleak future for the busters the bad economy generates boring, low-paying, noncareer-track jobs in the here and now. This was a major aspect of Douglas Coupland's novel, *Generation X: Tales for an Accelerated Culture* (which was published in 1991), and which provided the name that would henceforth label the cohort: Generation X. Coupland described his characters as working in "McJobs," a term that has by now gained a permanent place in the vocabulary. McJobs—"low-pay, low-prestige, low-dignity, no-future job[s] in the service sector" (Coupland 1991:5)—would be tedious and poorly paid by many people's standards, but they are particularly galling for Xers who have put in the time, effort, and money to gain an education that was supposed to yield something more rewarding in every sense.

In addition to encountering difficult economic conditions Generation X is described as encountering extremely problematic social conditions, including a soaring divorce rate, high rates of working mothers and latchkey children, ecological disaster, the AIDS epidemic, and more. This is particularly the theme of *13th Gen: Abort, Retry, Ignore, Fail* by Neil Howe and Bill Strauss, which came out in 1993 (see also *Business Week* 1992; Holtz 1995; Howe and Strauss 1992). Howe and Strauss are concerned to shift the blame for all these problems from the preceding boomer generation, where it is usually targeted, and which includes themselves (their e-mail moniker is "2boomers"). Instead, they spend a lot of time blaming the senior generations: "When Thirteeners [their term for Xers] were ready to enter the adult labor force, the politicians pushed every policy lever conceivable . . . to tilt the economic playing field away from the young and toward the old." (1993:78) They also specifically blame the parents of Xers (the pre-boomers), whom they see as having been self-indulgent, anti-child parents who sacrificed their children's psychological well-being for the fulfillment of their own selfish needs and desires.

Most other writers focus the blame not primarily on the parental generation but on the adjacent boomer generation. The boomers themselves are also very contradictorily portrayed, but this cannot be explored here. Suffice it to say that the category includes both the counterculture and antiwar generation, and the greedy Reagan/Bush generation, both hippies and yuppies. To someone who lived through both, and who thought first that the yuppies were a historically distinct cohort, and second that yuppie values were entirely antithetical to those of the counterculture and antiwar generation, the combination is rather startling.[4] Nonetheless, what unites them, in these arguments, is the notion of self-indulgence. And in at least some portrayals the hippies and political activists of the 1960s were even worse than the yuppies, because they claimed greater moral purity. It was this collective self-indulgence, in turn, that generated the economic, social, sexual, and psychological problems—everything from the deficit to the divorce rate to AIDS—that Gen Xers have inherited. Howe and Strauss call Generation X "the clean-up crew" (1993:12).[5]

Descriptions of Generation X then move from characterizations of the pathologies of the world to characterizations of the pathologies of Gen X consciousness. Living in a ruined world, Gen Xers manifest (it is claimed) a range of problematic attitudes. One set of attitudes clusters around anger and frustration over their plight; this shades into complaining and—as seen by others—"whining" (e.g., *Business Week* 1992; Martin 1993; Newman 1993). Another set of attitudes takes the form of ironic distancing from their situation, renouncing ambitions and ideals, becoming "slackers," and taking refuge in cyberspace and in a television-generated world of soap operas, quiz shows, and MTV. This is the stance portrayed in some of the most visible sites of Gen X expressive culture, including Coupland's novel *Generation X* (1991), Rushkoff's *Generation X Reader* (1994), and Richard Linklater's film *Slacker* (1991). A final set is organized around the idea that Gen Xers are truly damaged by the world in which they find themselves: they feel themselves to be worthless losers (one anthem of the generation is a song by Beck, of which the refrain is, "I'm a loser, baby, so why don't you kill me"; the band in *Slacker* is called "The Ultimate Losers") and are deeply depressed. The suicide of rock star Kurt Cobain (of the group Nirvana), and the empathetic responses to it, epitomize this cluster of images (Freedland 1994; O'Connell 1994).

As noted earlier, every one of these images has been contested. Among the journalists themselves there has been a fair amount of dissension as to whether Generation X has this or that characteristic. For example in June 1994 *Newsweek* came out with a cover story called "Generalization X," which argued that, although the world was indeed in bad shape, Generation X did not have all the bad attitudes that had been projected upon it (Giles 1994; see also

American Demographics 1993). On the contrary a poll was cited to show that there was virtually no difference in attitudes between Xers and boomers:

> Our extensive research shows *there are no significant national or personal mood differences separating young and old.* Twenty-five percent of the twenty-somethings polled said that they were unhappy with their lot in life; 26 percent of the baby boomers agreed. Sixty-three percent of the twenty-somethings said that they were "dissatisfied with the way things were going in the US"; 71 percent of boomers said the very same thing (Giles 1994:65).

Others have questioned the generational framing as well. In a piece in *The New Yorker* on Kurt Cobain following his suicide, Alex Ross called "the nation's ongoing symposium on generational identity . . . a fruitless project blending the principles of sociology and astrology" (Ross 1994:102; see also Ratan 1993). The most searching critique of the generational framing was offered by Alexander Star, whose remarks are worth quoting at length:

> This kind of generational packaging continues even as the actual bases of generational cohesion erode. Changing family roles and occupational hierarchies, the universal accessibility of the mass media to all age groups, early exposure to work and sex, gadgets and crime, have made age a less, not more, reliable indicator of taste, values, and behavior. The idea of generational culture is itself largely a by-product of the considerable leisure and prosperity that young people enjoyed in the '50s and '60s, together with the existence of overarching causes like Vietnam. Today, a generic youth culture has been assembled from above precisely because it doesn't exist down below. . . . As young people acquire adult responsibilities (and adult vices) at an earlier age, their distinctness as a group diminishes. They do not stamp a unique sensibility on society so much as mirror its disarray (Star 1993:25).

Yet these arguments perhaps go too far in the direction of denying that a Generation X consciousness exists. There is enough in both the public culture and in my ethnographic data to suggest that it is really out there in some part(s) of social space, and the question is one of locating it correctly rather than denying its existence. They also go too far in claiming that this consciousness is imposed from the top; popular thought and public culture exist in a fairly tight loop, each reworking the other in an ongoing process. I agree, however, that the idea of a single generational consciousness is highly implausible, especially in an era as conscious as this one about social difference.

It is perhaps time to declare my argument, which is that the idea of "Generation X" is an attempt to deal with profound changes in the U.S. middle class in the late twentieth century. Before getting to the class argument, however, a few words must be said about Generation X and racial identities.

The Whiteness of Generation X

Relatively early on in the baby buster literature, back in 1991, we were told that the economic downturns that were so problematic for the future of Generation X in fact hit minorities much harder than they hit whites. The 1991 *Business Week* article quoted above made it clear that the long decline in male wages may have put a squeeze on the white middle class, but had been "devastating"—its term—to many minorities (1991:80, 85).

Yet this point is never raised again within the framework of the Generation X public culture. Race is virtually absent from further discussions of the supposed characteristics of Generation X, except for some relatively flimsy references to "diversity." The first came in 1992, when *Business Week* pointed out that the baby buster generation was "more ethnically diverse, and they're more comfortable with diversity than any previous generation" (*Business Week* 1992:75). *Newsweek* made the same point in 1994:

> Generation X most certainly is not [white]. The stereotypical Xer, as he's trotted out in movies and in the media, is white and privileged and living in a suburb near you.[6] But twentysomethings are actually the most racially diverse of any generation to date: they're [only] 70% white. . . . Xers may also be the least racist. "We are the first generation to be born into an integrated society," writes Eric Liu, a foreign-policy speechwriter for President Clinton . . . (Giles 1994:65–66).

The point of these comments in both cases is quite unclear, as they never get integrated into some larger discourse about Generation X. They have a somewhat congratulatory tone, as if being demographically more diverse were some sort of (white) achievement, or as if it guaranteed a growth of tolerance, which may or may not be the case—no evidence is presented. In any event, despite these indications of greater diversity, the actual Generation X public culture—the journalism, the novels, the films—is almost entirely white. And despite the vast influence and popularity of African American performers in popular music, most of the musicians and groups taken as epitomizing Generation X (such as Nirvana, Beck, Hole, and Offspring) are white.[7]

For a long time it appears that nobody spoke to African Americans and other minorities about their relationship to this category. Finally the 1994 *Newsweek* article, which was concerned to sort the Gen X representations into "myths" and "realities," pointed out that the category had virtually no relevance for minorities:

> The phrase "Generation X" doesn't mean much to twenty somethings of color. . . . Allen Hughes, co-director of the inner-city coming-of-age story "Menace II Society" [said], "I mean, the media isn't aiming that at us. Our film had the same demographics as [the Gen X classic] "Reality Bites," but they didn't call it a Generation X film, they called it a damn gangsta film. Call it racist, or whatever, but we don't count when it comes to Generation X" (Giles 1994:66).

Or as rapper Dr. Dre put it, "I haven't heard anyone in my 'hood talking about [Generation X]. . . . The only X I know is Malcolm X" (quoted in Giles 1994:64).

My point is not so much that the Generation X representation "excludes" blacks, as if Generation X were some club to which African Americans or other minorities would like admission. Rather, it is that the racialization of the representation, white-not-racially-marked, hides more significant class divisions at work. In my own ethnographic data young African Americans in their twenties who were stuck in prime Gen X locations (I will get to what those are in a moment) sounded virtually indistinguishable from young white twenty-somethings in the same situation; it is the locations that are obscured by the racialization of the categories. This brings us finally to class.

The Transformations of the Middle Class

Whatever else Generation X has been about—social problems, ecological disasters, AIDS—it has always been, first and foremost, about identity through work: jobs, money, and careers. The issues have been economic from the very beginning: declining male wages and family incomes, working harder for less money, shrinking job markets, expensive degrees that lead nowhere, McJobs. And while one or another of these economic issues affects everyone in this society, it seems fairly clear that both the source and the target of the Generation X imagery is the middle class. That is, although poor people, mostly minorities, have actually been hit even harder than the middle class, the whiteness of the Gen X imagery just discussed indicates that these are not the people the public culture is worrying about. The centrality of the home ownership issue suggests the same thing.

Yet "the middle class" is not some empirical object that can be found lying around in the world, and this brings us back to the question of theory. By "theory" I mean a range of types of thought-frames—narratives, maps, categories, perspectives, positionalities—that operate as the conditions for allowing us to see and talk about social and cultural phenomena at all. Most theorizing in the late twentieth century is quite eclectic, drawing upon a variety of master theoretical narratives but rarely signing up for any one of them in full. Yet these master narratives, claiming to describe, explain, and represent how the social and cultural world is put together, and why things are the way they are and not otherwise, remain the (sometimes hidden) condition for the ongoing bricolage of contemporary theory-work. With respect to the questions for this essay I draw on theorizing about "late capitalism" and its entailments, about class reproduction as seen primarily from feminist perspectives, and most generally about the way in which public cultural representations operate in and through social practices and social anxieties. I begin with class transformations under late capitalism.

Recent theorizing of the postmodern condition, and the global or transnational turn, has somewhat overshadowed another major arena of theoretical activity, the attempt to retheorize late capitalism as a social structure, or in other words, to retheorize "class." A major part of this attempt derives from constructing a new narrative of capitalist transformation, which builds on Marxist theory but takes account of the further historical, institutional, and cultural changes that have taken place in the century and a half since Marx wrote.[8] The new narrative, in turn, constructs a new map of what Bourdieu (1984) has called "social space," a field of both locations and trajectories, possibilities of movement, defined by economic and cultural capital. Here, then, is a quick version of the story.

As a result of various forces unleashed by capitalism itself, as well as certain historical specifics of U.S. capitalism (e.g., the high proportion of illiterate immigrant labor), the notion of "management" and the emergence of a managerial class became a central aspect of the capitalist process starting relatively early in the twentieth century. As this class grew and became more powerful over the course of the century, theories of capitalist process had increasingly to take into account the dynamics of this class in itself—the middle class. Much of recent class theory has sought to understand what has happened to the middle class over the course of the century, and how changes in the middle class in turn have affected the structure of capitalism as a whole. The phenomenon that is called "late capitalism," including changes in relations between capital and labor and changes in the social characteristics of both the capitalist and working classes, is seen in many ways as a product of the expansion and transformation of the middle class.[9]

A major aspect of this expansion and transformation was generated at a certain point in time by boosting a large sector of the working class. Following the Second World War the GI Bill allowed thousands of veterans to go to college virtually free, and to get virtually free mortgages. The general level of prosperity in this period was extraordinarily high.[10]

This set of factors had many effects, which have all been well documented elsewhere. Here it is important to note that the home ownership program, along with changes in the occupational structure of the economy (the gradual reduction of "blue collar" jobs and the continual growth of "white collar" ones), created or vastly enlarged a zone in the class structure that the folk call the lower middle class. The lower middle class is really, one might argue, the working class in middle-class clothing (i.e., in its housing, as well as in other aspects of material culture); alternatively, it is the middle class with a working-class income.[11] Either way, it is a fundamentally insecure and interstitial place, and it is highly vulnerable to economic shifts.

Within the era of postwar prosperity, basically through the 1960s, people occupying this zone felt securely part of the middle class. They made good money. They were able to buy houses and consumer goods, and also to save for the future. They began to send their kids to college, and they bought heavily into "the American dream." They saw themselves mirrored in the new mass genre, television sitcoms, as the very type of what it means to be American (Lipsitz 1990). The culture of "the fifties," with its conservative politics and its repressive gender and sexual relations, was arguably their culture, hegemonized in part by the growth of television.

The popular image of "the middle class" as a large and relatively seamless whole, constituting the core of U.S. society, was created in this era and seemed infinitely sustainable. Starting in the 1970s, however, and accelerated by Reagan and Bush I policies in the 1980s, the middle class started pulling apart at the middle. The economy suffered a series of setbacks, and the overall level of prosperity began to slip. But Reagan and Bush I policies favored and protected the top of the structure. The top and the bottom of the middle class began pulling away from one another. Since that period the upper middle class has done better and better, while the lower middle class has been slipping down into more and more difficult straits. The old adage has absolutely applied: in this era "the rich got richer and the poor got poorer" (Duncan et al. 1992:38).

It is to this widening abyss in the middle class, I would argue, that the Generation X imagery is addressed. The most consistent aspect of the representations involves pointing at and constructing the characteristics of the social and economic abyss. Since the abyss is in many ways real, it takes no sleight of hand for the representations to be convincing. What is elided by the idea of "generation," however, is that people's relationships to the middle-class abyss are very different. Depending on which edge one is standing on, the configurations of anger, fear, anxiety, and resentment will vary. Yet all of Generation X can agree that it is "there." As a first move in the discussion, then, we need to look at the structures of feeling generated around this abyss. We begin with the view from the lower edge.

GENERATION X AS THE CHILDREN OF THE LOWER MIDDLE CLASS

Katherine Newman's *Declining Fortunes* (1993) was one of the pioneering works in establishing the argument that the generation that followed the baby boom was getting a raw deal.[12] Newman never uses the phrase "Generation X," but her portrait of "Pleasanton, New Jersey" maps almost perfectly onto one dimension of the Gen X literature. The book opens with (and contains throughout) quotes from informants that embody the anger and frustration over "declining fortunes" that are the hallmark of Generation X. For example:

> In Cathy's life, financial limitations create what she calls a "low burning thing," a subtext of constraint, a feeling that she is not free. This above all is the meaning of the intergenerational slide: the freedom to consume is cut short, the ability to plan for the long run is limited, and the bitter sense of rules turned inside out makes people feel, to use Cathy's words, like "it was all a big lie" (1993:20).

Or again, Newman quotes from "Lauren": "I'm living a lifestyle that's way lower than it was when I was growing up and it's depressing. . . . Even if you are a hard worker and you never skipped a beat, you followed all the rules, did everything they told you you were supposed to do, it's still horrendous. *They lied to me*" (1993:3). Newman's "Pleasanton" is described as embodying the full spread of the middle class, but various scattered indicators (e.g., occupational, ethnic) show that the bulk of the town, or perhaps the bulk of New-man's informants, were lower middle class. One indicator here is that there is a large Catholic sector of the population, and that "Jews were a decided minority" (1993:10); within the ethnic and religious spread of New Jersey, however, one knows that the Jews are strongly represented in the upper middle class, while the Catholics are the locus classicus of the lower middle class.

With respect to occupation the town is represented as "middle class," with occupations ranging from "white collar professionals [to] skilled blue-collar craftsmen" (Newman 1993:x). Nonetheless most of the informants quoted by Newman as specifically feeling the effects of "the withering of the American dream" (Newman's subtitle) seem to be upper working or lower middle class. Lauren's father was "a quiet man of working class origins and modest means" (1993:2); Simon Rittenberg was a salesman for security devices (12); "Martin's father was a blue-collar man through and through" (14).

Moreover, informants themselves were quite aware that the "middle-class" facade of the town contained an incipient split: "[My son] could always go to Michael's and play big shot over there. He made these friends. But I noticed that when he got in college . . . his friends seemed to be those who were more [like us]. Some did go to college, but one had a landscaping business, or an upholstery business. Some joined their fathers' trades." (Newman 1993:78) Another informant articulated a variant of the contradiction that is always lurking within the lower middle class, what I referred to above as the working class in middle-class clothing: She described her family as "a Sears Roebuck family living in a Bloomingdales' community" (1993:77).

It is worth noting that Newman's community is not only "lower middle class" but also white. I noted earlier the degree to which "Generation X" does not seem to embody a black referent (Coker 1994; James 1994; as well as interviewees quoted in Giles 1994). The whiteness of "Pleasanton" may explain particularly the sense of betrayal one hears in Newman's informants. African Americans are certainly just as angry as whites in this situation, if not more so, but they may never have felt that they had been promised more, that they had been "lied to" in the first place.

It makes sense that people who feel that they are slipping economically, despite their best efforts, would be frustrated and angry.[13] It is more of a puzzle to hear Gen X–type noises from the other side of the abyss, to which we now turn.

GENERATION X AS THE CHILDREN OF THE UPPER MIDDLE CLASS

As part of the larger project noted earlier, I had been interviewing Generation Xers in the early 1990s, that is, during the period in which the Gen X representation was taking shape and gaining visibility in the media. I was actually referred to the novel *Generation X* (Coupland 1991) by one of my interviewees, who recommended it to me as capturing important aspects of his own experience.

I interviewed about 50 people in their twenties, all of whom were children of my own high school classmates. They were scattered around the country, but most of the interviews were done in New York City, the New Jersey suburbs, Ann Arbor, and Los Angeles. Most of their parents, and most of these kids, are Jewish, although that will not play much of a role in the present discussion.[14] More important, for present purposes, are class factors: their parents, the Class of '58 of Weequahic High School in Newark, New Jersey, had been lower-to-middle middle class in the 1950s; many of them had done very well financially and were well up into the upper middle class by now. This meant in turn that many of their kids, the Xers I interviewed for the study, had grown up with a good bit of economic and cultural capital. Not all of them were either Jewish or had grown up in privileged circumstances, and the range of young people I interviewed had at least some diversity in terms of ethnicity, race, and class. I concentrate here, however, on the children of what is now the upper middle class.

What I found striking—astonishing, even—about these young people was that, despite all their capital (money, fine schools, self-assurance) they were just as upset about their economic situations as Newman's informants. Rather than being angry at the system, however, they expressed their distress as tremendous fear and insecurity about either achieving the level of success of their parents or holding on to what they had. While there are many Gen X aspects to these interviews, I select here a few passages that express this high level of economic anxiety and insecurity. Take, for example, David, the son of a wealthy businessman. He was 24 years old at the time of the interview (1993), living in New York and trying to launch a career as an artist.[15] David had gone to an elite college, was still being supported by his parents, and knew that he was very privileged. Every possible safety net was in place: his education, his parents' money, and a sense of plausible alternatives (law school, graduate

school) in case his career hopes did not work out. But David was still worried about the future:

> Look, I am willing to put in hard work, that has never been a problem. . . . There is this one guy, Edward, who is 29 I think, graduated years before me and he is [also trying to succeed as an artist]. He has these small shows, sometimes he gets a good crowd, sometimes not . . . and I look at him and I'm thinking, "Oh my God, I do not want to be 29, I do not want to be 30, I don't want to be 31 and still having no money at all and being no further along than I was when I was 24. . . ." To me that still sets in a panic attack of "Oh my God," and I try to think, that is not just my parents doing this to me, that's me.

David viewed his anxieties as specific to his Gen X positioning; it was he who recommended the novel *Generation X* (Coupland 1991) to me.

And then there was Karen, age 27, the daughter of a very successful doctor. She also went to an elite college, but at the time of the interview (1994) did not quite know what she wanted to do with her life. She had moved back in with her parents for a while after college while trying out various jobs in the New York–New Jersey area. But she came to feel that she needed to go someplace completely new and get a fresh start. Her parents agreed and were footing most of the bills for her to live in California while she figured out what she wanted to do. Karen had much the same configuration of anxieties about privilege, work, and success that we heard from David. In particular she felt guilty about her parents' unending flow of financial support, while at the same time she saw no real career possibilities for herself. She began by talking about a roommate who was also supported by his parents:

> [About] my roommate in New York—how did he not work for a whole year? How much money did his parents send him over that year? I mean how much does it take for a person to live, rent was nine to twelve thousand a year, cash. So we have a lot of guilt . . . [she thus insists on paying part of the rent herself] and my dad says "Are you sure, can you pay your rent?" and I say yes because I am working three jobs. And I could take the money [he offers] and party out here and go on hikes and write, do my thing, but I always know that I owe it to myself to keep making the effort to make my own living. . . .

Yet Karen too seemed to have little confidence that she would succeed. Although she was evidently an extremely talented writer, she was not pursuing a writing career. As I wrote in my summary of the interview, "The biggest part of her story was basically an unhappy history of boring and unfulfilling jobs. She [said that she] and her friends talk about Generation X all the time; they feel it really describes them."

As a final example, take Charles, 26, the son of a wealthy businessman. Charles went to an elite undergraduate college as well, and then went on to take an M.B.A. before joining his father's well-established and highly profitable business. At the time of the interview (1994) he had only been in the business for a year but he was doing very well, in terms of both making internal managerial improvements and bringing in new accounts. Moreover, not only were his own parents wealthy, but his fiancee's parents were also. Nonetheless he described himself as "terrified, absolutely terrified" of the possibility of financial ruin. Here is one of his many long riffs on the subject:

> Now my dad gave me his old Jaguar, I mean this is like a $50,000 car that I'm driving around. . . . I told my dad, I said, "Dad, look, this car is way beyond me, if you want this thing back I would not feel bad." . . . I don't care what the fuck I am driving, you just have got to produce something. Am I status conscious? Yeah. Do I feel great driving that car? Yeah. Does it make me feel good, do I love having good things and I am wearing a Rolex watch? Shit, that's great, I have had it since I was 15 years old, I mean, come on, this is the best life. But have I earned it? Have I deserved this? I am very aware of the fact that I deserve none of the shit that I have. I am very grateful. I am very aware of the fact that [my father] could fall over and die and then I am on my own and nobody is going to step in there and pick up. That's it, it's over.

I must confess at this point that for a long time I failed utterly to hear these texts as examples of Generation X anxiety. As I presented earlier versions of this piece as talks at various universities and colleges, I argued that these privileged and materially secure kids could not possibly be the "real" Generation Xers; that they have bought into representations that come from elsewhere and that do not really describe them; that what we were hearing in these texts was just recycled Protestant-ethic-type anxiety, soon to be well sublimated in hard work and more material success; that if they were Gen X at all it was only because any complaining from people with this much capital has to be heard as "whining."

Yet every time I gave a talk arguing that the real embodiment of Generation

X was the children of the lower middle class, and that the children of the upper middle class had been in effect terrorized by the media, there were howls of pain from the numerous Gen Xers (that is, graduate students) in my audiences. Finally I reminded myself of the cardinal rule of ethnography: the informant is always right. Even if, "objectively," these kids had nothing to worry about, there was something experientially real to them about the doomsaying forecasts of the Gen X literature, and this needed to be captured by the argument.[16]

Further Class Theorizing: Reproduction and Representations

At this point we must pull into this interpretive arena another active body of theorizing: the question of class reproduction via family and gender relations. This has become much more central to class theory than it used to be, a fact that may be seen as an effect of 25 years of feminist social and cultural thought. This includes, among other things, renewed attention to "youth culture" (Brake 1985; Gaines 1990; Hall and Jefferson 1976; Ortner 1992; Willis 1977). It also includes the recognition of the deep centrality of family politics, including gender and, most pertinent to the present article, generational politics, for understanding class reproduction. Although questions of family dynamics and politics in class reproduction are not missing from other recent works of class theorizing, like Bourdieu's *Distinction* (1984), they have been much more deeply explored in such feminist-inspired works as Barbara Ehrenreich's *Fear of Falling* (1989), Judith Stacey's *Brave New Families* (1990), and Elizabeth Traube's *Dreaming Identities* (1992a).

Let us start this time with the upper middle class. The characteristics of the upper middle class have by now been well described, because it is in some sense the growth of this class—what the Ehrenreichs call the "professional-managerial class," or the "PMC"—that is generally thought to have driven many of the transformations of late capitalism (Bourdieu 1984; Ehrenreich 1989; Ehrenreich and Ehrenreich 1979; Mandel 1978; Pfeil 1990; Walker 1979). Although the entire middle class is in some sense built on "managerial" functions (and hence is "white collar"), a large sector of the upper middle class specifically occupies those positions that depend on high levels of specialized education; they are the professionals of society—doctors, lawyers, judges, planners—as well as the managers of business and of finance.

As Ehrenreich and others have emphasized, the middle class in general and the upper middle class in particular cannot pass on its status to its children. This is distinctive of middle-class positionality: the lower classes find it all too easy to pass on their (low) status, while the upper classes have elaborate institutional means of preserving money and status for the group (e.g., Marcus 1992). Middle-class parents can only pass on to their children the means—economic, educational, and psychological—with which to (try to) reproduce their status. But ultimately the children must do it themselves.

The process is never secure. There are always some kids in danger of, as it is frequently put, getting off the track. Not every child can do well in school, not every child internalizes the work ethic or the commitment to "success." Although the upper middle class is down-classing slightly less than it did before 1980, the figure is still around 25 percent (Duncan et al. 1992), a figure well within the range documented for much of the twentieth century (see Lipset and Bendix 1957; Erikson and Goldthorpe 1985). Down-classing at the lower end of the middle class is surprisingly less likely overall (around 10 percent), although slightly more likely than it was before 1980 (Duncan et al. 1992). In any event it is clear that all middle-class parents have good reasons to worry about the trajectories of their particular children. But these anxieties are differently dealt with in the upper middle and the lower middle classes.

Among the upper middle class what comes through strongly in my ethnographic data is that parents will provide almost unlimited and unending support for their children, well into adulthood. It is important to remember that the postwar period, in which the parents of current twenty-somethings came of age, was a time of great prosperity, seemingly for all. Howe and Strauss call the parents of Generation X "the wealthiest generation in the history of America, maybe the world" (1993:39). This, of course, included the Class of '58 of Weequahic High School, my original ethnographic population, and the parents of the upper-middle-class Xers discussed here. These parents did very well indeed.

In turn, they told me stories of almost unlimited support for their kids.[17] The support took many forms, but certainly material benefits were front and center: a materially comfortable lifestyle while growing up, a college education, a professional education beyond that, a generous four- or five-figure wedding present, the down payment on a house, and perhaps a trust fund for the grandchildren's educations.[18]

In general parents spoke of these things as part of loving their children and wanting them to be happy, and there is no question in my mind that that was how they experienced what they were feeling and doing.[19] But at another level there was a kind of adaptationist logic behind this: several fathers said to me that they spoiled their kids by design, that they wanted them to become attached to the good things of life, so that they would want to work hard to get them. At the same time I also heard, from parents and grown children alike, about an amazing array of what I came to think of as "rescuing mechanisms" (Ortner 1992) on behalf of children who seemed to be in trouble: counseling, therapy, rehab programs, tutoring, booster courses, abortions for pregnant daughters, expensive legal services for sons in trouble with the law, and on and on.

The sum of these points is that upper-middle-class parents, in trying simply to do the best for their children out of the deepest sentiments of love and caring, were also enacting a refusal to let their kids slide down-class if they could possibly afford it. Virtually all the kids in my project, like the Xers of the public culture, had at least B.A. degrees and in some cases advanced (usually law) degrees. But those who were having trouble finding the jobs they wanted or hoped for, or having trouble starting on some career track that they sought, or finding it difficult to get a position consistent with their level of education and self-image, were being supported by their parents. In a few cases they were living at home, part of that large wave of "boomerang children" that is another piece of the Gen X picture. But for the most part these twenty-somethings were living on their own (at least physically), with a large part of the rent and other expenses covered by parents while they, the kids, sought the ideal (and not merely acceptable) job, or pursued the auditions and casting calls for careers in the arts or show business, or simply marked time till they decided what they wanted to do. The parental financial cushion, and their willingness to use it, meant that these young people had the luxury of a very extended period of uncertainty and openness about their own futures, and were not forced to lock themselves into McJobs. This is indeed cultural capital, backed up by the other, more old-fashioned, kind.

But all of this, which I found hard for a long time to view as anything but extreme privilege that should be protecting and defending these kids from anxiety, was also precisely the key to their anxieties. As the split opened up in the middle class, these kids felt like they were looking into the abyss, protected only by the safety net provided by their parents.[20] On the one hand they felt very grateful, which comes through in their texts. On the other hand they felt like they were in fact hanging over an abyss; hence the terror. As yet another Gen X informant said, "I adore working at [a certain upscale publishing house], but there's not a day when I don't think my happiness won't be pulled out from under me like a rug. And I have a trust fund!"

Let us return now to the lower middle class. We have seen that the upper middle class enacts a pattern of supporting their kids relatively lavishly, well into adulthood. The general idea, in a sense, is to front-load their potential for success, to go all out early in their careers and give them the strongest possible start. When we turn to the lower middle class, we see precisely the absence of this pattern of class reproduction. Here we must turn again to Katherine Newman's valuable ethnography of a lower-middle-class community. Newman discusses at length the fact that her informants grew up in nice houses with plenty of material comforts. They expected to do as well as, or better than, their parents. And now they realize (or fear) that they will not, which is why they are angry at the system.

Newman then raises the question of why the parents do not help out their kids. She argues that they cannot, that they are basically house-poor, and they need whatever resources they have to support their own retirements. At the same time she indicates that such massive aid to the next generation is in effect not part of the class culture, that there is a commitment to a much more classic kind of economic individualism:

> There are those—even in Pleasanton—who might ask why the postwar parents do not help out. Having benefited so much from the boom years, do they not have the resources to rescue their kids? *Even if Pleasanton parents were inclined toward rescue missions*, inclined to ignore the cultural prescription that calls for every generation to stand on its own two feet, they lack the wherewithal to prop up their adult children (1993:21, emphasis added).

I am not suggesting here that lower-middle-class parents do not adequately support their growing children. Nor am I suggesting that there is no variation; there is indeed a great deal of racial and ethnic variation that I have to gloss over here in the interests of space. But I am suggesting that the patterns are different. There is, as just indicated, a greater emphasis on the idea that kids should stand on their own two feet, and the earlier the better. Within that emphasis (and, of course, in a context of scarcer economic resources), help is more likely to take the form of sharing goods and pooling services than large transfers of cash.[21] There is also more emphasis on backing children up in case of failure rather than proactively endowing them with a lot of start-up capital and cultural boosting.

There are at least two ways in which these patterns would have worked well enough to produce "success" in times of prosperity and relative social stability, but would be problematic under 1990s' social and economic conditions. The first is simply that in better times the public sector picked up a bigger part of the tab, in the form of a better economic environment in general, and in the form of specific middle-class perks like student loans, for example.

But the second way in which lower-middle-class family economic practices have been rendered problematic relates to the specific patterns of the launching of adult children just discussed. The lower-middle-class pattern is heavily dependent on the maintenance of relatively stable family relations, on the availability of family members for backup child care, housing, and job connections. Yet the period in which the upper and lower middle class pulled apart economically was also the period of the tremendous growth of the two-earner family, the galloping divorce rate, the declining fortunes of divorced mothers, and so on. That is, what was attenuated in this period was not only a larger structure of economic resources and opportunities, but the specific form of the safety net upon which the lower middle class depended. This, then, is certainly a recipe for frustration and rage.

In the worst cases we see some social pathologies that are not normally recognized as part of the Generation X phenomenon, but that might fruitfully be looked at in that light. For example Joan Didion wrote a riveting piece on the "Spur Posse," a gang of youth in white, (lower-) "middle-class" Lakewood, California, who engaged in systematic gang rape and other forms of terrorism in their own community (1993). Didion situated the phenomenon within the massive unemployment generated by the collapse of the aerospace industry, including a large amount of white-collar unemployment. For another example Donna Gaines (1990) powerfully explored the dead-end conditions for lower-middle-class youth in Bergenfield, New Jersey, in order to understand what led four teenagers to collectively commit suicide there in 1987.

Lower-middle-class rage and depression, and upper-middle-class terror and whining, are thus two sides of looking into the same abyss, an abyss

portrayed in the public culture and theorized in accounts of class transformation and class reproduction. From the lower side this abyss seems increasingly
impossible to cross; from the upper side it seems all too easy.

At this point a shift in analytic strategy is called for. Thus far I have
portrayed the problematic as having three virtually independent pieces: the
public cultural representations, the ethnographic accounts of informants'
lives and talk, and a theoretical frame (or parts of one) that allows us to see
how class works and how it has been changing. This strategy has allowed us to
see a number of useful things: that the public culture hides social difference
even as it reveals (a certain picture of) social reality; that the amorphousness
of the representational process (Gen Xers are angry, depressed, whining, and
slacking, all at once) hides the ways in which different parts of the mix of
images actually apply to different and even antagonistic social locations; that a
theorized framework allows us to begin to sort out what goes where.

Yet this strategy itself obscures other questions. In particular I have so far
failed to ask in any systematic way about the production of these representations. In addition, apart from an early passing reference to "interpellating"
(Althusser 1971) or constituting Generation X, largely as a marketing target, I
have not asked what kinds of productive work these representations might in
turn be doing in the social process. Here we need to recall that the middle class
in general, and the upper middle class in particular, are not only the referents
and objects of Gen X imagery, but also its makers. Who after all writes the
screenplays, the novels, the advertising copy, the journalistic reports, the demographic surveys? If at one level the public culture stands over and against
what is going on on the ground, at another level it is one of the things that is
made on the ground. This brings us to the final section of this essay.

The Problem of the Slacker

In addition to the angry young lower-middle-class people with college degrees
working in McJobs, and the privileged but highly anxious children of the
upper middle class who come across as "whiners," there is one other classic
Gen X figure that needs to be addressed: the "slacker." The image of the slacker
derives from Richard Linklater's 1991 film by that name (published later as a
book: Linklater 1992), in which a series of seemingly bright, young, downwardly mobile twenty-somethings carom off one another ironically, absurdly,
funnily, for an hour and a half. All are either unemployed or working in jobs

that are beneath their abilities, educations, or parents' class positions. As Linklater said in an interview, "It's not that everyone in *Slacker* is unemployed, it's just that their little slave job isn't what's motivating them in the world" (quoted in Petrek and Hines 1993). This is classic Gen X stuff, another version of McJobs. But as Linklater himself says, most people think a slacker is simply "someone who's lazy, hangin' out, doing nothing" (quoted in Petrek and Hines 1993).[22]

Every Xer I have talked to across the class spectrum has hated the "slacker" label for their generation. All felt that they worked hard, and that their problems about their futures were not of their own making. Many, however, knew a slacker or two—recall Karen's roommate who lived in their expensive New York apartment and did not work for a whole year.

Let me suggest that the referent of the slacker image is the falling upper-middle-class child, but the power of the image is not simply in its referent. Recall here the figures for downward mobility in the upper middle class: one out of four kids will not make it, and in really bad times, one out of three. If, as we have seen, the kids are terrified about failure, their parents are equally (or more) frightened for their kids. One indicator of the depth of their fears is the degree to which it was difficult to get parents to acknowledge, no less discuss, children with serious problems. Along with criminality, this was certainly the most sensitive area of my fieldwork. Kids with serious problems were not the ones who sent back their questionnaires. And parent-talk about kids was almost entirely and unrelievedly upbeat: all the kids were reported to be doing unbelievably well at whatever it was they were doing. One is reminded of Garrison Keillor's Lake Wobegon, where all the children are above average. I do not think there was a single interview in which a parent actually volunteered a story about a child in trouble.

Yet one way or another I picked up fragments of the stories these middle-class parents did not tell, about the kids who got into drugs, who did poorly in school, who became pregnant at a young age, who got in trouble with the law, or who did not finish college and wound up as hairdressers or secretaries or mechanics. (These are, of course, perfectly respectable occupations, but from the point of view of the upper middle class, they represent failures of "achievement.") These kids are sources of great pain to their parents because the parents love them and do not want to see them damaged. They are also sources of conflict, as parents try to change their lives over and against the children's resistance. And they are sources of embarrassment verging on humiliation, as they stand in for and embody the parents' own anxieties about personal success in the world.

The degree to which upper-middle-class parents are sensitive about problems with and about their children, and the kinds of intense feelings generated around a problematic child, gives some sense of the anxieties behind the production and reception of a representation like the slacker. Slackers are images of (the possibility of) these kids as downwardly mobile and not even caring. More than markers of a social type, slackers are models of parental anxieties, pictures of upper-middle-class parents' worst fears for their kids. Moreover for these parents slackers are contradictions waiting to happen: When (if ever) does the parental support run out? When does one cut these kids loose financially? After all, the support was meant to be in the service of launching upward mobility, giving the kids the time to wait for the big break. If this period goes on too long, it becomes apparent to the parents that they have in fact financed downward mobility instead.

From the point of view of the anxious, young Gen Xers themselves, either locked into McJobs or hanging in the safety net, the slacker is a more complex figure—a figure of repulsion and resentment, but also of envy. Slackers' lives may be empty, but at least they have stopped feeling the pain. Or have they? Although the characters in the film *Slacker* appear to have adopted this stance, the characters in *Generation X* spend the entire novel in a desperate quest to fend off a sense of meaninglessness. As one of the characters says, "We know that this is why the three of us left our lives behind and came to the desert—to tell stories and to make our own lives worthwhile in the process" (Coupland 1991:8).

Some Conclusions

Anthropology increasingly operates in the midst of the contemporary world. Whereas once upon a time it was the hallmark of anthropologists to leave the world, to go far away, to seek the untouched and the premodern, it is now much more common for anthropologists to work in their home societies, or in sites of the "modern" wherever it happens to be. Even when they did not go far away, even when they worked in their home societies or on "modern" phenomena, the anthropological trick in the past was often to treat the community under study as if it were distant and exotic.

One implication of the shift to the here and now (or to recognizing the hereness and nowness of everything) is that anthropology becomes only one voice, one entry, within an enormously complex and multivocal universe of "public culture." In this context what—if anything—is its distinctive contribution? One obvious answer derives from the richness of ethnographic data, a product of doing long-term, in-depth, whole-self (or much-self) fieldwork. Ethnographic understanding is built up through density, "thickness" of observation, over an extended period of time. Perhaps the most extreme opposite of this kind of understanding is to be seen in some forms of television journalism, with its reliance on quick visual cuts and chopped sound bites. For all the attacks on elevated claims of "ethnographic authority" (some of which I agree with), I would still make the argument that classic long, deep ethnographic fieldwork produces some kinds of truth that a necessarily quicker and shallower journalism cannot produce.[23]

Yet in the end ethnography is not enough. Ethnography is not the whole of anthropology, and it is important for the field to resist being confined to that box. Ethnography always takes place in explicit or implicit interaction with theory, that is to say, with competing bigger pictures of how things are "really" put together (regardless of what the natives say) and why.

It is theory that allows us to map the world in such a way that we can understand the relationship between various journalistic and ethnographic claims, rather than engaging in a competitive struggle for authority. At least this is how I have proceeded in this chapter. I have argued that a range of recent theoretical thinking allows us to locate the diverse representations about twenty-somethings, including (diverse) representations of "Generation X" and my own ethnographic data, within a larger picture, a picture of changing class relations in the United States under "late capitalism." I have taken "theory" in a broad sense to include a variety of models, metaphors, arguments, and accounts that attempt to stand outside the "data" and provide some critical interpretive frames for understanding them, yet that do not fall into some sort of naive "objectivism." Thus I have drawn at different moments on rethought narratives of capitalist development in the late twentieth century, on feminist arguments concerning the centrality of intimate relations to the reproduction of all relations of inequality, including class, and (more implicitly) on theories of representation from Clifford Geertz and Louis Althusser to the present.

Theories of representation, in turn, compel us to think not only about the relationship between a signifier and its referent, but about representations as produced and consumed within a field of inequality and power, and shaped as much by those relations of production and consumption as by the nature of the supposed referent. Thus I have suggested, if only briefly, that the idea of Generation X tells us as much about the anxieties of upper-middle-class parents as it does about some set of young people out there in the world. We may think of the public culture on Generation X in part as the product of a cultural scouting expedition on behalf of these people, a trip to what to them is the edge of social space, and a set of postcards from that edge.

CHAPTER 5

Subjectivity and Cultural Critique

This essay considers the importance of the notion of subjectivity for a critical anthropology.[1] Although there is no necessary link between questions of subjectivity and questions of power and subordination, and although a great deal of work both inside and outside of anthropology explores subjectivity as a relatively neutral arena of inquiry, my particular interest is in extending those lines of work that do see a close linkage between subjectivity and power. Hence the significance of investigating subjectivity as part of "anthropology as cultural critique" (Marcus and Fisher 1986).

By subjectivity I mean the ensemble of modes of perception, affect, thought, desire, and fear that animate acting subjects. But I always mean as well the cultural and social formations that shape, organize, and provoke those modes of affect, thought, and so on. This essay will thus move back and forth between the examination of such cultural formations and the inner states of acting subjects.

A Brief History of the Debate over the Subject

Given that the idea of the subject is itself a bone of contention, it is worth first considering the history of the debate over it. One could look at the unfolding of social and cultural theory over the whole twentieth century and beyond as a struggle over the role of the social being—the person, subject, actor, or agent—in society and history. Although the origins of the struggle over the significance of the subject can be pushed back much further within philosophy, the twentieth-century version appears as a debate largely between the newly evolving social sciences on the one hand and certain lines of philosophic thinking on the other.[2] In the first half of the twentieth century the debate took shape as a philosophical reaction to the emergence of theories of social "constraint" (Durkheim) and "determinism" (Marx), with Sartre in particular arguing instead, in *Being and Nothingness* (1966 [1943]), for the primacy of human "freedom."

Responding directly to Sartre, in turn, Lévi-Strauss pushed Durkheim in new and more extreme directions, and also to some extent shifted the terms of the debate away from the categories of freedom and determinism. Where Durkheim argued for a level of "the social" which could be analyzed with little reference to subjects, nonetheless the subject (which he usually called the individual) remained important as a presence in the theoretical edifice, as that upon which and through which "society" does its work, and who even occasionally puts up a little struggle (Durkheim 1982:51). Lévi-Strauss took Durkheim's notion of the social fact that exists over and above the individual, and that almost has a life of its own, and sought to purify it of the presence of and necessity for subjects at all. Thus in the "Overture" to *The Raw and the Cooked* he famously wrote: "I therefore claim to show, not how men think in myths, but how myths operate in men's minds without their being aware of the fact. . . . It would perhaps be better to go still further and, disregarding the thinking subject completely, proceed as if the thinking process were taking place in the myths, in their reflection upon themselves and their interrelation" (Lévi-Strauss 1969: 12). Here it is no longer exactly a matter of freedom and constraint. It is not only the idea that the freedom of the subject is illusory, but that human thinking itself is simply an effect of, or a medium for, the pure play of structure. As Lévi-Strauss said in *The Savage Mind*, the aim of the human sciences was "not to constitute but to dissolve man" (1966:247). And as Nik Farrell Fox summarizes in a recent biography of Sartre: " . . . structuralism embarked upon a concerted critique of humanism and anthropocentrism, inverting humanist premises by prioritizing structure over the subject, the unconscious over the conscious, and the objective analyses of scientific laws over ego-based epistemologies" (2003:24).

The present landscape of social and cultural theory must be viewed against a backdrop of this history. There are in effect three lines of discussion. The first is so-called poststructuralism itself, which emphatically drops the Durkheimian positivism still present in Lévi-Strauss ("the objective analyses of scientific laws") and which focuses even more actively on "dissolving man." The terms of the critique take another slight turn here as the critique of the concept of "man" begins to emphasize not only its illusory qualities from a philosophical point of view (the self as an originary locus of coherence, intentionality, and creativity), but its ideological specificity. In the hands of feminist poststructuralists (e.g., Joan Scott 1988) the issue is its masked gendered nature: what pretends to be man in the universal sense is, literally, man in the gendered sense—men. In the hands of postcolonial poststructuralists (e.g., Spivak 1988) the issue is the location of the idea of a supposedly universal man in what is actually a specifically Western project of domination: (colonial) white men.

Looking at the issue in these terms, one can understand the continuing appeal of poststructuralism in many academic quarters, including major areas of anthropology. Nonetheless its antihumanism poses real problems for an anthropology that wishes to understand not just the workings of power but the attempts of subalterns (in the Gramscian sense) to attain to the privilege of becoming subjects in the first place.[3]

We must turn to a second important line of post-Lévi-Straussian (but not "poststructuralist") thinking, one that does attempt to restore a subject in some form to the center of social theory, but at the same time seeks to retheorize the subject in ways that do not reinstate the illusory universalism of "man." Here I would place the various versions of so-called practice theory, as seen in the work of Pierre Bourdieu (e.g., 1977, 1990, 2000), Anthony Giddens (esp. 1979), Marshall Sahlins (esp. 1981), William H. Sewell Jr. (1992), and several works of my own (e.g., Ortner 1984, 1996a, 1999a). Leaving aside my own work, which in any event I am trying to develop further here, we can see that the various thinkers just listed have a variety of theorizations of the subject. For Bourdieu the subject internalizes the structures of the external world, both culturally defined and objectively real. These internalized structures form a habitus, a system of dispositions that incline actors to act, think, and feel in ways consistent with the limits of the structure. While there are aspects of the concept of habitus that can be mapped onto a notion of subjectivity, especially "dispositions," the main emphasis of Bourdieu's arguments about habitus is on the ways in which it establishes a range of options and limits for the social actor. Sahlins, also influenced by French structuralist thought, and also at the same time resisting its antihumanism, constructs a subject very similar to Bourdieu's, very structurally driven. But, since Sahlins writes about real historical actors (e.g., Captain Cook), his descriptions of their actions sometimes show them to be subjectively more complex than he captures in his theoretical account of their actions.

For Giddens and Sewell though, while subjects are understood to be fully culturally and structurally produced, there is also an emphasis on the importance of an element of "agency" in all social subjects. As against Bourdieu's insistence on the deeply internalized and largely unconscious nature of social knowledge in acting subjects, Giddens emphasizes that subjects are always at least partially "knowing," and thus able to act on and sometimes against the structures that made them. And as against the heavy structural determinism of Bourdieu, Sewell marshalls his historian's perspective to argue that "in the world of human struggles and strategems, plenty of thoughts, perceptions, and actions consistent with the reproduction of existing social patterns fail to occur, and inconsistent ones occur all the time" (1992:15).

All of these thinkers who have in one way or another brought back the acting subject to social theory have significantly inspired my own thinking, and I have written about the importance of their work in many other contexts. Having said this let me suggest that there is a particular lack or area of thinness in all of their work that opens up the space of this essay: a tendency to slight the question of subjectivity, that is, the view of the subject as existentially complex, a being who feels and thinks and reflects, who makes and seeks meaning.[4]

Why does this matter? Why is it important to restore the question of subjectivity to social theory? In part it is important because it is a major dimension of human existence, and to ignore it theoretically is to impoverish the sense of the human in the so-called human sciences. But it is also important politically, as I said at the beginning of this essay. In particular I see subjectivity as the basis of "agency," a necessary part of understanding how people (try to) act on the world even as they are acted upon. Agency is not some natural or originary will; it takes shape as specific desires and intentions within a matrix of subjectivity—of (culturally constituted) feelings, thoughts, and meanings.

Let me offer a preliminary definition. By "subjectivity" I will always mean a specifically cultural and historical consciousness. In using the word "consciousness" I do not mean to exclude various unconscious dynamics as seen, for example, in a Freudian unconscious or a Bourdieusian habitus. But I do mean that subjectivity is always more than those things, in two senses. At the individual level I will assume, with Giddens, that actors are always at least partially "knowing subjects," that they have some degree of reflexivity about themselves and their desires, and that they have some "penetration" into the ways in which they are formed by their circumstances.[5] They are, in short, conscious in the conventional psychological sense, something that needs to be emphasized as a complement to, though not a replacement of, Bourdieu's insistence on the inaccessibility to actors of the underlying logic of their practices. At the collective level I use the word "consciousness" as it is used by both Marx and Durkheim: as the collective sensibility of some set of socially interrelated actors. Consciousness in this sense is always ambiguously part of people's personal subjectivities and part of the public culture, and this ambiguity runs through much of what follows. At times I will address subjectivity in the more psychological sense, in terms of the inner feelings, desires, anxieties, and intentions of individuals; but at other times I will focus on large-scale cultural formations.

The question of complex subjectivities in the more psychological (which is not to say acultural) sense is most often to be seen in studies of dominated groups. Questions not only of "agency" (and "resistance") but of pain or fear or confusion, as well as various modes of overcoming these subjective states, have been central to this kind of work. Examples would include Lila Abu-Lughod (1986, 1993) on Bedouin women's structures of feeling as shaped and expressed in poetry and narratives; José Limón (1994) on the sense of fragmentation among poor Mexican-Americans; Ashis Nandy (1983) on the disorientation and reorientation of Indian "selves" under colonialism; Purnima Mankekar (1999) on Indian women's complex reactions to television epics; and Tassadit Yacine (1992) on the gendered nature of fear among the Kabyle.[6] In all these cases there is an exploration of how the condition of subjection is subjectively constructed and experienced, as well as the creative ways in which it is—if only episodically—overcome.

In addition to this kind of investigation at the level of individual actors or groups of actors, there is also a tradition of research and interpretation at a broader cultural (and political) level, concerning the ways in which particular cultural formations shape and provoke subjectivities. At this point I want to shift to that level. I will begin by returning to some of the classic work by Clifford Geertz. Writing over the same period as Lévi-Strauss, Bourdieu, Sahlins, and others discussed earlier, Geertz was the only major social and cultural thinker to tackle the question of subjectivity in the sense discussed here.

Another Look at Geertz's Concept of Culture

In a few celebrated essays in the 1960s and 1970s Geertz drew on philosophy and literary theory to articulate a specifically cultural approach to subjectivity and, one could also say, a specifically subjectivity-oriented theory of culture.[7] The two are so closely interrelated that one cannot be discussed without the other. I will start with culture.

There are two identifiable dimensions to Geertz's theory of culture. On the one hand there is the classic American concept of culture, identified with Boas, Mead, Benedict, and others and defined substantively as the worldview and ethos of a particular group of people. On the other hand there is a philosophical and literary theory of the cultural *process*, inspired particularly by Wittgenstein, which emphasizes the construction of meaning, and of subjectivities, through symbolic processes embedded in the social world.

As anyone tuned into the anthropological literature over the past several decades will know, the concept of "culture" has come under severe attack. I have discussed the culture debate elsewhere (Ortner 1999b; introduction to this volume), but one cannot proceed with a discussion of Geertz's work without addressing it anew each time. I will, however, take the discussion in a somewhat different direction here.

If Geertz's concept of culture has two strands, it is fairly clear that the problematic strand is culture in the first, American, sense, that is, the idea that particular groups "have" particular cultures, each its own, and that this culture is "shared" by all members of the group. The critiques of culture in this sense take several forms. The first is that the culture concept is too undifferentiated, too homogeneous: given various forms of social difference and social inequality, how could everyone in a given society share the same view of the world and the same orientation towards it?[8] The second, and more fatal critique is that the homogeneity and lack of differentiation in the culture concept tied it closely to "essentialism," the idea that "the Nuer" or "the Balinese" had some single essence which made them the way they were, and which, moreover, explained much of what they did and how they did it. One can see the dangers of this position when one looks at the kinds of representations of "Arab culture" or "Muslim culture" that are being bandied about in the post-9/11 world. Geertz of course never subscribed to this kind of thinking. His interest in understanding cultural difference was precisely the opposite, as a way of opening up "conversations" across cultural lines. But the concept itself turned out to be more politically slippery than it had appeared in an earlier era.

Geertz's defense in *After the Fact* (1995) of what I am calling the American culture concept rests mainly on the grounds that culture is real, and that critics are burying their heads in the sand to deny it. I agree, but the critique calls for a more articulated defense in terms of the politics involved in using the concept. Thus, while recognizing the very real dangers of "culture" in its potential for essentializing and demonizing whole groups of people, one must recognize its critical political value as well, both for understanding the workings of power and for understanding the resources of the powerless.

Looked at on the side of power, first, one can recognize a cultural formation as a relatively coherent body of symbols and meanings, ethos and worldview, and at the same time understand those meanings as ideological, and/or as part of the forces and processes of domination. Perhaps the most important figure in recasting the culture concept in this direction has been Raymond Williams, with his adaptation of the Gramscian notion of hegemony.[9] Williams's work launched a virtual scholarly revolution, part of the creation of that enormous, fertile, and unruly field called "cultural studies." While the American version of cultural studies came to be dominated by (mostly French) literary theory, in Britain cultural studies was much more anthropological, involving ethnographic fieldwork (especially Paul Willis's classic *Learning to Labor* [1977]), and productively deploying Williams's view of culture as hegemony, that is, as an interworking of the American culture concept and the Marxist concept of ideology (Williams, 1977:108–9).[10] The discussions of postmodern culture as part of the larger hegemony of late capitalism, to be considered later in this article, will illustrate this kind of work.

Looked at from the side of the less powerful, culture in the American anthropological sense, but again with a more critical edge, lives on in studies of "popular culture." These are studies of the local worlds of subjects and groups who, however much they are dominated or marginalized, seek to make meaningful lives for themselves: race and ethnic cultures (e.g., Limón 1994), working-class cultures (e.g., Lipsitz 1994), and youth cultures (e.g., Amit-Talai and Wulff 1995; Taylor 2001; Thornton 1995). As in classic American anthropology, culture is here seen as being shared by a group, part of their collective form of life, embodying their shared history and identity, worldview and ethos. Studies of popular culture in this sense also tend to introduce, implicitly or explicitly, a Bakhtinian perspective, seeing culture as embodying some sort of resistance, some sort of mischief, or alternatively as playful and pleasurable, part of making a life on the margins of structures of domination. Robin D. G. Kelley's *Yo' Mama's Dysfunktional!* (1997) about African American popular culture is a wonderful example of this kind of work.

In sum "culture," even in something like the old American sense, is not *inherently* a conservative or dangerous concept; there is a kind of category mistake in seeing it as such. It is a flexible and powerful concept that can be used in many different ways including, most importantly, as part of a political critique.

The American-style culture concept was, however, only one dimension of Geertz's theory. The other was a set of ideas about how cultural processes work and what they do. Geertz argued that culture should be understood as public symbolic forms, forms that both express and shape *meaning for actors* engaged in the ongoing flow of social life. And, although the idea of "meaning" too may go off in many different directions, Geertz's specific interest has been in the forms of subjectivity that cultural discourses and practices both reflect and organize. This brings us back to subjectivity and consciousness.

The Cultural Construction of Subjectivity

In two of his most famous articles, "Person, Time, and Conduct in Bali" (1973c [1966]), and "Deep Play: Notes on the Balinese Cockfight" (1973d [1972]), Geertz provides powerful displays of his method at work, interpreting Balinese cultural forms—person terms, calendrical systems, rules of etiquette, cockfighting events—for the modes of consciousness they embody.

It is important to keep the interpretive method and the concern with subjectivity (historical and cultural consciousness) together. There are forms of cultural analysis today, mostly inspired by Foucauldian or other lines of poststructuralist thought, that emphasize the ways in which discourses construct subjects and subject positions, and that thus have a superficial resemblance to Geertzian interpretation. But the subjects in question in those kinds of analysis are defined largely in terms of political (usually subordinate) locations ("subject positions") and political (usually subordinate) identities—subaltern (in the colonial sense), woman, racialized other, and so on. This is not an unimportant exercise by any means, but it is different from the question of the formation of *subjectivities*, complex structures of thought, feeling, and reflection, that make social beings always more than the occupants of particular positions and the holders of particular identities.[11]

Geertz makes clear that he traces his ways of thinking about subjectivity back to Max Weber, and there is no better place to begin than with Weber's discussion of the ways in which Protestantism shaped the consciousness of early modern subjects. Starting from the Protestant doctrine of predestination and its assumption of the remoteness and inaccessibility of God, Weber argues that Calvinistic Protestantism instilled in its subjects a particular structure of feelings: "In its extreme inhumanity this doctrine must above all have had one consequence for the life of a generation which surrendered to its magnificent consistency. That was a feeling of unprecedented inner loneliness of the single individual" (1958:104).

Weber creates a picture of the ways in which Protestantism intensified religious anxieties at every turn. For example Calvinism allowed the practice of the "private confession" of sin to lapse, with the result that "the means to a periodical discharge of the emotional sense of sin was done away with" (Weber 1958:106). And of course the ultimate source of religious anxiety was the psychologically unbearable situation of having one's fate predestined, and yet having no means of discovering what that destiny is.

Weber's entire strategy for constructing the links between Protestantism and "the spirit of capitalism" rests on showing how specific Protestant doctrines and practices both induced these anxieties and prescribed solutions to them. The solutions—"intense worldly activity" (1958:112), "conduct [in worldly affairs] which served to increase the glory of God" (114), "systematic self-control" (115), and more—in turn were productive not merely of a certain kind of religious subject but, Weber famously argues, of an early capitalist subject as well. I will not follow Weber's argument about this connection further. My point here is simply that this culturally and religiously produced subject is defined not only by a particular position in a social, economic, and religious matrix, but by a complex subjectivity, a complex set of feelings and fears, which are central to the whole argument.

As for Weber, so for Geertz: Cultures are public systems of symbols and meanings, texts and practices, that both represent a world and shape subjects in ways that fit the world as represented. Geertz lays out the theoretical bases of this argument in "Religion as a Cultural System" (1973b [1966]) and also provides some brief examples there. But the fullest displays of both his point and his method are to be found in two extended interpretations of Balinese cultural forms.

The first, "Person, Time, and Conduct in Bali" (1973c [1966]), is a reading of multiple Balinese symbolic orders—one could perhaps call them discourses —to try to get at the kind of subjectivity they both reflect and shape. These include Balinese "orders of person-definition" (personal names, birth-order names, kinship terms, status titles, and more); Balinese discourses of time; and Balinese rules and patterns of social etiquette. Geertz interprets in detail all these forms, first individually, and then in terms of how they reinforce one another, all with an eye to understanding the kind of consciousness they converge to produce.

He argues (to jump to the conclusion of an enormously complex analysis) that the discourses of personhood are such as to produce a kind of "anonymization of persons," and that the systems of time reckoning are such as to produce an "immobilization of time" (1973c:398). Both, he argues, should be seen as cultural attempts to "block the more creatural aspects of the human condition—individuality, spontaneity, perishability, emotionality, vulnerability—from sight" (399). They converge, then, with a cultural passion for the "ceremonialization of social intercourse" which, ideally at least, has largely a parallel effect: of keeping many relationships in a "sociological middle distance" (399).

At one level all of this both enacts and induces a certain cultural style, what Geertz calls "playful theatricality" (1973c:402). But Geertz pushes further into the underlying shape of subjectivity involved, by examining the Balinese emotional category or state of *lek*, which he translates as "stage-fright . . . a diffuse, usually mild, though in certain situations virtually paralyzing, nervousness before the prospect (and the fact) of social interaction, a chronic, mostly low-grade worry that one will not be able to bring it off with the required finesse" (402). The elaborate cultural architecture, the interlocking discourses and practices, the person terms, the calendars, the rules of etiquette, both stoke and assuage this set of anxieties:

What is feared—mildly in most cases, intensely in a few—is that the public perfor-

mance that is etiquette will be botched, that the social distance etiquette maintains

will consequently collapse, and that the personality of the individual will then

break through to dissolve his standardized public identity. . . . *Lek* is at once the

awareness of the ever-present possibility of such an interpersonal disaster and, like

stage fright, a motivating force toward avoiding it (Geertz, 1973c:402).

What is interesting about the structure of feeling articulated here is its reflexive complexity. Cultural forms—discourses, practices—produce a certain kind of cultural mind-set—toward holding people at a distance, toward the ceremonialization of social intercourse—and at the same time create a set of anxieties about the ability to carry it off. The subjectivity in question has a certain cultural shape, but also a way of inhabiting that shape which is reflexive and anxious concerning the possibilities of one's own failures.

The second of Geertz's two major essays on culture and subjectivity is "Deep Play: Notes on the Balinese Cockfight" (1973d [1972]). Broadly speaking, the approach to the discussion is similar to that in "Person, Time, and Conduct." Geertz first carefully establishes the centrality of the cockfight to Balinese social life, cultural thought, and individual passions. He then performs a virtuosic interpretation of the cockfight as a public text. He spends a long time on the social organization of participation and betting, arguing that the cockfight, especially a "deep," or socially meaningful one, is "fundamentally a dramatization of status concerns" (1973d: 437). But then he asks, what does it mean for Balinese actors that the public dramatization of status rivalry takes the form of "a chicken hacking another mindlessly to bits?" (449). His argument follows his model of/model for distinction without explicitly invoking it. First, in the model of perspective, the cockfight is read as a text, a set of representations and orderings of cultural themes that endow them with particular meanings:

What [the cockfight] does is what, for other peoples with other temperaments and

other conventions, *Lear* and *Crime and Punishment* do; it catches up these themes—

death, masculinity, rage, pride, loss, beneficence, chance—and, ordering them into

an encompassing structure, presents them in such a way as to throw into relief a

particular view of their essential nature. It puts a construction on them, makes

them, to those historically positioned to appreciate the construction, meaningful—

visible, tangible, graspable—"real," in an ideational sense (1973d:443–44).

At the same time it is more than a text, or rather, texts do more than simply articulate and display meanings. Thus, and this is the model-for aspect, "attending cockfights and participating in them is, for the Balinese, a kind of sentimental education" (1973d:449). It is in this context that Geertz presents his most explicit theorization of the formation of subjectivity. He first talks about the ways in which participating in cockfights "opens [a man's] subjectivity to himself" (451). But then he moves to the stronger, constructionist position: "Yet, because . . . that subjectivity does not properly exist until it is thus organized, art forms generate and regenerate the very subjectivity they pretend only to display. Quartets, still lifes, and cockfights are not merely reflections of a pre-existing sensibility analogically represented; they are positive agents in the creation and maintenance of such a sensibility." (451) At the heart of this sensibility is once again a set of anxieties, different from, though not unrelated to, those brought out in "Person, Time, and Conduct." In this case the anxieties revolve around issues of the eruption of animality into human life: Geertz tells us that Balinese people are revolted and/or threatened, but also fascinated, by manifestations of animality in the human world, including most actual animals, animal-like human behavior, and vicious demons who all take animal forms (1973d:420).

I emphasize the centrality of anxieties in Geertz's analyses of subjectivity in part because this focus connects back very closely to Weber's anxiety-centered discussion of the Protestant ethic. But Geertz gives an even larger role to anxiety in his theoretical framework than we have seen thus far; it is one of the central axes not only of particular cultural subjectivities, but of the human condition as a whole, that is, the condition of being a cultural creature. To see this we must return to the essay that launched his theoretical project, "Religion as a Cultural System" (1973b [1966]). Geertz uses the religion essay to discuss what he sees as human beings' most basic fear, the fear of conceptual chaos. He begins by quoting Susanne Langer on the subject:

> [Man] can adapt himself somehow to anything his imagination can cope with; but he cannot deal with Chaos. Because his characteristic function and highest asset is conception, his greatest fright is to meet what he cannot construe—the "uncanny."
> . . . Therefore our most important assets are always the symbols of our general *orientation* in nature, on the earth, in society, and in what we are doing (Langer, in Geertz 1973b:99).

Geertz then sorts out the different kinds of fears embodied in this fear of chaos:

> There are at least three points where chaos—a tumult of events which lack not just interpretations but *interpretability*—threatens to break in upon man: at the limits of his analytic capacities, at the limits of his powers of endurance, and at the limits of his moral insight. Bafflement, suffering, and a sense of intractable ethical paradox are all, if they become intense enough or are sustained long enough, radical challenges to the proposition that life is comprehensible and that we can, by taking thought, orient ourselves effectively within it (1973b:100).

These anxieties of interpretation and orientation are seen as part of the generic human condition, grounded in the human dependency on symbolic orders to function within the world. Geertz had argued in an earlier article (1973a) that symbolic systems are not additive to human existence but constitutive of it. Because human beings are relatively open creatures, vastly unprogrammed compared to most other animals, they literally depend on external symbolic systems—including especially language, but more generally "culture"—to survive.

This larger foundational point concerning the core human anxieties, anxieties about the fragility of order and meaning, has taken a new turn in a major arena of cultural studies, studies of the "postmodern condition," argued (as we shall now consider) to be a powerful new configuration of the dominant culture.

From the Interpretation of Culture to Cultural Critique: Two Readings of Postmodern Consciousness

In this final section I present readings of two works on the cultural and subjective formations of late capitalism, with a number of objectives. First I want to display the point that a concern for complex structures of subjectivity persists beyond Geertz's foundational essays in the 1960s, flourishing in certain kinds of work up to the present. I want to contrast these kinds of work, in other words, with both the antihumanist (structuralist and poststructuralist) work I critiqued at the beginning of this article, and with the much more satisfactory work of the practice theorists, which nonetheless fails to attend to these issues of subjectivity. Second, I want to show both the continuity with, and the transformations of, the Geertzian interpretive method. The Geertzian method of interpreting public cultural forms to get at the *conscience collective* is still visible, but in the hands of the authors to be discussed here, it has taken what might be called the Raymond Williams turn—from the interpretation of culture to cultural critique.

There is in fact a certain irony here, namely, that while Geertz's "cultural-ism" has been increasingly cast as conservative, yet it has been the basis for a radical approach to cultural studies. Raymond Williams cross-fertilized a recognizably Geertzian version of the American culture concept with a Marx-ist conception of ideology to try to understand the ways in which culture forms and deforms subjectivities—what he called "structures of feeling"—in specific historical contexts of power, inequality, and commodification. In the discussions of the two works that follow, both of them in this critical cultural studies tradition, I want to show not only the general debt to Geertzian interpretive methods but also some surprising echoes of more specific elements of Geertz's worldview, particularly the centrality of issues of anxiety over meaning and order.

The first of the works in question is Fredric Jameson's classic essay, "Post-modernism, or the Cultural Logic of Late Capitalism," which was published (appropriately enough) in 1984. This was the launching point for a line of thinking about contemporary culture that is still going on, and the second work to be discussed, Richard Sennett's *The Corrosion of Character: The Personal Consequences of Work in the New Capitalism*, represents a further, and more recent (1998), development of some of the same issues.[12] I should say before continuing that, while I find both of these works quite interesting, I do not necessarily agree with everything in them. The following then is not meant to be a substantive exploration of the postmodern condition or a total endorsement of these two works. I present them here primarily to illustrate a certain form of contemporary cultural analysis, one that is centered, as is the work of Geertz, on questions of (anxious) subjectivity, and that turn Geertz-style cultural interpretation into cultural critique.

Jameson, first, sees postmodernism as a set of newly emerging styles in architecture, painting, literature, film, and academic theory, and at the same time as a newly emerging form of consciousness with particular characteristics. Both the styles and the consciousness are explicitly tied to "late capital-ism" in a variety of ways: through the commodification of "aesthetic produc-tion" (1984:4); as "the internal and superstructural expression of a whole new wave of American military and economic domination throughout the world" (5); and as an analog of "the great global multinational and decentered communicational network in which we find ourselves caught" (44).[13]

Jameson reads postmodern culture/consciousness (as in Geertz, or for that matter, in Durkheim or Marx, the boundary between the two is fuzzy) from a variety of public cultural forms and texts. He begins with a comparison of a painting of peasant shoes by van Gogh and Andy Warhol's painting "Diamond Dust Shoes." He argues that van Gogh's painting can, perhaps must, be read as responding to a particular real condition in the world, "the whole object world of agricultural misery" (1984:7), while the Warhol painting disallows this kind of reading: "There is . . . in Warhol no way to complete the hermeneutic gesture and restore to these oddments that whole larger lived context" (8). The Warhol embodies—according to Jameson, "perhaps the supreme formal feature of all . . . postmodernisms—flatness or depthlessness" (9, word order rearranged). This depthlessness is the first of Jameson's major "constitutive features of the postmodern," which also include "a consequent weakening of historicity, both in our relationship to public History and in the new forms of our private temporality . . . [and] a whole new type of emotional ground tone"—what he calls "intensities" (6).

Jameson goes on to compare Warhol's work to the Edvard Munch painting *The Scream*, "a canonical expression of the great modernist thematics of alienation, anomie, solitude, social fragmentation, and isolation" (1984: 11). These thematics, however, are grounded in what Jameson calls "depth models" of the subject, models which presume various kinds of complex subjectivities, including the distinction between an inner self and an outer world. Under postmodernism, however, "depth is replaced by surface" (12), and "the alienation of the subject is displaced by the latter's fragmentation" (14).[14] Jameson's interpretation is then punched home by a photograph of Wells Fargo Court, a building that appears to be "a surface unsupported by any volume" (13).

The postmodern subject, in short, has been drained of subjectivity in the modernist sense. Postmodernist cultural forms, including those lines of cultural theory which posit the irrelevance or "death" of the subject, reflect this flattened subjectivity and at the same time heighten the subject's sense of disorientation. At this point Jameson develops his famous interpretation of the Westin Bonaventure Hotel in Los Angeles.[15] Moving us, the readers, through its impossibly confusing spaces, Jameson talks of the ways the hotel "has finally succeeded in transcending the capacities of the individual human body . . . cognitively to map its position in a mappable external world" (1984: 44). He then locates the central anxiety that is modeled by this kind of environment:

> It may now be suggested that this alarming disjunction point between the body and its built environment . . . can itself stand as the symbol and analogon of that even sharper dilemma which is the incapacity of our minds, at least at present, to map the great global multinational and decentered communicational network in which we find ourselves caught as individual subjects (1984: 44).

Jameson here has both outlined what he sees as a new formation of culture/consciousness, and critiqued it as "the cultural logic of late capitalism." It is not an ideology in the common sense of the term, a set of ideas and perspectives imposed by dominant classes, but a *culture* looked at as ideology, as the "superstructural expression" of new forms of power in the world. Moreover, its central features constitute a Geertzian nightmare, disordering, disorienting, drained of meaning and affect. Postmodern subjects are disoriented in time (the "weakening of historicity") and space (metaphorically wandering the labyrinthine corridors of places like the Westin Bonaventure). Lacking a vocabulary of subjective depth and complexity (the end of "depth models"), their emotional lives are reduced to inchoate emotional bursts ("intensities") and featureless moods ("euphoria").

Given this interpretation grounded in anxieties of orientation and meaning, Jameson is consistent in terms of the kind of politics he calls for at the end. Although he gestures toward conventional radical politics, Jameson's final call is not to the barricades but to practices of conceptual ordering of the world, specifically the practice of "cognitive mapping": "The political form of postmodernism, if there ever is any, will have as its vocation the invention and projection of a global cognitive mapping" (1984: 54). In the course of such mapping "we may again begin to grasp our positioning as individual and collective subjects and regain a capacity to act and struggle which is at present neutralized by our spatial as well as our social confusion" (54).

Jameson's essay can be criticized on many grounds. In particular it is massively socially ungrounded. Postmodernity in the senses he has discussed is not linked to particular groups, classes, or forms of practice (e.g., work). It seems to float free of any location in the real world, existing as part of the ether of the late capitalist mode of production as a whole. Fred Pfeil has offered a brilliant critique of the essay in just these terms (1990 [1984]), and the Sennett book discussed below avoided many of these problems. Sennett's argument is developed more from ethnographic-type material than from texts, and that is part of the difference between them.[16] But leaving aside the flaws of Jameson's essay, my central point for present purposes is to emphasize how both Jameson *and* Sennett can be profitably read in terms of the (Geertzian) issues of culture and subjectivity, updated via Raymond Williams, that are central to this chapter.

Sennett's book, *The Corrosion of Character: The Personal Consequences of Work in the New Capitalism* (1998), is, like Jameson's essay, an exploration of the new forms of consciousness emerging under conditions of late capitalism. The texts for his discussion are not paintings and buildings but workplace scenes, structures of authority and responsibility in workplaces, and people's talk about work. If for Jameson "late capitalism" is largely seen in the form of multinationalism, "out there" and hard to grasp, for Sennett late capitalism is largely seen in the corporation and the workplace, "at home" but equally hard to grasp.[17]

Sennett argues that the conditions of work have radically changed under late capitalism, and that this has had profound effects on consciousness, which he calls "character." He sums up these changed conditions with the phrase "no long term." This means, first and foremost, that jobs are insecure, in part because of the increasing opacity of organizations, so that people never quite know what is expected of them, and in part because of the practices of "downsizing" and "reengineering" corporations, constantly throwing people out of work, even though there is no evidence that these practices actually increase productivity or profits. "No long term" means as well that work itself is not embedded in one's "job," a long-term relationship with a company that might become part of one's identity, but is cut up into "projects" which can be outsourced if necessary to contractors who themselves have no long-term relationship with the corporation. It means further a tremendous bias against older workers (over 50; in some places over 40; in advertising over 30); people who have been too long in the company are seen as too mired in past histories, too attached to past ways of doing things, too prone to talk back to a younger boss, and so on and so forth. In still other uses, "no long term" refers to the machines of production, which are and must be reprogrammable on short notice, the famous principle of just-in-time production (Harvey 1989). In sum the principle of "no long term" ramifies in myriad ways throughout the corporate culture of late capitalism.

Within this body of discourse, the positive spin on "no long term" is provided by the word "flexible." People must be flexible, machines must be flexible, corporations must be flexible. Sennett's book as a whole is about the kinds of subjectivities produced under the regime of flexibility. More careful than Jameson in locating who are the subjects in question, Sennett shows how flexibility plays itself out in different class locations. He makes several visits to a very high level annual symposium in Davos, Switzerland, for chief executive officers of major corporations. He concludes that people like Bill Gates and other members of the species "Davos Man" are comfortable with, and indeed flourish within, the mind-set of flexibility: "The capacity to let go of the past, the confidence to accept fragmentation: these are two traits of character which appear at Davos among people truly at home in the new capitalism" (Sennett 1998:63). But as he says next, "Those same traits of character . . . become more self-destructive for those who work lower down in the flexible regime. . . . [They] corrode the character of more ordinary employees who try to play by these rules" (1998:63).

Although from the point of view of the owners and executives, the flexible workplace is more productive, from the point of view of those who work "lower down," the organization and/or one's career within it appear "incoherent" (1998:48), "shapeless" (57), and "illegible" (86). Sennett gives a number of different, quite individualized, examples of how this plays out for people in different kinds of work environments and at different organizational levels. In one example, workers in a bakery that has been completely computerized, and with many flex-time workers on different schedules, were "indifferent" about their work (and none except the foreman were actually bakers). In another we learn about Rose, an older woman who went to work in an advertising agency. She quickly learned that performance "counted for less to employers than contacts and networking skills" (79); she felt vulnerable and continually at risk, partly because she lacked those skills, and partly because there was no clear way to read her own progress (84). A third example is of a factory with the increasingly popular "team" organization of work; here, where bosses represent themselves as simply other members of the team, workers feel the obscure workings of "power without authority" (114), while managers practice the skills of "deep acting" and the "masks of cooperativeness" (112). Even without downsizing, nobody stays very long at any given job.

Sennett sums up the corrosive effects of the many manifestations of flexible capitalism as follows:

> The culture of the new order profoundly disturbs self-organization. . . . It can divorce easy, superficial labor from understanding and engagement, as happened with the Boston bakers. It can make the constant taking of risks an exercise in depression, as happened to Rose. Irreversible change and multiple, fragmented activity may be comfortable for the new regime's masters, like the court at Davos, but it may disorient the new regime's servants (Sennett 1998:117).

Sennett thus arrives, from a different direction, at conclusions very similar to Jameson's. Jameson's "waning of affect" appears as the bakery workers' "indifference"; Jameson's "depthlessness" appears in the "masks of cooperativeness" that represent the primary skills of the contemporary manager; Jameson's emphasis on spatial disorientation is Sennett's emphasis on temporal disorientation: "Time's arrow is broken; it has no trajectory in a continually re-engineered, routine-hating, short-term political economy. People feel the lack of sustained human relations and durable purposes . . . register[ing] unease and anxiety" (1998:98).

The crisis of postmodern consciousness is once again a crisis of orientation within an uninterpretable, or what Sennett calls illegible, world.[18] In his final chapter Sennett writes of the necessity for human solidarity and community in order to effectively deal with that world politically. But as with Jameson there is in a sense a more fundamental need, a need for conceptual, cognitive, symbolic tools for reorienting and reconstituting the self within this new regime. Thus where Jameson talks of cognitive mapping, Sennett writes of the importance of narrative, of people being able to narrate their lives in a coherent and meaningful way. The capacity for coherent self-narration is constantly under assault in late capitalism and must be preserved or restored; the penultimate chapter considers the attempts of some downsized, unemployed IBM executives to narrate what happened to them and why, in ways that help them come to terms with the new conditions of their lives.[19]

Both Jameson and Sennett are performing what Raymond Williams called "epochal analysis," in which "a cultural process is seized as a cultural system, with determinate, dominant features: feudal culture or bourgeois culture" (Williams 1977:121) or, in this case, postmodern culture. But while this can be—is—very effective, it is never enough, and one must also, as Williams also argues, look for the countercurrents that exist within any given cultural formation. Before concluding this chapter I want to look briefly for such countercurrents.

What Williams was emphasizing as countercurrents was the question of alternative cultural formations coexisting with the hegemonic, what he calls the "residual" and the "emergent" (Williams 1977:121–22). For purposes of the present argument, however, I will not look at alternative cultural formations (though surely they are there to be found); instead I want to return to the question of complex subjectivities. I said above that I take people to be "conscious" in the sense of being at least partially "knowing subjects," self-aware and reflexive. Subjectivities are complex because they are culturally and emotionally complex, but also because of the ongoing work of reflexivity, monitoring the relationship of the self to the world. No doubt there are cultural subjects who fully embody, in the mode of power, the dominant culture ("Davos Man"), and no doubt there are cultural subjects who have been fully subjected, in the mode of powerlessness, by the dominant culture. By and large, however, I assume at the most fundamental level that for most subjects, most of the time, this never fully works, and there are countercurrents of subjectivity as well as of culture.

Thus while the two works just examined are primarily accounts of the dominant formation, we can also find in them evidence of these kinds of subjective countercurrents. Remember Rose, the older woman discussed by Richard Sennett who joined an advertising agency. Rose was, for Sennett, not primarily a victim of postmodern flattening but an informant. He uses her experience to write of the manipulative actors, and of the culture that rewards them, in the firm; he presents her reactions largely in terms of the ways in which she registers what is going on. And the fact of the matter is that Rose left the firm. She was somewhat "worn down" by the whole experience, but she returned to her former life (she owned a bar frequented by Sennett, and had leased it out in the interim), and she did so with a heightened critical consciousness about "slick uptown kids" and the queasy-making moral world of organizations like this (Sennett 1998:78). One could speak of this episode in terms of Rose's "agency," and that would not be inaccurate. But the idea of agency itself presupposes a complex subjectivity behind it, in which a subject partially internalizes and partially reflects upon—and finally in this case reacts against—a set of circumstances in which she finds herself.[20]

There are no individuals in the Jameson essay, so I cannot extract a story like Rose's to tell. But there is one place in Jameson's text in which we can see the *effects* of a critical subjectivity at work. Thus after powerfully communicating to the reader the disorienting spatial arrangements of the Westin Bonaventure Hotel, Jameson tells us that "color coding and directional signals have been added," obviously in response to people complaining that they were getting lost. Jameson sneers at these cognitive orienting tools, seeing them as evidence of "a pitiful and revealing, rather desperate, attempt to restore the coordinates of an older space" (Jameson 1984: 44). Maybe so. But I also like to think of them as political posters (in my imagination, someone goes around putting them up at night), both providing a way through the maze and conveying the message that arrogant architects and big capital can never fully get us down.

Again one could think in terms of the agency of those who successfully made demands for directional signs and color coding in the Bonaventure. But agency—unfortunately—has come to be associated with the problematic subject of humanism, and thus too easily dismissed. What I prefer to emphasize here are the complexities of consciousness even in the face of the most dominant cultural formations. This is not to say that actors can stand "outside of culture," for of course they cannot. But it is to say that a fully cultural consciousness is at the same time always multilayered and reflexive, and its complexity and reflexivity constitute the grounds for questioning and criticizing the world in which we find ourselves.

Some Very Brief Conclusions

Whether one agrees with their takes on postmodern consciousness or not, Jameson and Sennett show us that a critical reading of the contemporary world involves understanding not just its new political, economic, and social formations but its new culture, a culture in turn that is read by both authors in terms of the kinds of subjectivities it will tend to produce. This then returns us to the main thesis of this essay, which I would like to summarize briefly here.

I have argued for the importance of a robust anthropology of subjectivity, both as states of mind of real actors embedded in the social world and as cultural formations that (at least partially) express, shape, and constitute those states of mind. Clifford Geertz, carrying forward the tremendously important work of Max Weber, has been central here because of what I called earlier his subjectivity-oriented theory of culture. Moving beyond Geertz, however, I have been particularly interested in understanding subjectivity in its relations to (changing) forms of power, and especially—as in the Jameson and Sennett examples—the subtle forms of power that saturate everyday life, through experiences of time, space, and work. In short I have been concerned to explore the ways in which such an anthropology of subjectivity can be the basis of cultural critique, allowing us to ask sharp questions about the cultural shaping of subjectivities within a world of wildly unequal power relations, and about the complexities of personal subjectivities within such a world.

Power and Projects: Reflections on Agency

These reflections on "agency" are part of a larger project which centers on a concept I have called in other contexts "serious games" (Ortner 1996a, 1999a). The idea of serious games represented one attempt to build upon the important insights of "practice theory" but at the same time move beyond them. The fundamental assumption of practice theory is that culture (in a very broad sense) constructs people as particular kinds of social actors, but social actors, through their living, on-the-ground, variable practices, reproduce or transform—and usually some of each—the culture that made them. Reduced to bare bones like this, the idea sounds simple, but it is not. The theoretical elaboration and empirical application of the concepts of practice theory have both proven its power and shown its holes.

Responding to this the idea of serious games was meant to move questions of practice theory in several new directions. As in practice theory social life in a serious games perspective is seen as something that is actively played, oriented toward culturally constituted goals and projects, and involving both routine practices and intentionalized action. But the serious games perspective, as I will elaborate in part in this chapter, allows us to bring into focus more complex forms of social relations—especially relations of power—and more complex dimensions of the subjectivity of social actors—especially for present purposes, those involving "intentionality" and "agency."

A few notes before proceeding: First, I need to say immediately that serious games have nothing to do with formalistic game theory, popular in the harder social sciences.[1] Interpretations of social life by way of serious games involve neither game theory's formal modeling nor its assumption that a kind of universal rationality prevails in virtually all kinds of social behavior. On the contrary "serious games" are quite emphatically cultural formations rather than analysts' models. In addition a serious games perspective assumes culturally variable (rather than universal) and subjectively complex (rather than predominantly rationalistic and self-interested) actors.

I also need to say that the idea of (serious) games is not in any way meant to be a substitute for a theory of large-scale social and cultural processes. Despite its appearance of concentrating on micro-politics, its ultimate purpose is always to understand the larger forces, formations, and transformations of social life. In the normal course of the kinds of social and cultural analyses in which I am interested, one actually works in the opposite direction, starting with those larger formations and then trying to work backwards toward their underlying serious games.

This chapter, however, is focused on one particular piece of the serious games idea, namely the question of actors' agency and intentionality noted earlier. Serious games always involve the play of actors seen as "agents." Yet there is something about the very word "agency" that calls to mind the autonomous, individualistic, Western actor. The very categories historically standing behind practice theory, the opposition between "structure" and "agency," seem to suggest a heroic individual—The Agent—up against a Borg-like entity called "Structure." But nothing could be further from the way I envisage social agents, which is that they are always involved in, and can never act outside of, the multiplicity of social relations in which they are enmeshed. Thus while all social actors are assumed to "have" agency, the idea of actors as always being engaged with others in the play of serious games is meant to make it virtually impossible to imagine that the agent is free, or is an unfettered individual.

But the social embeddedness of agents, which is central to the idea of serious games, may take at least two forms. On the one hand the agent is always embedded in relations of (would-be) solidarity: family, friends, kin, spouses or partners, children, parents, teachers, allies, and so forth. It is important to note this point because some of the critics of the agency concept, those who see agency as a bourgeois and individualistic concept, focus largely on the ways in which the concept appears to slight the "good" embeddedness of agents, the contexts of solidarity that mitigate agency in its individualistic and selfish forms.

On the other hand the agent is always enmeshed within relations of power, inequality, and competition. Without ignoring relationships of solidarity, the omnipresence of power and inequality in social life is central to the very definition of serious games. (While earlier versions of practice theory did not wholly ignore questions of power, it is safe to say that those questions were not at the core of the framework; see the introduction to this volume.) This chapter focuses specifically on the relationship between agency and power.

The Agency Problem

The idea of "agency" is beset by many of the same problems as the idea of "the subject" (see chapter 5, this volume). There is a certain kind of antihumanist thinker or writer who has a knee-jerk antipathy to any allusions to either of these suspect phenomena. But for a more nuanced representation of the kinds of intellectual anxieties that these categories provoke, I will turn to the excellent introduction to *Ethnography and the Historical Imagination* (hereafter *EHI*) by John and Jean Comaroff (1992). The Comaroffs are not what are conventionally called "antihumanists." They are not interested in banishing the social subject from their theoretical models, nor individuals from their ethnographic histories. They are not interested in arguing for structural or discursive causation *as against* the effects of the actions of theoretically defined subjects and historical actors. Nonetheless the Introduction to *EHI* can be characterized as a kind of extended worry over "the humanist turn" (36) and "our current conceptual obsession with agency" (37).

In the introduction to *EHI* the Comaroffs are trying to develop a general theoretical framework for an anthropological history. They have two overarching concerns about an overemphasis on agency in anthropological and historical analysis. The first is that, unless very carefully handled, agency harks back to deep ethnocentrisms:

> Many anthropologists have been wary of ontologies that give precedence to individuals over contexts. For these rest on manifestly Western assumptions: among them, that human beings can triumph over their context through sheer force of will, [and] that economy, culture, and society are the aggregate product of individual action and intention (10).

The second concern, and one that is in some ways more central to their project, is that too much focus on the agency of individuals and/or groups results in a gross oversimplification of the processes involved in history. This oversimplification itself takes at least two forms. The first is simply that the social and cultural forces in play in any historical engagement are infinitely more complex than what can be learned from looking at actors' intentions: "The 'motivation' of social practice . . . always exists at two distinct, if related, levels: first, the (culturally configured) needs and desires of human beings; and second, the pulse of collective forces that, empowered in complex ways, work through them" (36). It is the close examination and analysis of the "pulse of collective forces" that, in the Comaroffs' view, begin to get slighted when the weight of analytic effort gets shifted to "agency," and that results in a deeply inadequate account of what was actually going on.

> [The problem] becomes particularly visible when we examine epochal movements like European colonialism, in which purposive, "heroic" action was a central motif, even a driving impulse. Yet, from our perspective, that impulse is not enough to account for the determination of the processes involved—or even to tell very much of the story (36).

The second dimension of lost complexity is in some ways an extension of the first. If an analysis that is too focused on the intentionalities of actors loses sight of large-scale social and cultural forces in play, it also—the Comaroffs fear—loses sight of the complex, and highly unpredictable, relationship between intentions and outcomes. Specifically they remind their readers of the importance, and prevalence, of unintended consequences in any historical process. Speaking of their *Of Revelation and Revolution* project (Jean and J. L. Comaroff 1991, J. L. and Jean Comaroff 1997) they emphasize the degree to which the processes of cultural transformation constantly worked in unanticipated ways: "The scattered signs retrieved in [the research] all pointed to wider social transformations borne *unwittingly* by the missionaries. In many respects these actually ran counter to their own desires and motives" (*EHI*, 36). The suggestion here is that "desires and motives," the stuff of intentionality and agency, are sometimes actually irrelevant to outcomes, but at the very least have a complicated and highly mediated relationship to outcomes. This complexity again, they fear, tends to get lost in the "obsession with agency."

Speaking for myself, but also I think for many other theorists interested in questions of agency, I can only agree that these dangers are always potentially real. And there are no doubt certain kinds of work that fall into the various traps the Comaroffs describe. But an important body of theoretical work has been developed precisely to theorize the "desires and motives" and practices of real people in the social process (1) without "giving precedence to individuals over contexts"; (2) without importing Western assumptions such as the idea "that human beings can triumph over their context through sheer force of will, [or] that economy, culture, and society are the aggregate product of individual action and intention"; (3) without slighting "the pulse of collective forces"; and (4) always recognizing the ever-present likelihood of unintended consequences. The reader will recognize here the framework with which I began this essay (and this volume), the framework of practice theory within which neither "individuals" nor "social forces" have "precedence," but in which nonetheless there is a dynamic, powerful, and sometimes transformative relationship between the practices of real people and the structures of society, culture, and history.

Interestingly the idea of agency was not much developed in two of the three key texts of early practice theory: Pierre Bourdieu's *Outline of a Theory of Practice* (1977) and Marshall Sahlins's *Historical Metaphors and Mythical Realities* (1981). Although there are discussions in Bourdieu that see actors as exhibiting what we would think of as "agency," the term is not theorized in this or in his later elaboration of the theory (1990). This omission may be intentional, but speculations on this point (e.g., on a lingering antihumanism in Bourdieu's work) would carry us far beyond the confines of this essay. It may also be relevant, however, that there is apparently no French term for what American and British social theorists mean by "agency," as I learned when I recently had a paper translated into French.[2] The term is also largely missing from Marshall Sahlins's book, in part I think because of the French influence on Sahlins's work, and in part because his interest in historical transformation led him to elaborate not on agents and agency, but on "events" and their dynamics.

Agency was however important to the third of the founding texts, Anthony Giddens's *Central Problems in Social Theory* (1979). And it has been important to the work of the Americans who have continued to work on practice theory: William H. Sewell Jr. and myself.[3] The Anglo-American bias toward agency in the practice theory literature lends some credence to the idea that agency is a form of Western individualism. Yet I think it would be a grave mistake to dismiss agency as merely a piece of American ethno-psychology not transferable to other cultural contexts, or even to "humanity" in general. Let me probe more deeply into its theoretical and philosophical underpinnings.

Defining Agency

The issues involved in defining agency are perhaps best approached by sorting out a series of components: (1) the question of whether or not agency inherently involves "intentions"; (2) the simultaneous universality and cultural constructedness of agency; and (3) the relationship between agency and "power." I will say a few words about how each of these has been approached by others, and also indicate my own position on each.[4]

Before continuing let me reiterate that "agency" is never a thing in itself but is always part of a process of what Giddens calls structuration, the making and remaking of larger social and cultural formations. As I focus on defining agency in this section it may seem to be a kind of freestanding psychological object, but that (mis)impression will be corrected in the final section of the essay.

INTENTIONALITY

I begin with the question of intentionality because in some ways it gets to the heart of what agency means. "Intentionality" here is meant to include a wide range of states, both cognitive and emotional, and at various levels of consciousness, that are directed forward toward some end. Thus intentionality in agency might include highly conscious plots and plans and schemes; somewhat more nebulous aims, goals, and ideals; and finally desires, wants, and needs that may range from being deeply buried to quite consciously felt. In short intentionality as a concept is meant to include all the ways in which action is cognitively and emotionally pointed *toward* some purpose.

On this question theorists tend to fall out along a continuum. At one end are what I think of as "soft" definitions of agency, in which intention is not a central component. Examples include "A sense that the self is an authorized social being" (Ortner 1996a:10); "the socioculturally mediated capacity to act" (Ahearn 2001b:112); "the property of those entities (i) that have some degree of control over their own behavior, (ii) whose actions in the world affect other entitities' . . . and (iii) whose actions are the object of evaluation . . ." (Duranti 2004:453); and "a stream of actual or contemplated causal interventions of corporeal beings in the ongoing process of events-in-the-world" (Giddens 1979:55).

In some cases people who provide such "soft" definitions do not address the question of intentionality at all. Giddens however does provide a discussion of the relationship between intentionality and agency. But it is in a sense a "soft" relationship. Giddens acknowledges "the intentional or purposive character of human behaviour," but at the same time he emphasizes " 'intentionality' as *process*. Such intentionality is a routine feature of human conduct, and does not imply that actors have definite goals consciously held in mind during the course of their activities" (1979:56). In other words acknowledging intentionality as a general disposition of humans as agents is an acceptable position; seeing intentionality as "definite goals consciously held in the mind" is more problematic.[5] This is so for several reasons: First, because what are presented discursively by actors as intentions are often after-the-fact rationalizations (57); second, because—and here the problematic word is "conscious" —Giddens wants to leave space for the Freudian unconscious in a theory of action (58); and finally because—as the Comaroffs also argued—too much focus on explicit intentions obscures the fact that most social outcomes are in fact *un*intended consequences of action (59).

I do not disagree with these points. One has to be careful with intentionality for all the reasons Giddens (and the Comaroffs) noted. Yet if one is too soft on intentionality, one loses a distinction that I think needs to be maintained, between routine practices on the one hand, and "agency" seen precisely as more intentionalized action on the other.

On the other end of the continuum are thinkers who make intention (in various senses) much more central to their concept of agency. For example, Charles Taylor, not in his paper on agency (1985a) but in "The Concept of a Person" (1985b:99) says, "To say that things matter to agents is to say that we can attribute purposes, desires, aversions to them. . . ." But the most developed presentation of this position is to be found in William H. Sewell Jr.'s by now classic paper, "A Theory of Structure: Duality, Agency, and Transformation" (1992). Sewell's definitions of agency are always full of intentions in the broadest sense, that is, always seem to be projected forward, if not toward "definite goals," then at least in ways more actively motivated than is the case for routine practices. Thus he first defines agency as "the strivings and motivated transactions that constitute the experienced surface of social life" (2). He later defines "a capacity for agency" as a capacity "for desiring, for forming intentions, and for acting creatively" (20). Finally, in a discussion of the ways in which agency can be collective as well as individual, he says that "agency entails an ability to coordinate one's actions with others and against others, to form collective projects, to persuade, to coerce . . ." (21).[6]

I share Sewell's "hard" conception of agency for the reason given above, namely, that it is the strong role of active (though not necessarily fully "conscious") intentionality in agency that, in my view, differentiates agency from routine practices. Of course there is not some hard and fast boundary between them; rather there is a kind of continuum between routine practices that proceed with little reflection and planning, and agentive acts that intervene in the world with something in mind (or in heart). But it seems worthwhile to try to maintain the distinction that defines the two ends of the spectrum.

THE CULTURAL CONSTRUCTION OF AGENCY

There is general agreement across all theorists that agency in some sense is universal, and is part of a fundamental humanness. William Sewell says explicitly that "a capacity for agency . . . is inherent in all humans" (1992:20). Alessandro Duranti points out that "all languages have grammatical structures that seem designed to represent agency" (2004:467). Charles Taylor simply uses "agent" interchangeably with person, self, and human being (1985a passim).[7]

At the same time there is general agreement that agency is always culturally and historically constructed. Sewell uses the analogy of the capacity for language. Just as all humans have the capacity for language but must learn to speak a particular language, so all humans have a capacity for agency, but the specific forms it takes will vary in different times and places.

The authors vary in emphasizing different domains of social life as shapers of agency. Charles Taylor in a very general way, and Laura Ahearn and Alessandro Duranti in much more specific ways, focuses on the relationships between language and agency. For Giddens the most relevant level is that of social practices and interactions. Sewell importantly invokes "the schemas that are part of any cultural repertoire" that are both imposed and drawn upon in shaping forms of desire, courses of action, and so forth (1992:8). The notion of cultural schemas in this sense has been central to some of my own work as well, from my early discussion of "key scenarios" (Ortner 1973) to my work on (Sherpa) cultural schemas in *High Religion* (1989a). And finally, agency is differentially shaped, and also nourished or stunted, under different regimes of power, which brings us to the final dimension of defining agency.

THE RELATIONSHIP BETWEEN AGENCY AND POWER

A number of theorists of agency do not spend much time on questions of power,[8] beyond a sort of general notion that agency is the capacity to affect things. In my own view, however, agency and social power in a relatively strong sense are very closely linked. Thus here I will quickly survey only those authors who give this question some systematic attention.

Laura Ahearn, first, opens her essay on "Language and Agency" (2001b) with the question, "why agency now?" and answers it in part by relating it to the emergence of social and political movements starting in the 1970s. This is to say that the emergence of a problematic of "agency" had its roots in questions of power from the outset.

Partly as a result of that history, "agency" came to be equated in many people's minds with the idea of "resistance." Ahearn rightly asserts, however, that "oppositional agency is only one of many forms of agency" (2001b:115). Yet it is clear that questions of power more broadly conceived are central to Ahearn's thinking about agency. Her point is not that domination and resistance are irrelevant, but that that human emotions, and hence questions of agency, within relations of power and inequality are always complex and contradictory (2001b:116; see also chapter 1, this volume).

Where Ahearn addresses the complexity of motivations and intentionalities generated in relations of power, Giddens moves the discussion of agency and power back into his larger theory of structuration (1979). On the one hand he argues that "the concept of action [a term he sometimes uses interchangeably with agency] is *logically tied* to that of power, where the latter notion is understood as transformative capacity" (88). On the other hand the transformative capacity of agents is only one dimension of how power operates in social systems. It also operates as what he distinguishes as "domination," that is, power as it is built into objectified structures like institutions and discourses. The two in turn are interconnected through his notion of the "duality of structure" (91–92), as mediated by "resources." But here the discussion gets rather murky.

In his discussion of Giddens's notion of resources, Sewell assures us first that the confusion is not entirely in the mind of the reader: "I agree with Giddens that any notion of structure that ignores asymmetries of power is radically incomplete. But [using] an undertheorized notion of resources . . . succeeds merely in confusing things" (1992:9). He then clarifies what is meant by resources, how these are implicated in power, and how all of this ties up with what we mean by agency:

> However unequally resources may be distributed, some measure of both human and nonhuman resources are controlled by all members of society, no matter how destitute and oppressed. Indeed, part of what it means to conceive of human beings as agents is to conceive of them as empowered by access to resources of one kind or another (1992:9–10).

Sewell returns to issues of power in the article's section entitled "Agency." He argues (here in agreement with Giddens) that "agency is not opposed to, but . . . constituent of, structure" (1992:20). It is here that he makes the point noted above about the universality of human agency. But he goes on to talk about power differentials and the ways in which they affect people's capacities for, and forms of, agency:

> It is . . . important . . . to insist that the agency exercised by different persons is far from uniform, that agency differs enormously in both kind and extent. What kinds of desires people can have, what intentions they can form, and what sorts of creative transpositions they can carry out vary dramatically from one social world to another. . . . Structures . . . empower agents differentially, which also implies that they embody the desires, intentions, and knowledge of agents differentially as well. Structures, and the human agencies they endow, are laden with differences of power (20–21).

Ahearn on the one hand and Giddens and Sewell on the other approach the nexus of agency and power quite differently. But my point is not so much to draw out the contrast (although that might be an interesting exercise), as simply to agree with all of them that a strong theory of agency (and more broadly a transformed theory of practice) must be closely linked with questions of power and inequality. The question for the rest of this chapter is the nature of that linkage.

Please note: Many of the major examples in the discussion that follows are drawn from the realm of gender. This was not entirely intentional; I did not initially set out to write an essay about agency as a gendered issue. There is no question, however, that in a great many cases the most vivid examples of the relationships between agency and power turn out to be found in the realm of gender relations. But of course questions of agency also go far beyond gender relations. Thus gender here stands not only for itself but for a range of other forms of power and inequality, as will become clear in the course of the discussion.

Three Mini Essays on Agency and Power

Broadly speaking the notion of agency can be said to have two fields of meaning, both of which have been signalled in the preceding discussion. In one field of meaning "agency" is about intentionality and the pursuit of (culturally defined) projects.[9] In the other field of meaning agency is about power, about acting within relations of social inequality, asymmetry, and force. In fact "agency" is never merely one or the other. Its two "faces"—as (the pursuit of) "projects" or as (the exercise of or against) "power"—either blend or bleed into one another or else retain their distinctiveness but intertwine in a Moebius-type relationship. Moreover, power itself is double-edged, operating from above as domination and from below as resistance. The Moebius helix therefore becomes even more complex. All of this may seem rather dense; the examples to come are meant to play out what these points look like in practice.

THE TEXTUAL CONSTRUCTION OF AGENCY

I begin with an interpretation of some Grimms' fairy tales.[10] I said above that, while in some sense agency is a capacity of all human beings, its form and, as it were, its distribution are always culturally constructed and maintained. Sub stantively, then, this exercise will allow us to see in some detail what might be called the politics of agency, the cultural work involved in constructing and distributing agency as part of the process of creating appropriately gendered, and thus among other things differentially empowered, persons.[11]

The brothers Grimm reworked and wrote down the tales in a particular time and place—early-nineteenth-century Germany. One could certainly ask questions about the relationship between their acts of inscription and its historical context but that would be a very different exercise. One could also ask questions about the variable ways in which these tales were heard, interpreted, and used in ordinary social practice, but again that would be a very different exercise. Here I have a more modest purpose: I am simply interested in looking at what might be called the narrative politics involved in the construction of agency in a particular body of stories, something which, at least for me, virtually leaps out of the texts.

As we shall see agency or its absence in the tales is expressed largely through an idiom of activity and passivity. Activity involves pursuing "projects"; passivity involves not simply refraining from pursuing projects, but refraining in a sense from even desiring to do so. I should note first that for the most part the only consistently active female characters in the tales are wicked—the wicked stepmothers and witches who have evil projects and seek by evil means to carry them out. I will return to them below. Here I want to focus on the heroines, the little girls and young princesses who are the protagonists of their stories.[12] Most of these heroines are in the mode of what the folklorist V. I. Propp (1968) calls "victim heroes": Although they are the protagonists the action of the story is moved along by virtue of bad things happening to them rather than by their initiating actions as in the case of the majority of male heroes. Thus passivity is to some extent built into most of these girls from the outset.

Yet a closer look at the tales shows that even many of these victim heroines take roles of active agency in the early parts of their stories. Though their initial misfortunes may have happened to them through outside agency, they sometimes seize the action and carry it along themselves, becoming—briefly— heroines in the active questing sense usually reserved for male heroes. But— and this is the crux of the (gendered) politics of agency—they are invariably punished for this. The action of the tales systematically, and often ruthlessly, forces them to renounce this active stance, forces them to renounce the possibility of formulating and enacting projects, *even when those projects are altruistic.*

At the simplest level I take these stories to be tales of "passage," of moving from childhood to adulthood. For the boy heroes passage generally involves the successful enactment of agency—solving a problem, finding a lost object, slaying the dragon, rescuing the damsel in distress. For all of the female protagonists, however, passage almost exclusively involves the *renunciation* of agency. Agentic girls, girls who seize the action too much, are punished in one of two ways. The less common form of punishment, first, is the denial of passage to adulthood. Five of the tales have heroines who are fully active and fully successful in enacting their projects. In one version of "Little Red Riding Hood," for example, the girl and her grandmother get up on the roof and successfully kill the wolf and turn him into sausage. Or in "Hansel and Gretel" it is Gretel who kills the witch. In these and other cases of active and specifically successful heroism on the part of the heroine, the girl does not achieve what the vast majority of Grimms' heroines achieve—the mark of female adulthood, marriage.[13] Instead she returns to her natal home at the end of the story, and does not achieve passage.

In the more common female tale the heroine gets married at the end. But if she has been at all active in the early part of the tale (and sometimes even if she has not), she must invariably pass through severe trials before being worthy of marrying the prince, or by implication, any man at all. These trials always involve symbols and practices of utter passivity and/or total inactivity, as well as practices of humility and subordination. In "Sweetheart Roland,"[14] she cleverly saves her skin at the beginning, and then saves both herself and her lover, but for her pains her lover betroths another woman. In response the heroine turns herself first into a stone (utterly inert), then into a flower (in which form she says she hopes to be stepped on and crushed), and finally cleans house for some time for a shepherd before marrying her sweetheart in the end. In "The Twelve Brothers" and "The Six Swans,"[15] the heroine actively sets out on a quest to rescue her brothers. Despite her good intentions, however, she causes her brothers damage as a result of her efforts to save them and goes through a seven year period of complete silence and solemnity (including in one case making shirts for her brothers and in the other case simply spinning for seven years) before getting married at the end.

If any sort of agency must be punished, even for "good" girls, the punishment is even worse for "bad" female characters, the witches and wicked stepmothers. These women are highly agentic: they have projects, plans, plots. Needless to say they all come to terrible ends. After trying and failing to kill Snow White, for example, the stepmother/witch is invited to the wedding of

Snow White and the Prince, but once there she is forced to dance in red-hot slippers until she falls down dead. Since she and similar characters have done wicked things, their punishments seem justified on moral grounds, yet within the general pattern of punishing any sort of female agency, it seems fair to suggest that they are punished as much for their excessive agency as for its moral content.

In sum we can see these tales as cultural formations that construct and distribute agency in particular ways, as part of the cultural politics of creating appropriately gendered persons in that particular time and place. From the actor's point of view, the "project" of the story is the project of growing up, of doing the appropriate things to become an adult man or woman. Within the cultural politics of gender difference and inequality that informs the tales, however, growing up means that both parties in this ultimately unequal relationship cannot "have" agency. This is couched in a language of (the complementarity of) activity and passivity. The prince cannot be a hero if the princess can rescue herself.[16] Even worse the prince cannot be a hero if the princess can rescue *him*.[17]

But an examination of texts like the Grimms' fairy tales has narrowed our focus to the cultural construction of social subjects as agents (or not), that is, it has narrowed our focus to the culturally constituted psychology of players within serious games. For the rest of this chapter, however, I want to move to the broader level at which the relationship(s) between agency and power are organized into the serious games of culture and history in the first place.

PROJECTS ON THE EDGE OF POWER

I have long been interested in the question of how people sustain a culturally meaningful life in situations of large-scale domination by powerful others, including prominently slavery, colonialism, and racism. This was a central theme, for example, of *Life and Death on Mt. Everest* (Ortner 1999a), where I discussed the ways in which Sherpas, despite having been greatly affected by a century of intimate involvement in Himalayan mountaineering, nonetheless retain arenas of culturally "authentic" life. By this I mean not that those arenas are untouched by the massive presence of mountaineering, but simply that they are shaped less by the mountaineering encounter and more by the Sherpas' own social and political relations, and by their own culturally constituted intentions, desires, and projects. We may shorthand this idea as cultural life "on the margins of power."

During this extended moment when the often linked histories of anthropology and colonialism are being worked out, and when the very practices of anthropology in light of those histories are being rethought, it seems important to pay attention to this question of cultural "authenticity" in the shadow of massive, and culturally (as well as physically) hostile, forms of power. One response by many anthropologists has been to emphasize the degree to which colonialism so formed and deformed the societies in question that what anthropologists have seen in later fieldwork has virtually no cultural authenticity at all, that it is largely a Western and/or colonial product. Clearly this position in its extreme form would tend to replicate at an intellectual level the sins of historical colonialism itself.[18] As against this position it seems important to seek different ways of thinking about these questions.[19]

The example of "power" for present purposes is colonialism in southern Africa, as discussed by Jean and John Comaroff in *Of Revelation and Revolution*, Volumes 1 and 2.[20] The Comaroffs brilliantly explore the "long conversation" between Methodist missionaries and Tswana subjects, and the ways in which over time Tswana consciousness has been transformed by the ideas and practices introduced by the missionaries.

Here however I wish to draw something different out of their material. In looking at their data I found it useful to distinguish broadly between two modalities of agency, as broached at the beginning of this section. In one modality agency is closely related to ideas of power, including both domination and resistance; in another it is closely related to ideas of intention, to people's (culturally constituted) projects in the world and their ability to engage and enact them. I must emphasize again that these are not two different "things," although I despair of a terminology that may seem to render them as such. At an epistemological level the contrast is between what I called earlier two fields of meaning. At the ethnographic level, however, what is at stake is a contrast between the workings of agency *within* massive power relations, like colonialism or racism, as opposed to the workings of agency in contexts in which such relations can be—however momentarily, however partially—held at bay. Here it is less a matter of things than a matter of contexts.

Let us return for a moment to the categories and say a bit more about agency as power. In probably the most common usage "agency" can be virtually synonymous with the forms of power people have at their disposal, their ability to act on their own behalf, influence other people and events, and maintain some kind of control in their own lives. Agency in this sense is relevant for both domination and resistance. People in positions of power "have"—legitimately or not—what might be thought of as "a lot of agency," but the dominated too always have certain capacities, and sometimes very significant capacities, to exercise some sort of influence over the ways in which events unfold. Resistance then is also a form of "power-agency," and by now we have a well-developed theoretical repertoire for examining it. It includes everything from outright rebellions at one end, to various forms of what James Scott (1985) so well called "foot dragging" in the middle, to—at the other end—a kind of complex and ambivalent acceptance of dominant categories and practices that are always changed at the very moment they are adopted. Instances across the whole spectrum of "resistance" (although the Comaroffs eschew the term) can be found throughout the *Revelation and Revolution* opus, but it is the last type that is most central to it and most fully developed: ambivalent acceptance by many Tswana people of missionary categories and practices, together with a constant recasting and reframing of them in terms of their own ways of seeing and acting in the world.

The agency of (unequal) power, of both domination and resistance, may be contrasted with the second major mode of agency noted earlier, that of intentions, purposes, and desires formulated in terms of culturally established "projects." This agency of projects is from certain points of view the most fundamental dimension of the idea of agency. It is this that is disrupted in and disallowed to subordinates, as in the example of what happens to active, intending girls in the Grimms' fairy tales. It is also this that flourishes *as* power for the powerful, whose domination of others is rarely an end in itself but is rather in the service of enacting their own projects. And finally it is this—an agency of projects—that the less powerful seek to nourish and protect by creating or protecting sites, literally or metaphorically, "on the margins of power."

What, then, would such cultural projects look like? Many are simple "goals" for individuals, as in the case of the fairy tale heroine who wishes to grow up, marry the prince, and live happily ever after. Here the notion of agency as individual "intention" and "desire" comes to the fore, although one must never lose sight of the fact that the goals are fully culturally constituted. But many projects are full-blown "serious games," involving the intense play of multiply positioned subjects pursuing cultural goals within a matrix of local inequalities and power differentials.

As an example of the latter let me turn to the extensive discussions of precolonial Tswana politics, kinship, and marriage (see especially J. L. Comaroff and Jean Comaroff 1981, J. L. Comaroff 1987, and Jean and J. L. Comaroff 1991: chapter 4). Here we see the strong cultural value invested in male political careers, in which Tswana men seek to better their positions in relation to royal families, local rivals, and the like. We learn how these men seek to "eat" their rivals and to establish themselves as patrons with arrays of clients in their service. We see how kinship relations and marriage transactions are managed in relation to the furtherance of these careers.

This is an example first of all of agency primarily in the sense of the pursuit of (cultural) projects. It is not about heroic actors or unique individuals, nor is it about bourgeois strategizing; nor on the other hand is it entirely about routine everyday practices that proceed with little reflection. Rather it is about (relatively ordinary) life socially organized in terms of culturally constituted projects that infuse life with meaning and purpose. People seek to accomplish valued things within a framework of their own terms, their own categories of value.

But this is also not free agency. The political rivalries are themselves generated by various orders of social and political asymmetries and/or rivalries between chiefs and commoners, free men and serfs, fathers and sons, men and women, agnates and affines, and so on and so forth. The cultural desires or intentions, in other words, emerge from structurally defined differences of social categories and differentials of power. Thus as I stated above these cultural projects are themselves serious games, the social play of cultural goals organized in and around local relations of power. The point is thus not that the pursuit of cultural projects is something wholly innocent of power relations; quite the contrary, as we have just seen in the example of Tswana men's politics. But the point of making the distinction between agency-in-the-sense-of-power and an agency-in-the-sense-of-(the pursuit of) projects is that the first is organized around the axis of domination and resistance, and thus defined to a great extent by the terms of the dominant party, while the second is defined by local logics of the good and the desirable and how to pursue them.

For a second, and slightly more complicated, example let us look at Tswana women. We learn from earlier Comaroff writings that women had some significant disadvantages within Tswana society. In the traditional division of labor women did all the agricultural work. The work was fairly laborious in itself, and its laboriousness was compounded by certain kinds of chiefly powers and chiefly demands in relation to agriculture. In addition women were culturally viewed and ritually remade as inferior and subordinate (Jean Comaroff 1985). It was a specific feature of the initiation rites that young girls were trained in "passive obedience" and "docile endurance" (Jean Comaroff 1985:115, 116). The data here have very strong resonances with the European fairy tales discussed above. The Tswana rites constructed the girls precisely as subjects from whom any vestige of agency was ideally drained out.

Under these circumstances much of the "agency" of women that appears even in the earlier works is reactive to power, is an agency of "power-as-resistance." For example during the initiation rites, even as the women were constructed as docile bodies ready for sex, marriage, and hard agricultural labor, they expressed "resistance to established gender relations: provocative song and dance, intrusive noise and explicit accusation" (Jean Comaroff 1985:117). And, although in the traditional context such gestures appear to have had relatively minor impact, Jean Comaroff suggests that they represented "a suppressed, but continuing undercurrent of female discontent in the precolonial system" that played a significant role in the "enthusiastic response of [Tswana] women to the Methodist mission" (1985:118). Here, then, the agency of power-as-resistance moves toward the status of something more active, something resembling a "project." In embracing Methodism it would seem that many Tswana women began to embrace a vision of an alternative world that went beyond the reactive opposition to male and/or chiefly domination.

In addition, however, we can perhaps tease out an agency of projects, a sense of women enacting their own (culturally constituted) intentions, even in the precolonial context. This is more difficult to see, in part because women were, as just noted, precisely not supposed to have agency in this sense. Yet there are hints in the texts that one could see women's relationship to their agricultural work, for example, in this light. Women not only did all the agricultural work, but they also "held fields in their own right as daughters or wives" (Jean Comaroff 1985:64). They seem to have invested much pride and planning in their agricultural activities; occasionally they tried to evade or resist chiefly regulation of agricultural activities (J. L. Comaroff and Jean Comaroff 1997:128); and finally, when the missionaries actively sought to make agriculture men's rather than women's work, the women strongly resisted this change (ibid.: 136–37). I call attention here less to the resistance itself, than to the likelihood that the resistance signaled an important arena of women's projects of pride and identity, with which the missionaries were interfering. Perhaps resistance is always of this nature: protecting projects, or indeed the right to have projects. I note again that the distinction between an agency of power and an agency of projects is largely heuristic. In practice they are often inseparable.

Both of these examples—of men's political practices and women's practices of fertility (there was a close cultural link between agricultural and physical fertility [Jean Comaroff 1985:65])—are examples of what I am calling agency as (the pursuit of) projects. The agency of projects is not necessarily about domination and resistance, although there may be some of that going on. It is about people having desires that grow out of their own structures of life, including very centrally their own structures of inequality; it is in short about people playing, or trying to play, their own serious games even as more powerful parties seek to devalue and even destroy them.

I said earlier that in some ways the notion of projects is perhaps the most fundamental dimension of the idea of agency. In the discussion of the Grimms' fairy tales "power" consisted of destroying the girls' agency precisely in the sense of their capacity to actively enact projects. In the present section I set the discussion at a different level, contrasting the forms of agency seen within the dialectics of domination and resistance, and the forms of agency seen when actors are engaged in cultural projects, serious games whose terms are not primarily set by the power dialectic. At issue once again is the importance of questioning the totalizing effect of formations like colonialism or racism, and of attempting to see the ways in which dominated actors retain "agency" in either mode—by resisting domination in a range of ways, but also by trying to sustain their own culturally constituted projects, to make or sustain a certain kind of cultural (or for that matter, personal) authenticity "on the margins of power."

THE ELEMENTARY STRUCTURE OF AGENCY

In the previous section I looked at agency-as-power and agency-as-projects almost as if they occupied two different spaces. This was an intentional move as I tried to think about the dynamics of local agency in the face of domination by outsiders and powerful others. Here however I wish to look at the organization of "projects" themselves and think about something that was hinted at in the case of Tswana men's politics: the ways in which the agency of projects, the agency involved in pursuing significant cultural ends, almost always, and almost necessarily, involves *internal* relationships of power. Marx saw the point quite clearly: very schematically, for capitalists to play the serious game of capitalism, to make a profit and defeat the competition, they had to subordinate and exploit workers. The agency of project intrinsically hinges on the agency of power.

This little structure interrelating projects and power is extremely widespread. That is why I am calling it, with only slight tongue in cheek, "the elementary structure of agency." In this final section of the chapter I will begin by simply illustrating the way in which this structure plays out in a number of diverse ethnographic and historical cases. After presenting a few examples, however, I will complicate the picture by considering the instability of power relations, and thus the ways in which "resistance" lurks within this elementary structure, even if it is not always enacted.

An example that is probably familiar to most anthropologists can be seen in the games of honor played between men in many cultures. The man's honor vis-à-vis his opponents' is enhanced or diminished depending on his ability to maintain his authority and control over "his" women and, to a lesser extent, "his" junior males. Success in the public arenas of honor depends on power in the private arenas of gender, family, and kinship.[21]

But not all cultural games are men's games (though, given a widespread masculinist bias cross-culturally, many are), and not all cultural games hinge on control of women (though, by the same reasoning, many do).[22] An example that hinges on a different power axis, and again one which could be drawn, with variations, from any number of cultures, would be the phenomenon of arranged marriage. The case I will use here is from Laura Ahearn's work (2001a) among some Magar people of Junigau village in Western Nepal.[23] Traditionally the people of the area in which Ahearn worked recognized three types of marriage: arranged marriage (the most prestigious); elopement (which entailed some loss of prestige for the family); and marriage-by-capture, a violent, barely legitimate affair held in very low esteem in which a man's kin group kidnapped the prospective "bride" and brought her home for rape/consummation by the groom. A family gained prestige and respect in the community by arranging a good match for their child; this is "the (ideal) game." One could proceed to focus on the intricate politics of the negotiations between bride's and groom's kin, that is, on the game as it is played *between* the families. There is certainly a good deal of this, and it is indeed complex and delicate. But this focus diverts one's attention from the underlying power relations that make it possible: parents must have enough control and authority over their children to have them go along with the arrangements, and children have to be willing to accept the parents' choice of spouse.

It should be noted that the power differentials within what are supposed to be groups or social entities (here families) with shared goals are also the basis of the ultimate instability of all games. And it is here that we must introduce the third piece of the "elementary structure," the ever-present possibility of "resistance." The possibility of resistance is a more shadowy and of course not always realized part of the structure, but it is part of the structure nonetheless. This is true because subordinated actors are never wholly drained of agency except perhaps in fairy tales.

It is no doubt the case that playing the game tends to reproduce both the public structures of rules and assumptions, and the private subjectivity/consciousness/habitus of the players, and thus that playing the game—as Bourdieu unhappily and critically insists[24]—almost always results in social reproduction. Yet ultimately games do change, sometimes because of the entry of some externality that cannot be digested, but sometimes too because of the instability of the internal power relations on which successful play depends. Indeed, the externalities may prove indigestible precisely because they empower some of the normally subordinated subjects, and open up the possibility of rebellions, great and small.

The Magar case nicely illustrates all this as well. The power and authority of parents over children is clearly unstable, since even within the traditional system young people could and did elope and foil their parents' plans, or a stubborn daughter could resist an arrangement and open herself up to capture. But Ahearn traces the injection into the system of a new technology, one that gave even more power to young people, and that further undermined the parents' abilities to control their children's marriages: writing. As younger Magar men and women became better educated, and gained control of the tool of literacy, the unprecedented social phenomenon of love letters burgeoned. Even though young men's and women's physical behavior was still closely monitored, letters could be exchanged, and young men and women were more and more able (and, in a sense, incited) to "arrange" their own marriages. Clearly the game was changing.[25]

And one final example, in this case involving yet other power differentials:

class and ethnicity. I draw the case from Nicole Constable's study of Filipina domestic workers in Hong Kong (1997). The dominant game here is the game of capitalist success, with ambitious young Hong Kong couples out in the workplace and in the market making money and seeking to establish very upscale lifestyles. This being the late modern, haute bourgeoisie, both husbands and wives have time-consuming careers, and their success depends on hired domestic labor for cleaning, entertaining, and most of all, child care. Enter the Filipina domestic workers, who of course have their own projects, pursuing the higher wages of Hong Kong to make better lives for their own families. The financial success of the power couple no doubt depends on their own hard work, social networking, and so forth. But it also depends, though much more invisibly, on their ability to control their domestic workers. In the Hong Kong case, as in many others, the power differential is exacerbated by the weak legal position of many of the workers, who either came in illegally, or overstayed their visa, or in some other way are vulnerable to the power of the state. At the same time the control of the workers by their bosses can be quite literal—Filipina maids are sometimes physically struck, sometimes locked in their rooms, or otherwise abused. The power of the employers seems virtually total.

And yet, again, it is unstable, as all power relations ultimately are. While employers can be highly controlling, they also see themselves as enlightened modern subjects, and not as slave owners. Thus Filipina and other foreign domestic workers are given one day off a week, usually Sunday, and they have developed a practice of gathering in a particular square on Sundays. These gatherings have all the characteristics of Bakhtinian carnivals. Sociability is enjoyed, and cultural commonalities are celebrated. At the same time stories about the often unhappy working conditions are shared, mutual support is exchanged, and—most of all—information about "rights" and organizations that support them is made collectively available. Many of the women have become involved in organizations such as the Asian Domestic Workers Union or the United Filipinos in Hong Kong. Constable quotes various journalists complaining that the workers' power has grown too strong (1997:164). While these views are greatly exaggerated, there is no doubt that many of the workers are no longer willing to tolerate bad treatment and have learned to stand up for their rights, individually and collectively. Once again, then, the game is changing.

These examples are meant to make several points. The first, which I emphasized at the outset, concerns the ways in which games are not simply engagements between opposing families, groups, or classes, but are built upon power relations at a micro-level. These are often invisible in anthropologies that remain at the level of large-scale political formations—colonialism, the state, etc.—and do not as it were touch the ground. The second follows from the first: the internal power relations are so heavily policed precisely because they contain the potential to disrupt particular plays of the game in the case of individuals, and the very continuity of the game as a social and cultural formation over the long run. Yet finally we must come back to the distinction, yet also articulation, between an agency of projects and an agency of power. We have seen here how the exercise of power over subordinates is normally in the service of the pursuit of some project. Power is rarely an end in itself. But subordinates inevitably have projects of their own. These may be quite overt, as in the case of subordinated cultures under colonialism, or that of workers like the Filipina maids under global capitalism. Or they may be covert, as in the case of the "hidden transcripts" of slaves so well discussed by James Scott (1990), or in the more inchoate forms of dissatisfaction of women and wives often seen in apparently stable gender systems (see again Jean Comaroff 1985, Ahearn 2000; see also Ortner 2003, chapter 11). Thus if power and the subordination of others is always in the service of some project, so too is resistance; the entire domination/resistance dialectic itself makes sense as the clash of people's projects, their culturally constituted intentions, desires, and goals.

By Way of Conclusion

We have seen that at one level agency is a kind of property of social subjects. It is culturally shaped by way of the characteristics that are foregrounded as "agentic"—for example, activity versus passivity in the Grimms' fairy tales, or wild versus tame in American high school social classifications (Ortner 2003). And agency is almost always unequally distributed—some people get to "have" it and others not; some people get to have more and others less. In the first instance it thus appears largely as a quality invested in individuals.[26]

Yet individuals or persons or subjects are always embedded in webs of relations, whether of affection and solidarity, or of power and rivalry, or frequently of some mixture of the two. Whatever "agency" they seem to "have" as individuals is in reality something that is always in fact interactively negotiated. In this sense they are never free agents, not only in the sense that they do not have the freedom to formulate and realize their own goals in a social vacuum, but also in the sense that they do not have the ability to fully control those relations toward their own ends. As truly and inescapably social beings, they can only work within the many webs of relations that make up their social worlds.

Further, while agency in the abstract sense appears as a property of (differentially empowered) subjects, it is best seen (again) less as a psychological property or capacity unto itself, and more as a disposition toward the enactment of "projects." From the point of view of the subject this disposition toward the enactment of projects appears as issuing from one's own desires: "I will . . ." But from the point of view of the cultural analyst it is the projects that define the desires in the first place. Thus the anthropology of "agency" is not only about how social subjects, as empowered or disempowered actors, play the games of their culture, but about laying bare what those cultural games are, about their ideological underpinnings, and about how the play of the game reproduces or transforms those underpinnings.

Finally there is the question of the relationship between agency and power that has been the central theme of this chapter. At one level agency itself may be defined as a form of power; "agents" could easily be shorthanded simply as "empowered subjects." This point would work for the relatively simple Grimms' fairy-tale analysis where boys are constructed precisely as empowered subjects, "agents," while girls are systematically disempowered by having their agency deconstructed.

But subsequent sections of this chapter revealed more complex relations between the two phenomena. In the section using the Comaroffs' material on Tswana men and women, I tried to make a distinction between Tswana agency as it plays out within the missionary-cum-colonial relationship, and agency as it plays out "on the margins" of that relationship. I called the first an "agency of power," because it tends to be defined almost entirely by the domination-resistance dialectic, and thus almost entirely in the terms of the dominant party. I called the second an "agency of (cultural) projects," because I was calling attention to the ways in which Tswana men and women could or should be seen to be playing, or trying to play, their own serious games, defined more by their own values and ideals despite the colonial situation.

I find it useful to distinguish, and not just in situations of colonial domination, between agency as a form of power (including issues of the empowerment of the subject, the domination of others, the resistance to domination, and so forth) and agency as a form of intention and desire, as the pursuit of goals and the enactment of projects. I find it useful because, at the simplest level, they seem to me quite distinct usages of the term, distinct "fields of meaning." But I find it useful as well because, having pulled them apart, one can examine their articulations with one another. That is what I tried to show in the final section of this essay, in which I argued that, in the context of what I have been calling serious games, the pursuit of projects for some often entails, necessarily, the subordination of others. Yet those others, never fully drained of agency, have both powers and projects of their own, and resistance (from the most subtle to the most overt) is always a possibility. Both domination and resistance then are, it seems to me, always in the service of projects, of being allowed or empowered to pursue culturally meaningful goals and ends, whether for good or for ill.

NOTES

Introduction: Updating Practice Theory

Thanks first to Timothy Taylor for speedy, insightful, and extremely helpful comments on several drafts of this introduction. In addition I presented earlier versions of this introduction, then titled "Serious Games," to the Department of Anthropology at Stanford University and to the "Cultures of Capitalism" group at UCLA. In both cases I received very probing comments (that also reinforced some questions raised by one of the anonymous press readers), and that caused me to change the direction of the essay substantially. I thank them all.

1. Because of the longstanding historical opposition between "structure" and "agency" in the social sciences, and the ways in which this opposition seems to function as a deep structure in the Lévi-Straussian sense, there was and continues to be a tendency to view practice theory itself as a kind of covert revival of theories that underemphasize the real and deeply sedimented constraints under which people live. I have been opposing this view at least since my monograph on the founding of Sherpa monasteries, *High Religion* (1989:11–18) and can only say again that nothing could be further from the truth. Indeed most readers of (especially the early works of) Bourdieu and Giddens would argue that in the end both of these pioneers of practice theory tended to *overemphasize* structural constraint, even as they viewed structures as *produced* through (never-free) social practices.

2. Marshall Sahlins kindly sent me the manuscript of *Historical Metaphors . . .* when I was writing that paper. At the time I read it mainly for "data." It was only on a later rereading that I focused on his theoretical framework and its resonances with other practice theory work coming out in that era. I made the connections in Ortner 1984.

3. Scott casts his argument against an exaggerated version of Gramsci's position on hegemony, taking "hegemony" to be something that totally controls the minds of the dominated party.

4. Most recently William H. Sewell Jr.'s very important *Logics of History* (2005) has provided a theorization of "events" that not only illuminates Sahlins's "possible theory of history" (as Sahlins had called it), but provides a powerful theorization of the relationship between historical thinking and social and cultural theory much more broadly.

5. The degree to which the media attend to issues of class varies a great deal over time. Recently, for example, the *New York Times* ran a multi-part series on class in America. But at the level of popular consciousness, "class" is virtually unthought and untalked about. See Ortner 2003.

6. Bourdieu later (2000) shifted and/or defended his arguments to some degree. Throughout this essay I refer primarily to the early works in which his basic outlines of a theory of practice (to coin a phrase) were laid out: 1978 and 1990.

1. Reading America: Class and Culture

This paper was written while I was a visiting member at the Institute for Advanced Study in Princeton, New Jersey, supported by funds from the University of Michigan and the National Endowment for the Humanities. Arjun Appadurai, Nicholas B. Dirks, and Elliot Shore read the first draft on short notice and gave me extremely useful comments. Later drafts were read by Nancy Chodorow, Salvatore Cucchiari, Richard Fox, Abigail Stewart, and Peter van der Veer, all of whom provided excellent insights and suggestions. There was also very constructive and stimulating discussion of the paper in the Thursday night seminar of the Program in the Comparative Study of Social Transformations, which nourished and provoked me intellectually at the University of Michigan throughout the late '80s and early '90s.

1. Ethnographic work by sociologists began to diminish in the 1950s, presumably coinciding with the achievement of hegemony of quantitative research in that field.

2. Schneider and Smith's *Class Differences and Sex Roles in American Kinship and Family Structure* (1973) is one of the rare anthropological works on America with "class" in its title, but it is not a monograph. There are also some older review articles by Goldschmidt (1950, 1955). A review article by Raymond Smith on "Anthropological Studies of Class" (1984) focuses largely on the study of third world societies.

3. Television sitcoms of both white and black lower-class families (such as *All in the Family* and *Sanford and Son*) have long followed the tradition of representing both groups as endearing ethnic others.

4. It will be no surprise to the anthropologists that Lloyd Warner, whose work with Australian aborigines focused on kinship terms—that is, on native categories of social relationships—was essentially the founding father of the second—native category—approach.

5. It might be argued that "middle class" is not a class term at all, since it is not generally seen as part of a class *structure*, that is, as a positional or relational category vis-à-vis other classes. In ordinary discourse it seems simply to mean a general allegiance to the nation and to large, overarching values like freedom and individualism.

6. This is the so-called multiple domination position, with which I am in basic agreement. One of the clearest statements of this position is to be found in Cohen (1982). Another version is developed in Laclau and Mouffe (1985). Feminist theory in general also tends toward a multiple domination position; see, for example, Sacks (1989).

7. There is a problem of terminology here. The terms for the lower end of the class structure are to some extent racially coded. The term "working class" seems nor-

mally to refer to whites. For black people one more often sees "lower class." I will use the terms interchangeably for both.

8. There seems to have been more introjection in the nineteenth century, when the split between the middle class and the working class was played out *within* middle-class gender relations (see Smith-Rosenberg 1986).

9. The authors also identify an important ethnographic category: "nobody," as in, "Her? Oh, she's nobody." More work needs to be done on nobodies.

10. In Willis's account of the discourse of the nonconformist (i.e., the most "hoody") working-class lads, they claim this greater sexual experience and knowledgeability for themselves, and Willis thinks it is probably true that they have more active sex lives than the ear'oles.

11. I am indebted to Arjun Appadurai for putting these particular pieces together. Some of my students have argued that this sexual-cum-class division no longer applies, because even middle-class kids are having a lot of sex in high school. Although I accept my students as valid informants, the question needs to be investigated more closely. I suspect that the situation is similar to that described by Eckert in her high-school study with respect to drugs: both middle-class and working-class kids do drugs, but the use of drugs plays an entirely different role in their respective symbolic economies (Eckert 1989).

12. The phrase is from Claude Lévi-Strauss (1966).

13. A little known but very interesting example is Raymond Sokolov's 1975 novel *Native Intelligence*.

14. This also suggests that they were socialists, but Roth does not develop the political contrasts in the story.

15. Another painful irony with respect to hidden injuries of class: while the middle class endows the working class with a free and imaginative sexuality, sociologists tell us that sex as actually practiced in the working class is just the opposite: repressed, unimaginative, and—according to informants—largely unsatisfying (see Reiche 1971).

2. Resistance and Ethnographic Refusal

1. An earlier and very different version of this essay was written for "The Historic Turn" Conference organized by Terrence McDonald for the Program in the Comparative Study of Social Transformations (CSST) at the University of Michigan. The extraordinarily high level of insightfulness and helpfulness of critical comments from my colleagues in CSST has by now become almost routine, and I wish to thank them collectively here. In addition for close and detailed readings of the text, I wish to thank Frederick Cooper, Fernando Coronil, Nicholas Dirks, Val Daniel, Geoff Eley, Ray Grew, Roger Rouse, William H. Sewell Jr., Julie Skurski, Ann Stoler, and the excellent readers who reviewed this work when it was first published in *Comparative Studies in Society and History* (37:1 [1995]: 173–93). I have incorporated many of their suggestions and know that I have ignored some at my peril. Finally, for valuable comments as well as for the heroic job of organizing the conference, I wish especially to thank Terrence McDonald.

2. Scott was of course drawing on a wealth of earlier scholarship.

3. The notion of ambivalence has become central to colonial and postcolonial studies more generally and is worth a paper in itself. See for example Hanks (1986) and Bhabha (1985).

4. A parallel to the monolithic portrayal of resistors is the monolithic portrayal of the dominants. This is beginning to be broken down, as for example in Stoler (1989).

5. The absence of gender considerations in generic resistance studies and some implications of this absence have been addressed particularly by O'Hanlon (1989). See also White (1986). But for valuable ethnographic studies of gender resistance per se, see Abu-Lughod (1986) and Ong (1987).

6. The beginnings of (Franco-British) structural Marxism in anthropology were also contemporary with the beginnings of British (Marxist) cultural studies. The impact of structural Marxism on anthropology, as well as the fact that the field was still mired in the split between materialism and idealism in that era, probably accounts in good part for the delayed impact of British cultural studies. See Ortner (1984) for a review of anthropological theory from the 1960s to the '80s.

7. Some important early feminist anthropology was directly drawing on structural Marxism. See especially Collier and Rosaldo (1981).

8. The work of the British cultural studies scholars is seemingly a major exception to this point. I would argue if I had time, however, that in much of the work in this field the treatment of both culture and ethnography is also "thin" (Willis 1977 is a major exception). In any event my focus in this section is on influential work that is much more obviously problematic with respect to the thickness of culture.

9. The Subaltern Studies school is complex, and a variety of tendencies appear within it. Shahid Amin's "Gandhi as Mahatma" (1988) is more fully cultural than many of the other writings, as is Gyanendra Pandey's "Peasant Revolt and Indian Nationalism" (1988).

10. The same is true of other postcolonial historiographies (African studies, for example), but I am less familiar with their literatures. Indian anthropology and history touch upon my own long-term research in Nepal.

11. For another strong work on Gandhi's cultural genius, see Fox (1989).

12. See for example the quite different disclaimer in Don DeLillo's fictionalization of the Kennedy assassination, *Libra* (1989).

13. I am indebted to Nick Dirks for pushing me on this point.

14. Nandy (1983) and Comaroff (1985) make a point of discussing the ways in which subalterns may effectively draw on, and take advantage of, some of the latent oppositional categories and ideologies of Western culture.

3. The Hidden Life of Class

Thanks to Louise Lamphere for extensive and detailed comments. Thanks also to Dan Segal, Lawrence G. Straus, and Timothy D. Taylor for valuable readings and comments. This paper was first published in the *Journal of Anthropological Research* 54(1):1–17, 1998.

1. In contrast, see Gregory and Sanjek 1994.

2. In chapter 1 I discussed the ways in which American categories of gender and sexuality are deeply "classed" as well.

3. It is not clear whether the float of the battle involving Benedict Arnold was ever built.

4. About 100 with my classmates and about 50 with their grown (in their twenties) children. For an account of the fieldwork for the project, see Ortner 1997.

5. People are actually getting more Jewish than they were when I and my classmates were growing up, which was—I now see—a particularly secularist time. Many of my classmates describe themselves as more observant now than when we were growing up, and many of their children declared themselves more observant than their parents, my contemporaries.

6. I begin to tackle the question of slippage between popular and academic categories in the next chapter on Generation X.

7. Warner and Lunt (1941) used the fine folk gradations of classes in 1930s Yankee City (upper upper, upper middle, etc.) as analytic categories. In effect they translated (as the natives tend to do) "class" into "social status." Many view Warner's work as part of the beginnings of "bourgeois social science" in the United States.

8. Weiss (1996), summarizing a variety of scholarly studies, presents a remarkable picture of Jewish "success" in the late twentieth century. Michael Lind (1995) includes WASPs and Jews as the dominant groups in the "white overclass" that has been developing since the 1970s.

9. It has not totally waned. I received some anti-Semitic hate mail as I was drafting this essay.

10. The other arena in which generic "middle-class" values are presumed, articulated, and transmitted is education, in which again the Jews have been disproportionately represented.

11. Woody Allen in film and Philip Roth in fiction are more or less contemporary; both mark a shift from Jewish artists doing generically "American" work (at least if they wanted to reach a broad American public) to doing ethnically "Jewish" work and succeeding in making it of broad (though by no means universal) appeal.

12. A similar argument has recently been made with respect to the "disappearance" of contemporary American Jewry. The Jews in America are said to be proportionally declining in American society, down from 4 percent to 2 percent since 1950. And one of the reasons offered for that is that Jewish culture is being absorbed into the dominant culture: "Many of the key ingredients in the ethnic alchemy that produce the Jewish persona have been soaked up and absorbed by the larger culture. As a result, the secular Jewish world is losing its distinctiveness. Jewish humor, the Jewish perspective, the Jewish sensibility, are all being subtly blended into the American mainstream" (Horowitz 1997:33).

13. The wording of the statement here is open to another interpretation. African Americans may "assert" a working-class identity as a kind of political statement, a statement of solidarity with the majority of the group. Questions of African American internal class categories have not been well explored, as far as I know. But see Bell 1983 for at least some ethnographic address of these issues.

14. A seeming exception to this point would be the idea of "the culture of poverty," which tried to explain that poor people get into a vicious cycle of objective poverty and dysfunctional social practices. While the intent of the idea was not necessarily "racist" and was apparently meant both to denaturalize this cycle and to open it to would-be well-meaning intervention, it was virtually impossible for those who generated the idea, as well as for those who heard it, not to invest it with a racial subtext. It thus became another way of linking racial and ethnic blame, on the one hand, and popular "bootstrap" theory, on the other.

4. Generation X

Funding for the larger project of which this is a part came from the University of Michigan, the Wenner-Gren Foundation for Anthropological Research, the University of California at Berkeley, and the John D. and Catherine T. MacArthur Foundation. I am extremely grateful to all these sources. For excellent library searches, thanks to Lynn Fisher, and for amazing Internet searches, thanks to Tim Taylor. For insightful comments on earlier drafts of this essay, I wish to thank James Faubion, Marc Flacks, Judith Rothbard, Roger Rouse, Dan Segal, Judith Stacey, Tim Taylor, the members of the School of American Research seminar organized by George Marcus on Power/Knowledge Shifts in America's Fin de Siècle, and the anonymous readers for *Cultural Anthropology*. And finally a special vote of thanks to Rick Perlstein, Xer native, generous commentator, and vociferous critic—if I still have not gotten it right, it is not his fault. This paper was first published in *Cultural Anthropology* 13(3): 414–40, 1998.

1. The ethnography of New Jersey is building up nicely. Donna Gaines's (1990) youth study was in Bergenfield, not far from Katherine Newman's "Pleasanton" (1993) and not far from the epicenter (though not the only site) of my study. Michael Moffatt's *Coming of Age in New Jersey* (1989) should also be mentioned. David Halle's study of chemical workers (1984) was done in Elizabeth; *The Class of '66* was based in a town on the south Jersey shore (Lyons 1994; Lyons is a graduate of Weequahic High School, Class of 1960); the research for *Ritual Healing in Suburban America* was conducted in Essex County (McGuire 1988). Varenne et al. (1998) worked in New Jersey and have a similar footnote to this one, listing yet other New Jersey–based ethnographic work.

2. See Bourdieu 1984, particularly on the inflation and devaluation of higher educational certification.

3. There is some question as to whether the idea of Gen X is still alive. Although I think it has died down somewhat in the press, my sense is that many Gen Xers still feel that the issues involved remain highly relevant to their lives. Moreover, no other image or idea seems to have replaced it in the public culture. I will thus continue to use the present tense about the phenomenon in this chapter.

4. Some famous hippies and antiwar political activists later became yuppies, of course. But this was a secondary convergence.

5. Writers vary on the degree to which they acknowledge the counterculture and antiwar generation as having made any positive changes. Most recognize to some degree that that generation produced some important kinds of social and cultural progress:

social advances for women, gays, and minorities; the ecology movement; the legit-
imation of rock music and many other forms of contemporary popular culture. But
depending on the writer's political stripe (which is quite variable) these are either not
really gains, or they are gains that are irrelevant to today's world, and Xers are tired of
hearing about them (see Rushkoff 1994 for the more appreciative end, Howe and
Strauss 1993 for the more negative end).

6. Despite the male pronoun Generation X does not seem to be particularly gendered.

7. Thanks to in-house music consultants Gwen Kelly and Tim Taylor. The genre is
sometimes called "whiny white boy rock."

8. The discussion begins with Mandel 1978. See also Harvey 1989, Lash and Urry 1987,
and Rouse 1995.

9. The other major force in the emergence of "late capitalism" is globalization, which
gives the economy its increasingly decentered and transnational character. This aspect of the question cannot be pursued here.

10. As several observers have pointed out (e.g., Sacks 1994), today's "middle class" is not
aware of, or does not wish to recognize, the degree to which it was created by what
would now be seen as "government handouts." The minority scholarships, fellow-
ships, and other forms of affirmative action created in the 1970s and 1980s are clearly
analogues of those earlier programs, and they have had analogous positive effects.
They are currently (and foolishly, in my opinion) being dismantled.

11. Working-class studies frequently—and correctly in my view—differentiate between
the home-owning and non-home-owning working class (e.g., Chinoy 1955; Halle
1984). See chapter 1 of this volume, on this split within the working class.

12. Although it is clear from context that Newman is talking about the group that came
to be called the "baby busters," or Generation X, she locates them as the latecomers
or tail end within the baby boomers, which she sees as a split generation. This
produces some confusion for readers (e.g., Callinan 1993), as her classification is out
of sync with what have now become the established categories. This does not affect
the present argument.

13. For an excellent portrayal of lower-middle-class rage in this era, from a different
angle, see Rieder 1985.

14. See chapter 3 of this volume, on the relevance and nonrelevance of the Jewish factor
in the project.

15. Quite a few of the twenty-somethings in this project were trying to "make it" in one
or another of the arts.

16. Thanks to tremendously responsive and thoughtful audiences at Princeton; University of California, Berkeley (Sociology); and University of California, Santa Cruz. In
the same way, thanks to my Practice Theory seminar at UC Berkeley in the spring of
1996.

17. I benefited from a goodly level of this sort of privilege myself, and take this opportunity to thank my parents again for everything they have done for me.

18. It may be suspected—given the Jewish bias in my ethnographic data, as well as
various folk beliefs about these matters—that the extremes of (financial) support for

grown children is a particularly "Jewish" pattern, and not characteristic of the upper middle class as a whole. While I do think there are some subcultural differences between ethnicities, including Jews, in the United States, I would resist an argument posed in terms of Jewish exceptionalism. Again see chapter 3 of this volume.

19. On love and American kinship, see Schneider 1980.

20. The idea of the safety net is central to the *Generation X* novel. Coupland (1991) uses it to signify several different points: that being a Gen Xer can be a pose, when one really has parents and resources one can fall back on, but also that all upper-middle-class kids carry around the idea of safety nets that may not in reality be available any more (Carden n.d.; Coupland 1991: 113 et passim).

21. I am grateful to Judith Stacey for stressing this point in her comments to me.

22. This article was downloaded from the Web, where it was reprinted by permission of the authors and the editor of the magazine. Both quotes are from the unpaginated first page of the interview.

23. There are of course some great ethnographic journalists. Frances FitzGerald is at the top of my personal list, which also includes Jane Kramer. *The New Yorker* in general has long supported this kind of work.

5. Subjectivity and Cultural Critique

I would like to thank Lila Abu-Lughod, Roy D'Andrade, Clifford Geertz, Steven Gregory, Paul Rabinow, Steven Sangren, and Timothy D. Taylor for excellent critical comments on earlier drafts of this piece. I also received valuable comments when I presented it as a paper at the Glasscock Center for the Humanities at Texas A&M University; the Society for Psychological Anthropology 2003 annual meetings; the Department of Anthropology at UCLA; the Department of Anthropology and also Jeffrey Alexander's Cultural Sociology seminar at Yale; the conference on "Blurred Boundaries: Rethinking 'Culture' in the Context of Interdisciplinary Practices" at the Institute of Ethnology, Academia Sinica, Taiwan (with formal comments by Ding-tzann Lii); and finally at the École des Hautes Études en Sciences Sociales in Paris. I also want to thank James Rosenheim at Texas A&M, Allen Chun in Taiwan, and Tassadit Yacine in Paris for hospitality above and beyond the call of duty.

1. This essay first appeared in *Anthropological Theory* 5:1 (2005):31–52.

2. See Bourdieu (2000) and Fox (2003) for discussions of this history.

3. As Abdul JanMohamed and David Lloyd put it in a discussion of "minority discourse":

> Where the point of departure of poststructuralism lies within the Western tradition and works to deconstruct its identity formations "from within," the critical difference is that minorities, by virtue of their very social being, must begin from a position of objective *non-identity* which is rooted in their economic and cultural marginalization vis-à-vis the "West." The non-identity which the critical Western intellectual seeks to (re)produce discursively is for minorities a given of their social existence. But as such a given it is not yet by any means an index of liberation.... On

the contrary, the non-identity of minorities remains the sign of material damage to which the only coherent response is struggle, not ironic distanciation (1987:16).

I have used this quotation from JanMohamed and Lloyd before (Ortner 1996a:8), but as the poststructuralist, antihumanist project continues unabated in some quarters, it seems worth quoting again. See also Hartsock (1990).

4. See an excellent essay by Throop and Murphy (2002) that raises some of the same questions. See also Meneley (1999).

5. James Scott (1990, esp. chapter 4) considers the question of the knowledgeability of dominated subjects and argues strongly against seeing them as hegemonized in a deep Gramscian sense, or subjected in the deep Foucauldian sense. I sympathize with his position but I think he goes too far. On this point I am more closely in agreement with Giddens, who argues that there is "no circumstance in which the conditions of action can become *wholly* opaque to agents" (1979:144, emphasis added).

6. Yacine was a student of Bourdieu's. I find it interesting that she has located her own ethnographic work in this area of subjectivity that was lacking in his framework.

7. I consider almost exclusively Geertz's foundational essays in this article. For a recent overview of his work as a whole, see Inglis (2000). For a very interesting interview, see Panourgiá (2002). For a collection of essays taking stock of, and extending, Geertz's work, see Ortner (ed., 1999).

8. My own empirical work has primarily responded to this version of the critique and has for a long time emphasized the articulation of cultural forms with social differentiation and inequality. See esp. Ortner 1999a and 2003.

9. Williams can be thought of as having effected the rapprochement between anthropology and literature from the literature side, as Geertz did from the side of anthropology.

10. Crehan (2002) has criticized Williams's adaptation of Gramsci's notion of hegemony and also the extensive use of Williams's version of the concept in anthropology. She raises interesting questions, but these cannot be pursued here.

11. See for example my discussion of Shahbano in chapter 2 of this volume.

12. I do not mean to privilege nonanthropologists here. I choose the Jameson and Sennett works because they illustrate best the points I wish to make about Geertz's approach to subjectivity. Anthropologists have addressed various aspects of late capitalism, especially globalization (Appadurai 1996; Hannerz 1996; Ong 1999). On questions specifically of postmodern consciousness, among the closest work would be that of Traube (1992b), Martin (1994) and Comaroff and Comaroff (2001a).

13. To show how fast the language of theory and politics changes, the term "globalization" was not yet in currency when Jameson wrote his essay and used the term "multinational."

14. On the basis of a small set of interviews she conducted in the United States, Claudia Strauss (1997) has questioned Jameson's arguments, and my amendments to those arguments, about the fragmented self (Ortner 1991). It is not clear that these kinds of interviews with individuals can be used to respond to Jameson's and my points, which are pitched at a cultural level, but it would take me too far afield to address these questions here.

15. Having moved from New York to Los Angeles, I have to say that there is something strange to a New Yorker about the design of many buildings in LA. Here I specifically refer to apartment houses. Many of them, for example, do not really have an obvious entry door, or some kind of recognizable entry space or lobby. In my own building and many others in my new neighborhood one has to enter through the garage, or through a nonobvious side door which puts one directly into a hallway of apartments. This is all to say that the Westin Bonaventure may be "postmodern," but it may also represent an exaggerated version of some local architectural culture.

16. It is possible to distinguish certain kinds of textually based cultural studies work that are more successful in dealing with the social location problem, even without ethnographic data or research. See for example Traube (1992b) and Bordo (1993), also on postmodern consciousness.

17. The third major site for mapping postmodern culture and consciousness is the family, for which see Judith Stacey's outstanding *Brave New Families* (1990).

18. Sennett rejects the term "postmodern," but he is clearly talking about the same phenomena that Jameson gathers under that term.

19. I actually disagree with Sennett's interpretation of their stories. But I completely agree with his general point about the rupturing and reconstitution of narrativity; in fact I wrote a paper, which for various reasons I never published, making much the same point (Ortner 1991). See also Salman Rushdie's wonderful children's book, *Haroun and the Sea of Stories* (1990).

20. Actually, in the context of this story. Rose's first act of agency was taking the job. The whole Rose story is fascinating but I cannot pursue it here.

6. Reflections on Agency

I would like to thank Oscar Salemink and his colleagues and students at the Vrije Universiteit of Amsterdam for warm hospitality and helpful comments on an earlier draft of this paper. I would also like to thank Laura Ahearn, Andrew Apter, Alessandro Duranti, Antonius C. G. Robben, and Timothy Taylor for additional, extremely valuable and supportive, comments.

1. For a recent example within anthropology, however, see Acneson and Gardner 2004.

2. Given this, the occasional appearance of the term in English translations of Bourdieu's works may represent the translator's choice of terms. I believe the closest approximation in French for "agency" is "action," which carries a somewhat different set of connotations. Bourdieu does however use the term "agent" interchangeably with actor; this does not seem to represent any significant theoretical point on his part.

3. There is also a growing body of work on agency in American archaeology, in which it has become something of a hot topic. See, e.g., Dobres and Robb (2000) and Dornan (2002).

4. I have not been able to cover all the thinkers who have tackled one or another aspect of the agency question. But I would mention in particular Keane (2003).

5. Duranti 2004 largely follows Giddens on this point. But in a forthcoming paper (2006) he moves toward the harder end of the spectrum.

6. Somewhere in between these softer and harder views of the role of intentionality in agency lies the question of improvisation, which has been a central category in practice theory from the beginning. In Bourdieu it represents the idea that the *habitus*, the internalized system of cultural dispositions toward action, is not a set of hard and fast rules, but rather a set of limits within which an actor can improvise. Yet improvisation itself has what can be thought of as a soft end and a hard end. At the soft end it is akin to improvisation in jazz—a kind of playing with the possibilities inherent in the musical form, for the sheer emotional and aesthetic pleasure of that play. But at the hard end it is closely tied to intentionality. The actor has some intention in mind; there is perhaps a standard cultural way of realizing that intention, but for some reason it is blocked; the actor thus improvises an alternative solution in order to realize that intention. Improvisation here is more like Lévi-Strauss's *bricolage*, the creative use of possibilities at hand to realize some goal or purpose. It is worth noting that most of Bourdieu's examples of improvisation are of this latter nature. See also the well-discussed story of the woman who climbed up a house in Holland et. al. 1998.

7. See also Mohanty 1989.

8. I will not try to define power in any systematic way or this essay will be endless. My various uses of the term will be clear, I hope, from context.

9. I use "projects" in the Sartrean sense, especially as discussed in *Search for a Method* (Sartre 1968). This important book moves decisively away from Sartre's early emphasis on the freedom of the acting subject.

10. A condensed version of this discussion was published as a section of Ortner 1996a. The present, fuller, version of this discussion harks back to an unpublished working paper (Ortner 1991).

11. The tales have been interpreted many times over (see especially Bettelheim 1977); much of the more recent work has specifically focused on gender issues (e.g., Bottigheimer 1987, Barzelai 1990, Zipes 1993, Orenstein 2003).

12. Interestingly the tales divide almost evenly between those with male and those with female protagonists.

13. In "The Seven Ravens" the girl goes to seek her brothers, and finds and rescues them with great resourcefulness, virtually unassisted. In "The Robber Bridegroom" the girl is helped by an old woman, and between the two of them they bring about the execution of the robber and his band. And in "Fundevogel" the girl actively and resourcefully saves her brother from a wicked old woman.

14. A variant of "Fundevogel."

15. Variants of each other and of "The Seven Ravens."

16. See also my discussion of Shahbano in chapter 1 of this volume.

17. It is worth reflecting for a moment on the different loci of power in the tales, and power's different relationships to "agency." Agency is directly equated with power in the case of the wicked stepmothers, but in the case of the boys and girls, princes and princesses, the relationship between agency and power is more oblique and indirect. The "power" that endows boys with agency and drains it out of girls is not in the

hands of any particular agent but is built into the larger cultural order as encoded, among other things, in the fairy tales. This provides a clear illustration of Giddens's distinction between power, which is interpersonal, and domination, which is structural. Obviously the two levels or modalities feed off one another—practices of power reproduce structural domination, while structural domination enables and, one might say, empowers, practices of power.

18. Said (1978) made the point that much of Western scholarship carries forward colonialist assumptions. Yet he probably did not envision the ironic situation that these kinds of colonialist assumptions are sometimes re-created by well-meaning scholars who are precisely trying to overcome them.

19. Probably the best body of work along alternative lines is Robin D. G. Kelley's work on African American popular, political, and musical culture (e.g., 1997).

20. This section is drawn from a paper called "Specifying Agency: The Comaroffs and their Critics." It was presented at the 1998 American Anthropological Association meetings on a panel devoted to *Of Revelation and Revolution*, Vol. 2. The Comaroffs wrote a response to all the papers, and the papers and the response were published as a special issue of *interventions* (2001). In the meetings version, and later the published version, of my paper, I formulated my comments as a critique of some of the discussions of the book. I do not wish to continue in that vein, in part because I am persuaded by some of the Comaroffs' defenses of their text in their rejoinder, and in part because, in the long run, I feel that we are on the same side of the intellectual and political issues in question, even if we approach them differently.

21. The classic references here are from the Mediterranean area as it was studied and interpreted in the sixties—see especially Peristiany 1966. I am aware of the critiques of the honor and shame literature, to the effect that honor and shame have been used to homogenize and stereotype an entire region (see especially Appadurai 1996). Nothing I say here is intended to stereotype the region, but only to illustrate through an ethnographically familiar pattern the ways in which one part of a cultural game—the competition between men—hinges on the subordination of others for its success.

22. See Ortner 1981 for another example of the pattern, and also for an early attempt on my part to theorize the idea of an underlying "game." I am struck now by the coincidence of the date of that paper with the early practice theory literature.

23. Ahearn primarily examines the case in terms of issues of female agency; see also Kratz 2000. I am using Ahearn's material here to develop a slightly different point.

24. See, for example, the discussion of working class habitus in *Distinction* (1984).

25. Although from a historical or processual point of view one can say that "the game is changing," from an ethnographic point of view, at one point in time, it will appear as a *conflict* of cultural or historical games between parents and children (Ahearn, personal communication).

26. Or groups. The question of group agency is less problematic than it appears. While groups do not have agency in the psychological sense (like individuals), groups surely have both "projects" and "power."

REFERENCES CITED

Abu-Lughod, Lila. 1986. *Veiled sentiments: Honor and poetry in a Bedouin Society*. Berkeley: University of California Press.

———. 1990. "The Romance of resistance: Tracing transformations of power through Bedouin Women." *American Ethnologist* 17(1):41–55.

———. 1993. *Writing women's worlds: Bedouin stories*. Berkeley: University of California Press.

Acheson, James M. and Roy J. Gardner. 2004. "Strategies, conflict, and the emergence of territoriality: The case of the Maine lobster industry." *American Anthropologist* 106(2): 296–307.

Ahearn, Laura. 2000. "Agency." *Journal of Linguistic Anthropology* 9(1–2):12–15.

———. 2001a. *Invitations to love: Literacy, love letters, and social change in Nepal*. Ann Arbor: University of Michigan Press.

———. 2001b. "Language and agency." *Annual Review of Anthropology* 30:109–37.

Alexander, Jeffrey. 2004. "The cultural pragmatics of social performance: Symbolic action between ritual and strategy." *Sociological Theory* 22 (4):527–73.

Althusser, Louis. 1971. *Lenin and philosophy and other essays*. Trans. Ben Brewster. New York and London: Monthly Review Press.

American Demographics. 1987. "Baby bust incomes." October: 70.

———. 1992. "Hanging out with American youth." February: 24–33.

———. 1993. "The dream is alive." August: 32–37.

Amin, Shahid. 1988. "Gandhi as Mahatma," in R. Guha and G. C. Spivak, eds., *Selected Subaltern Studies*, 288–350. New York: Oxford University Press.

Amit-Talai, Vered and Helena Wulff, eds. 1995. *Youth cultures: A cross-cultural perspective*. London: Routledge.

Appadurai, Arjun. 1996. *Modernity at large: Cultural dimensions of globalization*. Minneapolis: University of Minnesota Press.

Appiah, Kwame Anthony and Henry Louis Gates Jr., eds. 1995. *Identities*. Chicago: University of Chicago Press.

Applebaum, Herbert. 1981. *Royal blue: The culture of construction workers*. New York: Holt, Rinehart, Winston.

Arens, William, and Susan P. Montague, eds. 1976. *The American dimension: Cultural myths and social realities*. Port Washington, N.Y.: Alfred Publishing.

Barzelai, Shuli. 1990. "Reading 'Snow White': The mother's story." *Signs* 15(1):515–34.

Bell, Michael J. 1983. *The world from Brown's Lounge: An ethnography of black middle class play*. Urbana: University of Illinois Press.

Bellow, Saul. 1975. *Humboldt's gift*. New York: Viking Press.

Bettelheim, Bruno. 1977. *The uses of enchantment: The meaning and importance of fairy tales*. New York: Vintage Books.

Bhabha, Homi K. 1985. "Signs taken for wonders: Questions of ambivalence and authority under a tree outside Delhi." *Critical Inquiry* 12(1):144–65.

Bloch, Maurice. 1975. *Marxist analyses and social anthropology*. New York: Wiley.

Bordo, Susan. 1993. " 'Material Girl': The effacements of postmodern culture." In her *Unbearable weight: Feminism, Western culture, and the body*, 245–76. Berkeley and Los Angeles: University of California Press.

Bottigheimer, Ruth B. 1987. *Grimms' bad girls and bold boys: The moral and social vision of the tales*. New Haven: Yale University Press.

Bourdieu, Pierre. 1977. *Outline of a theory of practice*. Trans. R. Nice. Stanford: Stanford University Press.

——. 1984. *Distinction: A social critique of the judgment of taste*. Trans. R. Nice. Cambridge, Mass.: Harvard University Press.

——. 1990. *The logic of practice*. Trans. R. Nice. Stanford: Stanford University Press.

——. 2000. *Pascalian meditations*. Trans. R. Nice. Stanford: Stanford University Press.

Brake, Michael. 1985. *Comparative youth cultures*. London: Routledge and Kegan Paul.

Business Week. 1991. "What happened to the American dream?" August 19: 80–85.

——. 1992. "Move over, Boomers. The Busters are here—and they're angry." December 14:74–82.

Butler, Judith. 1997. *The psychic life of power: Theories in subjection*. Stanford: Stanford University Press.

Callinan, Kevin. 1993. "Baby Boomer blues." Letter to the Editor, Book Review Section. *New York Times*. July 25: 31.

Carden, Amy. n.d. "Generation and class in the watching of 'Melrose Place.' " Course paper, University of California, Berkeley. Unpublished MS.

Chinoy, Eli. 1955. *Automobile workers and the American dream*. Garden City, N.Y.: Doubleday.

Christopher, Robert C. 1989. *Crashing the gates: The dewASPing of America's power elite*. New York: Simon and Schuster.

Clendinnen, Inga. 1987. *Ambivalent conquests: Maya and Spaniard in Yucatan, 1517–1570*. Cambridge: Cambridge University Press.

Clifford, James. 1986. "Introduction: Partial truths" in J. Clifford and G. Marcus, eds. *Writing culture: The poetics and politics of ethnography*, 1–26. Berkeley: University of California Press.

——. 1988. *The predicament of culture: Twentieth century ethnography, literature, and art*. Cambridge, Mass.: Harvard University Press.

——. 1997. *Routes: Travel and translation in the late twentieth century*. Cambridge, Mass.: Harvard University Press.

Clifford, James, and George E. Marcus, eds. 1986. *Writing culture: The poetics and politics of ethnography*. Berkeley: University of California Press.

Cohen, Jean L. 1982. *Class and civil society: The limits of Marxian critical theory*. Amherst, Mass.: University of Massachusetts Press.

Cohn, Bernard S. 1980. "History and anthropology: The state of play." *Comparative Studies in Society and History* 22:198–221.

Coker, Cheo H. 1994. "Ice Cube," in Douglass Rushkoff, ed., *The Gen X reader*. 89–98. New York: Ballantine Books.

Coleman, Richard P., and Lee Rainwater. 1978. *Social standing in America: New dimensions of class*. New York: Basic Books.

Collier, Jane, and Michelle Z. Rosaldo. 1981. "Politics and Gender in Simple Societies," in S. Ortner and H. Whitehead, eds., *Sexual meanings: The cultural construction of gender and sexuality*, 359–409. Cambridge and New York: Cambridge University Press.

Comaroff, Jean. 1985. *Body of power, spirit of resistance: The culture and history of a South African people*. Chicago: University of Chicago Press.

Comaroff, Jean, and John L. Comaroff. 1991. *Of revelation and revolution: Christianity, colonialism, and consciousness in South Africa*, Vol. 1. Chicago: University of Chicago Press.

———. 2001a. "Millennial capitalism: First thoughts on a Second Coming" in J. and J. L. Comaroff, eds., *Millennial capitalism and the culture of Neoliberalism*. 1–56. Durham, N.C.: Duke University Press.

———. 2001b. "Revelations upon *Revelation*: After shocks, afterthoughts." *interventions* 3(1):100–126.

Comaroff, John L. 1987. "*Sui Generis*: Feminism, kinship theory, and structural 'domains,'" in J. F. Collier and S. J. Yanagisako, eds., *Gender and kinship: Essays toward a unified analysis*. 53–85. Stanford: Stanford University Press.

Comaroff, John L., and Jean Comaroff. 1981. "The management of marriage in a Tswana chiefdom" in E. J. Krige and J. L. Comaroff, eds., *Essays on African marriage in Southern Africa*. 29–49. Capetown: Juta and Company.

———. 1992. *Ethnography and the historical imagination*. Boulder: Westview Press.

———. 1997. *Of revelation and revolution: The dialectics of modernity on a South African frontier*, Vol. 2. Chicago: University of Chicago Press.

Constable, Nicole. 1997. *Maid to order in Hong Kong: Stories of Filipina workers*. Ithaca, N.Y.: Cornell University Press.

Cooper, Frederick. 1992. "The dialectics of decolonization: Nationalism and labor movements in post-war Africa." Paper prepared for the Power Conference, Program in the Comparative Study of Social Transformations. Ann Arbor: University of Michigan.

Coronil, Fernando. 1994. "Listening to the subaltern: The poetics of subaltern states." *Poetics Today* 15(4):643–58.

Coupland, Douglas. 1991. *Generation X: Tales for an accelerated culture*. New York: St. Martin's Press.

Crehan, Kate. 2002. *Gramsci, culture, and anthropology*. Berkeley and Los Angeles: University of California Press.

Davis, Natalie Zemon. 1997. "Religion and capitalism once again? Jewish merchant culture in the seventeenth century" in Sherry B. Ortner, ed., *The "Fate of Culture": Geertz and beyond*. Special issue of *Representations* 59 (summer):56–84.

de Certeau, Michel. 1984. "Foucault and Bourdieu" in his *The practice of everyday life*. Trans. S. F. Rendall. Berkeley: University of California Press.

de Lauretis, Teresa. 1984. *Alice doesn't: Feminism, semiotics, cinema*. Bloomington: Indiana University Press.

de Lauretis, Teresa, ed. 1986. *Feminist studies, Critical studies*. Bloomington: University of Indiana Press.

DeLillo, Don. 1989. *Libra*. New York: Penguin Books.

de Mott, Benjamin. 1990. *The imperial middle: Why Americans can't think straight about class*. New York: William Morrow and Company.

Deutschman, Alan. 1990. "What 25-year-olds want." *Fortune*. August 27: 42–47.

——. 1992. "The upbeat generation." *Fortune*. July 13: 42–53.

Didion, Joan. 1993. "Trouble in Lakewood." *The New Yorker*. July 26:46–65.

di Leonardo, Micaela. 1984. *The varieties of ethnic experience: Kinship, class and gender among California Italian-Americans*. Ithaca: Cornell University Press.

Dirks, Nicholas B., Geoff Eley, and Sherry B. Ortner. 1994. "Introduction" in their *Culture/Power/History: A reader in contemporary social history*. 3–46. Princeton: Princeton University Press.

Dobres, M., and J. Robb, eds. 2000. *Agency in archaeology*. Routledge: London.

Dornan, Jennifer L. 2002. "Agency and archaeology: Past, present, and future directions." *Journal of Archaeological Method and Theory* 9(4):303–29.

Duncan, Greg J., Timothy M. Smeeding, and Willard Rogers. 1992. "The incredible shrinking middle class." *American Demographics*. May:34–38.

Duranti, Alessandro. 2001. "Intentionality" in A. Duranti, ed., *Key terms in language and culture*. 129–31. Malden, Mass.: Blackwell.

——. 2004. "Agency in language" in A. Duranti, ed., *A companion to linguistic anthropology*. 451–73. Malden, Mass.: Blackwell.

——. 2006. "The social ontology of intentions." *Discourse Studies* 8(1):31–40.

Durkheim, Emile. 1982. *Rules of the sociological method*. Trans. W. D. Halls. New York: Free Press.

Eckert, Penelope. 1989. *Jocks and burnouts: Social categories and identity in the high school*. New York: Teachers College Press.

Edmondson, Brad. 1987a. "This is a baby bust town." *American Demographics*. March: 22.

——. 1987b. "Colleges conquer the baby bust." *American Demographics*. September: 26–31.

Ehrenreich, Barbara. 1989. *Fear of falling: The inner life of the middle class*. New York: Harper Collins.

Ehrenreich, Barbara, and John Ehrenreich. 1979. "The professional-managerial class," in Pat Walker, ed., *Between labour and capital*. 5–48. Hassocks, England: Harvester Press.

Erikson, Robért, and John H. Goldthorpe. 1985. "Are American rates of social mobility exceptionally high? New evidence on an old issue." *European Sociological Review* 1(1):1–22.

Errington, Frederick. 1987. "Reflexivity deflected: The festival of nations as an American cultural performance." *American Ethnologist* 14(4):654–67.

Fanon, Frantz. 1967 [1952]. *Black skin, white masks.* Trans. C. L. Markmann. New York: Grove Press.

Fegan, Brian. 1986. "Tenants' non-violent resistance to landowner claims in a central Luzon village." *Journal of Peasant Studies* 13(2): 87–106.

Foucault, Michel. 1978. *The history of sexuality, part I.* Trans. R. Hurley. New York: Vintage Books.

Fox, Nik Farrell. 2003. *The new Sartre: Explorations in postmodernism.* New York and London: Continuum.

Fox, Richard G. 1985. *Lions of the Punjab: Culture in the making.* Berkeley: University of California Press.

——. 1989. *Gandhian utopia: Experiments with culture.* Boston: Beacon Press.

——. 1999. "Editorial: Culture—A second chance?" *Current Anthropology* 40(S1):1–2.

Fox, Richard G., ed. 1991. *Recapturing anthropology: Working in the present.* Santa Fe: School of American Research Press.

Freedland, Jonathan. 1994. "Generation Hex." *Washington Post.* April 24: G1–G6.

Friedrich, Paul. 1970. *Agrarian revolt in a Mexican village.* Englewood Cliffs, N.J.: Prentice-Hall.

Fussell, Paul. 1983. *Class.* New York: Ballantine Books.

Gabler, Neal. 1988. *An empire of their own: How the Jews invented Hollywood.* New York: Anchor/Doubleday.

Gaines, Donna. 1990. *Teenage wasteland: Suburbia's dead end kids.* New York: Harper Collins.

Gans, Herbert J. 1962. *Urban villagers: Group and class in the life of Italian-Americans.* New York: Free Press.

Geertz, Clifford. 1973a [1962]. "The growth of culture and the evolution of mind" in his *The interpretation of cultures.* 55–83. New York: Basic Books.

——. 1973b [1966]. "Religion as a cultural System" in his *The interpretation of cultures.* 87–125. New York: Basic Books.

——. 1973c [1966]. "Person, time, and conduct in Bali" in his *The interpretation of cultures.* 360–411. New York: Basic Books.

——. 1973d [1972]. "Deep play: Notes on the Balinese cockfight" in his *The interpretation of cultures.* 412–453. New York: Basic Books.

——. 1980. *Negara: The theater state in nineteenth century Bali.* Princeton: Princeton University Press.

——. 1995. *After the fact: Two countries, four decades, one anthropologist.* Cambridge, Mass.: Harvard University Press.

Genovese, Eugene D. 1976. *Roll, Jordan, roll: The world the slaves made.* New York: Vintage Books.

Giddens, Anthony. 1973. *The class structure of the advanced societies.* London: Hutchinson.

——. 1979. *Central problems in social theory: Action, structure and contradiction in social analysis.* Berkeley: University of California Press.

Giles, Jeff. 1994. "Generalization X." *Newsweek.* June 6:62–72.

Ginsburg, Faye D., Lila Abu-Lughod, and Brian Larkin, eds. 2002. *Media worlds: Anthropology on new terrain*. Berkeley: University of California Press.

Ginzburg, Carlo. 1985. *The night battles: Witchcraft and agrarian cults in the sixteenth and seventeenth centuries*. Trans. J. and A. Tedeschi. New York: Penguin Books.

Goffman, Erving. 1959. *The presentation of self in everyday life*. New York: Anchor Books/ Doubleday.

——. 1967. *Interaction ritual: Essays in face-to-face behavior*. Garden City, N.Y.: Anchor Books.

Goldschmidt, Walter. 1950. "Social class in America—A critical review." *American Anthropologist* 52:483–98.

——. 1955. "Social class and the dynamics of status in America." *American Anthropologist* 57:1209–17.

Gregory, Steven, and Roger Sanjek, eds. 1994. *Race*. New Brunswick, N.J.: Rutgers University Press.

Grimm, Jacob, and Wilhelm Grimm. 1945. *The complete Grimm's fairy tales*. Trans. E. V. Lucas, L. Crane, and M. Edwards. New York: Grosset and Dunlap.

Guha, Ranajit. 1988. "The prose of counter-insurgency" in R. Guha and G. C. Spivak, eds. *Selected subaltern studies*, 45–88. New York: Oxford University Press.

Gupta, Akhil, and James Ferguson. 1992. "Beyond 'culture': Space, identity, and the politics of difference." *Cultural Anthropology* 7(1):1–23.

——. 1997. *Anthropological locations: Boundaries and grounds of a field science*. Berkeley: University of California Press.

Hall, Stuart. 1988. "The toad in the garden: Thatcherism among the theorists" in C. Nelson and L. Grossberg, eds. *Marxism and the interpretation of culture*, 35–57. Urbana: University of Illinois Press.

Hall, Stuart, and Tony Jefferson, eds. 1976. *Resistance though rituals: Youth subcultures in post-war Britain*. London: Hutchinson.

Hall, Stuart, Dorothy Hobson, Andrew Lowe, and Paul Willis, eds. 1980. *Culture, media, language*. London: Hutchinson.

Halle, David. 1984. *America's working man: Work, home, and politics among blue collar property owners*. Chicago: University of Chicago Press.

Hanks, William F. 1986. "Authenticity and ambivalence in the text: A colonial Maya case." *American Ethnologist* 13(4):721–44.

Hannerz, Ulf. 1969. *Soulside: Inquiries into ghetto culture and community*. New York: Columbia University Press.

——. 1996. *Transnational connections: Culture, people, places*. New York: Routledge.

Hartsock, Nancy. 1990. "Rethinking modernism: Minority vs. majority theories" in A. R. JanMohamed and D. Lloyd, eds. *The nature and context of minority discourse*. 17–36. New York: Oxford University Press.

Harvey, David. 1989. *The condition of postmodernity: An enquiry into the origins of cultural change*. Oxford: Blackwell.

Hebdige, Dick. 1979. *Subculture: The meaning of style*. London: Methuen.

Holland, Dorothy, William Lachicotte Jr., Debra Skinner, and Carol Cain. 1998. *Identity and agency in cultural worlds*. Cambridge, Mass.: Harvard University Press.

Holtz, Geoffrey T. 1995. *Welcome to the jungle: The why behind "Generation X."* New York: St. Martin's Griffin.

Horowitz, Craig. 1997. "Are American Jews disappearing?" *New York Magazine.* July 14:30–37, 101, 108.

Howe, Neil, and William Strauss. 1992. "The new generation gap." *Atlantic Monthly.* December: 67–89.

——. 1993. *13th Gen: Abort, retry, ignore, fail.* New York: Vintage Books.

Inglis, Fred. 2000. *Clifford Geertz: Culture, custom and ethics.* Cambridge: Polity Press.

Jacobs, Jerry. 1974. *Fun City: An ethnographic study of a retirement community.* New York: Holt, Rinehart, Winston.

Jain, Sharada, Nirja Misra, and Kavita Srivatava. 1987. "Deorala episode: Women's protest in Rajasthan." *Economic and Political Weekly* 22:45 (November 7): 1891–94.

James, Darius. 1994. "Negrophobia" in Douglass Rushkoff, ed. *The Gen X reader.* 129–40. New York: Ballantine Books.

Jameson, Fredric. 1984. "Postmodernism, or the cultural logic of late capitalism." *New Left Review* 146 (July–August):53–92.

JanMohamed, Abdul R., and David Lloyd. 1987. "Introduction: Minority discourse— What is to be done?" *Cultural Critique* 7 (fall):5–18.

Kaplan, Martha. 1990. "Meaning, agency and colonial history: Navosavakadua and the Tuka movement in Fiji." *American Ethnologist* 17(1):3–22.

Kaplan, Martha, and John Kelly. 1994. "Rethinking resistance: Dialogics of 'disaffection' in colonial Fiji." *American Ethnologist* 21(1):123–51.

Katznelson, Ira, and Aristede Zolberg. 1986. *Working class formation: Nineteenth-century patterns in western Europe and the United States.* Princeton, N.J.: Princeton University Press.

Keane, Webb. 2003. "Self-interpretation, agency, and the objects of anthropology: Reflections on a genealogy." *Comparative Studies in Society and History* 45(2): 222–48.

Keiser, R. Lincoln. 1969. *The vice lords: Warriors of the streets.* New York: Holt, Rinehart, Winston.

Kelley, Robin D. G. 1997. *Yo' mama's dysfunktional! Fighting the culture wars in urban America.* Boston: Beacon Press.

Kratz, Corinne A. 2000. "Forging unions and negotiating ambivalence: Personhood and complex agency in Okiek marriage arrangement" in I. Karp and D. A. Masolo, eds. *African philosophy as cultural inquiry.* 136–71. Bloomington and Indianapolis: Indiana University Press.

Kugelmass, Jack. 1987. *The miracle of Intervale Avenue: The story of a Jewish congregation in the South Bronx.* New York: Schocken Books.

Laclau, Ernesto, and Chantal Mouffe. 1985. *Hegemony and socialist strategy: Towards a radical democratic politics.* London and New York: Verso.

Lamphere, Louise, Patricia Zavella, and Felipe Gonzales, with Peter B. Evans. 1993. *Sunbelt working mothers: Reconciling family and factory.* Ithaca: Cornell University Press.

Lash, Scott, and John Urry. 1987. *The end of organized capitalism.* Madison: University of Wisconsin Press.

Lévi-Strauss, Claude. 1966. *The savage mind.* Chicago: University of Chicago Press.

——. 1969. *The raw and the cooked: Introduction to a science of mythology*. Trans. J. and D. Weightman. New York: Harper and Row.

Limón, José E. 1994. *Dancing with the devil: Society and cultural poetics in Mexican-American south Texas*. Madison: University of Wisconsin Press.

Lind, Michael. 1995. *The next American nation: The new nationalism and the fourth American Revolution*. New York: Free Press.

Linklater, Richard. 1992. *Slacker*. New York: St. Martin's Press.

Linklater, Richard, director. 1991. *Slacker* (film). 97 minutes. Detour Film Productions.

Lipset, Seymour Martin, and Reinhard Bendix. 1957. *Social mobility in industrial society*. Berkeley: University of California Press.

Lipsitz, George. 1990. "The meaning of memory: Family, class, and ethnicity in early network television" in his *Time passages: Collective memory and American popular culture*. 77–98. Minneapolis: University of Minnesota Press.

——. 1994. " 'Ain't nobody here but us chickens': The class origins of rock and roll" in his *Rainbow at midnight: Labor and culture in the 1940s*. 303–33. Urbana: University of Illinois Press.

Lyons, Paul. 1994. *Class of '66: Living in suburban middle America*. Philadelphia: Temple University Press.

Mandel, Ernest. 1978 [1972]. *Late capitalism*. London: Verso.

Mani, Lata. 1987. "Contentious traditions: The debate on Sati in colonial India." *Cultural Critique 7* (fall):119–56.

Mankekar, Purnima. 1999. *Screening culture, viewing politics: An ethnography of television, womanhood, and nation in postcolonial India*. Durham, N.C.: Duke University Press.

Marcus, George E. 1986. "Contemporary problems of ethnography in the modern world system" in James Clifford and George E. Marcus, eds. *Writing culture: The poetics and politics of ethnography*. 165–93. Berkeley: University of California Press.

Marcus, George E., and Michael M. J. Fischer. 1986. *Anthropology as cultural critique: An experimental moment in the human sciences*. Chicago: University of Chicago Press.

Marcus, George E., with Peter Dobkin Hall. 1992. *Lives in trust: The fortunes of dynastic families in late twentieth-century America*. Boulder: Westview Press.

Martin, David. 1993. "The whiny generation." My Turn column. *Newsweek*. November 1: 10.

Martin, Emily. 1994. *Flexible bodies: Tracking immunity in American culture from the days of polio to the age of AIDS*. Boston: Beacon Press.

Marx, Karl. 1967 [1867]. *Capital, Vol. I. A critical analysis of capitalist production*. New York: International Publishers.

——. 1975 [1843]. "On the Jewish question" in his *Early writings*. Trans. R. Livingstone and G. Benton. New York: Vintage Books.

McDonald, Terrence J., ed. 1996. *The historic turn in the human sciences*. Ann Arbor: University of Michigan Press.

McGuire, Meredith B. 1988. *Ritual healing in suburban America*. New Brunswick, N.J.: Rutgers University Press.

Meillassoux, Claude. 1981. *Maidens, meal and money: Capitalism and the domestic community*. New York: Cambridge University Press.

Meneley, Anne. 1999. "Introduction: Possibilities and constraints in the shaping of subjectivities." *Social Analysis* 43(3):3–5.

Moffat, Michael. 1989. *Coming of age in New Jersey: College and American culture.* New Brunswick, N.J.: Rutgers University Press.

Mohanty, Chandra. 1988. "Under Western eyes: Feminist scholarship and colonial discourse." *Feminist Review* 30 (autumn):61–88.

Mohanty, S. P. 1989. "Us and them: On the philosophical bases of political criticism." *Yale Journal of Criticism* 2(2):1–31.

Myerhoff, Barbara. 1978. *Number our days.* New York: Simon and Schuster.

Nandy, Ashis. 1983. *The intimate enemy: Loss and recovery of the self under colonialism.* Delhi: Oxford University Press.

Nelson, Rob, and Jen Cowan. 1994. *Revolution X: A survival guide for our generation.* New York: Penguin.

Neville, Gwen Kennedy. 1987. *Kinship and pilgrimage: Ritual of reunion in American Protestant culture.* New York: Oxford University Press.

Newman, Katherine S. 1988. *Falling from grace: The experience of downward mobility in the American middle class.* New York: Free Press.

——. 1993. *Declining fortunes: The withering of the American dream.* New York: Basic Books.

Newton, Esther. 1972. *Mother camp: Female impersonators in America.* Englewood Cliffs, N.J.: Prentice-Hall.

O'Connell, Kathleen M. 1994. "Kurt Cobain reached people who had a lot to be mad about." *Los Angeles Times.* April 14:37.

O'Hanlon, Rosalind. 1989. "Cultures of rule, communities of resistance: Gender, discourse, and tradition in recent south Asian historiographies." *Social Analysis* 25 (September):94–114.

Ong, Aihwa. 1987. *Spirits of resistance and capitalist discipline: Factory women in Malaysia.* Albany: State University of New York Press.

——. 1999. *Flexible citizenship: The cultural logics of transnationality.* Durham, N.C.: Duke University Press.

Orenstein, Catherine. 2003. *Little Red Riding Hood uncloaked: Sex, morality, and the evolution of a fairy tale.* New York: Basic Books.

Orlove, Benjamin S. 1991, "Mapping reeds and reading maps: The politics of representation in Lake Titicaca." *American Ethnologist* 18(1):3–38.

Ortner, Sherry B. 1973. "On Key Symbols." *American Anthropologist* 75: 1338–46.

——. 1981. "Gender and sexuality in hierarchical societies: The case of Polynesia and some comparative implications" in S. Ortner and H. Whitehead, eds. *Sexual meanings: The cultural construction of gender and sexuality.* 359–409. Cambridge and New York: Cambridge University Press.

——. 1984. "Theory in anthropology since the sixties." *Comparative Studies in Society and History* 26(1):126–66.

——. 1989a. *High religion: A cultural and political history of Sherpa Buddhism.* Princeton: Princeton University Press.

——. 1989b. "Categories of un-modernity: Community." Paper delivered at the 88th annual meeting of the American Anthropological Association, Washington, D.C.

Ortner, Sherry B. 1991. "Narrativity in history, culture, and lives." Working Paper 66, Program in the Comparative Study of Social Transformations. Ann Arbor: University of Michigan.

——. 1992. "Resistance and class reproduction among middle class youth." Working Paper 71, Program in the Comparative Study of Social Transformations. Ann Arbor: University of Michigan Press.

——. 1994. "Ethnography among the Newark: The Class of '58 of Weequahic High School." *Michigan Quarterly Review* 32 (summer): 410–29.

——. 1996a. "Making gender: Toward a feminist, minority, postcolonial, subaltern, etc., theory of practice" in S. B. Ortner, *Making gender: The politics and erotics of culture*. 1–20. Boston: Beacon Press.

——. 1996b. "Gender hegemonies." In S. B. Ortner, *Making gender: The politics and erotics of culture*. 139–72. Boston: Beacon Press.

——. 1997. "Fieldwork in the postcommunity" in "Fieldwork revisited: Changing contexts of ethnographic practice in the era of globalization." Edited by Joel Robbins and Sandra Bamford. Special issue of *Anthropology and Humanism* 22(1):61–80.

——. 1999a. *Life and death on Mt. Everest: Sherpas and Himalayan mountaineering*. Princeton: Princeton University Press.

——. 1999b. "Introduction." In S. B. Ortner, ed. *The fate of "culture": Geertz and beyond*. 1–13. Berkeley: University of California Press.

——. 2001. "Specifying agency: The Comaroffs and their critics." *interventions* 3(1):76–84.

——. 2003. *New Jersey dreaming: Capital, culture, and the Class of '58*. Durham, N.C.: Duke University Press.

Ortner, Sherry B., ed. 1999. *The fate of "culture": Geertz and beyond*. Berkeley: University of California Press.

Ortner, Sherry B., and Harriet Whitehead. 1981. "Introduction: Accounting for sexual meanings" in S. B. Ortner and H. Whitehead, eds. *Sexual meanings: The cultural construction of gender and sexuality*. 1–28. Cambridge and New York: Cambridge University Press.

Ortner, Sherry B., and Harriet Whitehead, eds. 1981. *Sexual meanings: The cultural construction of gender and sexuality*. Cambridge and New York: Cambridge University Press.

Pandey, Gyanendra. 1988. "Peasant revolt and Indian nationalism" in R. Guha and G. C. Spivak, eds. *Selected Subaltern Studies*. 233–87. New York: Oxford University Press.

Panourgiá, Neni. 2002. "Interview with Clifford Geertz." *Anthropological Theory* 2(4):421–31.

Pathak, Zakia, and Rajeswari Sunder Rajan. 1989. " 'Shabhano.' " *Signs* 14(3):558–82.

Peristiany, John G., ed. 1966. *Honour and shame: The values of Mediterranean society*. Chicago: University of Chicago Press.

Petrek, Melissa, and Alan Hines. 1993. "Withdrawing in disgust is not the same as apathy." Electronic document. *Mondo 2000*, no. 9. http://www.hyperweb.com/linklater/mondo.html.

Pfeil, Fred. 1990 [1984]. " 'Makin' flippy-floppy': Postmodernism and the Baby-Boom

PMC" in his *Another tale to tell: Politics and narrative in postmodern culture*. 97–125. London: Verso.

Pilcher, William. 1972. *The Portland longshoremen*. New York: Holt, Rinehart, Winston.

Poulantzas, Nicos. 1974. *Classes in contemporary capitalism*. London: New Left Books.

Powdermaker, Hortense. 1939. *After freedom: A cultural study in the Deep South*. New York: Viking Press.

———. 1950. *Hollywood the dream factory: An anthropologist looks at the movie-makers*. Boston: Little, Brown and Company.

Propp, V. I. 1968. *Morphology of the folktale*. Trans. L. Scott. Austin: University of Texas Press.

Public Culture. 1988. "Editors' comments" 1(1):1–4.

Ratan, Suneel. 1993. Review of *13th Gen: Abort, retry, ignore, fail*, by Neil Howe and Bill Strauss. *Fortune*. July 26: 142.

Reiche, Reimut. 1971. *Sexuality and class struggle*. Trans. S. Bennett. New York: Praeger.

Rieder, Jonathan. 1985. *Canarsie: The Jews and Italians of Brooklyn against Liberalism*. Cambridge, Mass.: Harvard University Press.

Ringer, Benjamin B., and Elinor R. Lawless. 1989. *Race-ethnicity and society*. New York: Routledge.

Rogin, Michael. 1996. *Black face, white noise: Jewish immigrants in the Hollywood melting pot*. Berkeley: University of California Press.

Ross, Alex. 1994. "Generation Exit." *New Yorker*. April 25:102–6.

Roth, Philip. 1960. *Goodbye, Columbus and five short stories*. New York: Meridian Books.

———. 1967. *Portnoy's complaint*. New York: Random House.

———. 1988a. *The counterlife*. New York: Penguin Books.

———. 1988b. *The facts: A novelist's autobiography*. New York: Penguin Books.

Rouse, Roger. 1995. "Thinking through transnationalism: Notes on the cultural politics of class relations in the contemporary United States." *Public Culture* 7:353–402.

Rushdie, Salman. 1989. *The satanic verses*. New York: Viking Press.

———. 1990. *Haroun and the sea of stories*. London: Granta Books.

Rushkoff, Douglas, ed. 1994. *The Gen X reader*. New York: Ballantine Books.

Sacks, Karen Brodkin. 1989. "Toward a unified theory of class, race, and gender." *American Ethnologist* 16(3):534–50.

———. 1994. "How did Jews become white folks?" in S. Gregory and R. Sanjek, eds. *Race*. 78–102. New Brunswick, N.J.: Rutgers University Press.

Sahlins, Marshall. 1981. *Historical metaphors and mythical realities: Structure in the early history of the Sandwich Islands Kingdom*. Ann Arbor: University of Michigan Press.

———. 1985. *Islands of history*. Chicago: University of Chicago Press.

———. 2000. *Culture in practice: Selected essays*. New York: Zone Books.

Said, Edward. 1978. *Orientalism*. New York: Vintage Books.

Sanjek, Roger. 1994. "Intermarriage and the future of races in the United States" in S. Gregory and R. Sanjek, eds., *Race*. 103–30. New Brunswick, N.J.: Rutgers University Press.

Sartre, Jean-Paul. 1966 [1943]. *Being and nothingness: A phenomenological essay on ontology*. Trans. H. E. Barnes. New York: Washington Square Press.

———. 1968. *Search for a method*. Trans. H. E. Barnes. New York: Vintage Books.

Scase, R. 1992. *Class*. Minneapolis: University of Minnesota Press.

Schneider, David M. 1980. *American kinship: A cultural account*. Chicago: University of Chicago Press.

Schneider, David M. and Raymond T. Smith. 1973. Class differences and sex roles in American kinship and family structure. Englewood Cliffs, N.J.: Prentice-Hall.

Schwartz, Gary, and Don Merten. 1975. "Social identity and expressive symbols" in J. P. Spradley and M. A. Rynkiewich, eds. *The Nacirema: Readings on American culture*. 195–212. Boston: Little, Brown.

Scott, James C. 1985. *Weapons of the weak: Everyday forms of resistance*. New Haven: Yale University Press.

———. 1990. *Domination and the arts of resistance: Hidden transcripts*. New Haven: Yale University Press.

Scott, James C., and Benedict J. Tria Kerkvliet, eds. 1986. "Everyday forms of peasant resistance in South-East Asia." Special issue of *Journal of Peasant Studies* 13:2 (January).

Scott, Joan. 1988a. "On language, gender, and working-class history" in her *Gender and the politics of history*. 53–67. New York: Columbia University Press.

———. 1988b. *Gender and the politics of history*. New York: Columbia University Press.

Segal, Daniel A. 1998. "The hyper-visible and the masked: Observations of 'race' and 'class' in the contemporary U.S." in Carol Greenhouse, ed. *Democracy and ethnography*. Albany: SUNY Press.

Sennett, Richard. 1998. *The corrosion of character: The personal consequences of work in the new capitalism*. New York: W. W. Norton and Company.

Sennett, Richard, and Jonathan Cobb. 1972. *The hidden injuries of class*. New York: Vintage Books.

Sewell, William H., Jr. 1980. *Work and revolution in France: The language of labor from the Old Regime to 1848*. Cambridge: Cambridge University Press.

———. 1992. "A theory of structure: Duality, agency, and transformation." *American Journal of Sociology* 98(1):1–29.

———. 2005. *Logics of history: Social theory and social transformation*. Chicago: University of Chicago Press.

Smith, Raymond T. 1984. "Anthropology and the concept of social class." *Annual Reviews of Anthropology* 13:467–94.

Smith-Rosenberg, Carroll. 1986. "Writing history: Language, class and gender" in T. de Lauretis, ed. *Feminist studies, critical studies*. 31–54. Bloomington: Indiana University Press.

Sokolov, Raymond. 1975. *Native intelligence*. New York: Harper and Row.

Somers, Margaret Ramsay. 1989. "Workers of the world, compare!" *Contemporary Sociology* 17(3):325–29.

Spivak, Gayatri Chakravorty. 1988a. "Can the subaltern speak?" in C. Nelson and L. Grossberg, eds. *Marxism and the interpretation of culture*. 271–313. Urbana and Chicago: University of Illinois Press.

———. 1988b. "Subaltern studies: Deconstructing historiography" in R. Guha and G. C. Spivak, eds. *Selected Subaltern Studies*. 3–34. New York: Oxford University Press.

Spradley, James P., and Michael A. Rynkiewich, eds. 1975. *The Nacirema: Readings on American culture*. Boston: Little, Brown.

Stacey, Judith. 1990. *Brave new families: Stories of domestic upheaval in late twentieth century America*. New York: Basic Books.

Stack, Carol B. 1974. *All our kin: Strategies for survival in a black community*. New York: Harper and Row.

Star, Alexander. 1993. "The Twentysomething myth." *New Republic*. January 4: 22–26.

Stedman Jones, Gareth. 1983. *Languages of class: Studies in English working-class history 1832–1982*. Cambridge: Cambridge University Press.

Steinberg, Stephen. 1989. *The ethnic myth: Race, ethnicity, and class in America*. 2nd ed. Boston: Beacon Press.

Strauss, Claudia. 1997. "Partly fragmented, partly integrated: An anthropological examination of 'postmodern fragmented subjects.'" *Cultural Anthropology* 12(3):362–404.

Stoler, Ann. 1986. "Plantation politics and protest on Sumatra's East Coast." *Journal of Peasant Studies* 13(2):124–43.

——. 1989. "Rethinking colonial categories: European communities and the boundaries of rule." *Comparative Studies in Society and History* 31(1):134–61.

Talbot, Margaret. 1997. "Getting credit for being white." *New York Times Magazine*. Nov. 30:116–19.

Taylor, Charles. 1985a. "What is human agency?" in *Human Agency and Language: Philosophical Papers* 1:1–44. Cambridge: Cambridge University Press.

——. 1985b. "The concept of a person" in *Human Agency and Language: Philosophical Papers* 1:97–114. Cambridge: Cambridge University Press.

Taylor, Timothy. 2001. *Strange sounds: Music, technology, and culture*. New York: Routledge.

Terray, Emmanuel. 1972. *Marxism and "primitive" societies*. Trans. M. Klopper. New York: Monthly Review Press.

Thompson, E. P. 1966. *The making of the English working class*. New York: Vintage Books.

Thornton, Sarah. 1995. *Club cultures: Music, media, and subcultural capital*. Cambridge: Polity Press.

Throop, C. Jason, and Keith M. Murphy. 2002. "Bourdieu and phenomenology: A critical assessment." *Anthropological Theory* 2(2): 185–207.

Traube, Elizabeth. 1992a. *Dreaming identities: Class, gender, and generation in 1980s Hollywood movies*. Boulder: Westview Press.

——. 1992b. "Secrets of success in postmodern society" in her *Dreaming identities: Class, gender, and generation in 1980s Hollywood movies*. 67–97. Boulder: Westview Press.

Turner, Terence. 1991. "Representing, resisting, rethinking: Historical transformations of Kayapo culture and anthropological consciousness" in George Stocking, ed. *Postcolonial situations: The history of anthropology*, 7:285–313. Madison: University of Wisconsin Press.

——. n.d. "The Mebengokre Kayapo: History, social consciousness and social change from autonomous communities to inter-ethnic system." Unpublished manuscript.

Vanneman, Reeve, and Lynn Weber Cannon. 1987. *The American perception of class*. Philadelphia: Temple University Press.

Varenne, Hervé. 1977. *Americans together: Structured diversity in a Midwestern town*. New York: Teachers College Press.

Varenne, Hervé, Shelley Goldman, and Ray McDermott. 1998. "Racing in place" in George Spindler, ed. *Successful failure: The school America builds*. 106–31. Boulder: Westview Press.

Von Neumann, John, and Oskar Morgenstern. 1953 [1944]. *The theory of games and economic behavior*. New York: Wiley.

Walker, Pat, ed. 1979. *Between labour and capital*. Hassocks, England: Harvester Press Limited.

Wallace, Anthony F. C. 1972. *Rockdale: The growth of an American village in the early industrial revolution*. New York: W. W. Norton.

Warner, W. Lloyd. 1961. *The family of God: A symbolic study of Christian life in America*. New Haven: Yale University Press.

Warner, W. Lloyd, and Paul S. Lunt. 1941. *The social life of a modern community*. New Haven: Yale University Press.

Weber, Max. 1958 [1904–5]. *The Protestant ethic and the spirit of capitalism*. Trans. Talcott Parsons. New York: Scribners.

Weiss, Philip. 1996. "Letting go: A personal inquiry." *New York Magazine*. January 29:24–33.

White, Christine Pelzer. 1986. "Everyday resistance, socialist revolution and rural development: The Vietnamese case." *Journal of Peasant Studies* 13(2):49–63.

Williams, Monci Jo. 1985. "The baby bust hits the job market." *Fortune*. May 27:122–35.

Williams, Raymond. 1977. *Marxism and literature*. Oxford: Oxford University Press.

Willis, Paul. 1977. *Learning to labor: How working-class kids get working-class jobs*. New York: Columbia University Press.

Wilson, William Julius. 1978. *The declining significance of race*. Chicago: University of Chicago Press.

——. 1987. *The truly disadvantaged*. Chicago: University of Chicago Press.

Wolf, Eric R. 1982. *Europe and the people without history*. Berkeley: University of California Press.

Wray, Matt, and Annalee Newitz, eds. 1997. *White trash: Race and culture in America*. New York: Routledge.

Wright, Eric Olin. 1985. *Classes*. London and New York: Verso.

Yacine, Tassadit. 1992. "Anthropologie des affects: La peur dans les rapports hommes-femmes" in her *Amour, phantasmes, et sociétés en Afrique du nord et au Sahara*. Paris: L'Harmattan-Awal.

Zipes, Jack. 1993. *The trials and tribulations of Little Red Riding Hood*. New York: Routledge.

INDEX

Abu-Lughod, Lila, 46, 111

Actors and subjectivity, 111–12. *See also* Agency

Adas, Michael, 44

African Americans: class associated with, 64, 77; Generation X and, 88–89; studies on communities of, 21–22. *See also* Race

After the Fact (Geertz), 112

Agency: construction of, 57–58, 139–42; context of history and, 132; culture and, 136–37, 151–52; defining, 134–39; elementary structure of, 147–51; ethnocentricity and, 131–32; in Grimms' fairy tales, 138–42; informants and, 126–27; intentionality and, 134–36; power and, 129–53; practice theory and, 133–34; problem of, 131–34; "serious games" and, 130; structure of, 147–51; subjectivity and, 110–11; as term, 143–44

Ahearn, Laura, 136–38, 148

Althusser, Louis, 105

Ambivalent Conquests: Maya and Spaniard in Yucatan (Clendinnen), 46–48, 53

"American Dream" and image of middle class, 91–92

American ideology and class discourse, 20

American Perception of Class, The (Vanneman and Cannon), 74

Anthropologists, backgrounds of, 68–69

Anthropology, American: class ignored by, 20–22; class in, 19–20, 66; culture in, 12–13, 105, 114; ethnography vs., 81–82, 105; feminist, 49; subjectivity in, 127–28

Antihumanists, 119–20, 131

Anti-Semitism, 76. *See also* Jewish culture

Anxiety, 115, 118–19, 120, 122

Appiah, Kwame Anthony, 63

Authenticity, 45–46; in relationships of power, 52–53; of subalterns, 50, 62

Bakhtin, Mikhail, 53, 150

Bali, ethnographic study of, 114–19

Being and Nothingness (Sartre), 108

Bendix, Reinhard, 23, 25

Birmingham cultural studies school, 12–13, 19–20, 52

Body of Power, Spirit of Resistance (Comaroff), 53

Bourdieu, Pierre, 2, 72, 78, 97, 109–10, 133; on culture, 11; on habitus, 16–17; on importance of time, 9; on psychological depth of power, 7–8

Brave New Families (Stacey), 97

Calvinism, 115

Cannon, Lynn Weber, 74

16–18; inequality and, 14; interpretation of, 119–27; power and, 14; "power shift" and, 13; in practice theory, 11–16, 18; reinterpretation of, 3–4; studies of, 113–14; in the United States, 19–41; Williams on, 52. *See also* Anthropology, American

"Davos Man," 124
Declining Fortunes (Newman), 92
"Deep Play: Notes on the Balinese Cockfight" (Geertz), 114, 117
"Diamond Dust Shoes" (Warhol), 121
Didion, Joan, 101
Di Leonardo, Micaela, 64, 73
"Discursive turn," 65–66
Distinction (Bourdieu), 97
Domination and resistance, 44–46
Dr. Dre, 89
Dreaming Identities (Traube), 97
Duranti, Alessandro, 136
Durkheim, Emile, 108, 111

Eckert, Penelope, 22, 33
Ehrenreich, Barbara, 31–32, 97
"Epochal analysis," 125–26
Ethnic difference vs. class difference, 73
Ethnic discourse, 64, 73–74. *See also* Class discourse
Ethnicity: class and, 64–66, 77; dominance of categories of, 66–69; race and, 77
Ethnocentricity and agency, 131–32
Ethnographic inquiry and public culture, 80–106
Ethnographic refusal: fiction metaphor and, 60–61; illustrated by "Shahbano," 54–56; resistance and, 42–62; thickness and, 43–44
Ethnographic thickness, 43–44
Ethnographic thinness, 61–62. *See also* Cultural thinning; Ethnographic thickness

Ethnography: anthropology vs., 81–82, 105; "historical imagination" and, 42–43; possibility of, 59–60. *See also* Anthropology, American
Ethnography and the Historical Imagination (John and Jean Comaroff), 131
Europe and the People without History (Wolf), 8, 49, 51–52

Family dynamics, 97–101. *See also* Children, middle-class; Parent-child relations
"Fear of falling," 31–32
Fear of Falling (Ehrenreich), 97
Fegan, Brian, 44–45
Feminist poststructuralism, 109
Fiction as ethnography, 35–41. *See also* Roth, Philip, fiction of
Fiction metaphor and ethnographic refusal, 60–61. *See also* Ethnographic refusal
Filipina domestic workers, 150
Foucault, Michel, 3–8, 40–41, 44
Fox, Nik Farrell, 108
Fox, Richard, 49, 51–52
Freud, Sigmund, 40
Functionalism, 1–2
Fussell, Paul, 24

Gaines, Donna, 101
Games. *See* Cultural games; "Serious games"
Gandhi, Mahatma, 58
Gans, Herbert, 27–30
Gates, Bill, 124
Gates, Henry Louis, 63
Geertz, Clifford, 105, 128; concept of culture and, 112–14; on cultural construction of subjectivity, 114–19; on culture as enabling, 15; on fears, 118–19; interpretive method of, 119–20; practice theory and, 1; on "thickness," 43

Gender, 4–7, 26–41, 48, 139

Gender discourse, 20, 26–34, 41. *See also* Class discourse; Ethnic discourse

Generation X, 80–106; as attempt to deal with changes in U.S. middle class, 88–92; as children of lower middle class, 92–93, 97; as children of upper middle class, 94–97; consciousness of, 86; demographic definition of, 83–84; economic characteristics of, 84–85, 89–92; as ideal type, 82–83; pathologies of, 101–2; portrayals of, 86; as public culture, 82–88; representations of, 11, 15–16, 81, 83; the Slacker and, 102–4; social conditions for, 85–86; as white, 88–89, 93. *See also* "McJobs"; Middle class

Generation X: Tales for an Accelerated Culture (Coupland), 85–86, 94–95, 104

Generation X Reader (Rushkoff), 86

Genovese, Eugene, 53

Giddens, Anthony, 2, 7–8, 11, 23, 109–11, 133–38

Ginzburg, Carlo, 59

Girls: in Grimms' Fairy Tales, 140–42; high school, language of class difference for, 72–73. *See also* Children, middle-class

Goffman, Erving, 2

Goodbye, Columbus (Roth), 36, 38, 40

Gramsci, Antonio, 6

Grimms' fairy tales, interpretation of, 139–42, 147

Guha, Ranajit, 50–51, 53, 59

"Habitus," 16–17, 78–79

Halle, David, 24, 29, 70

Hannerz, Ulf, 28–30

"Hansel and Gretel," 141

High Religion (Ortner), 9–10

High schools: ethnographies of, 20; language of class difference for girls in, 72; middle-class, 33–34; social categories in, 33–34; working-class, 27–29. *See also* Children, middle-class; New Jersey Dreaming project

Historical Metaphors and Mythical Realities: Structure in the Early History of the Sandwich Islands Kingdom (Sahlins), 2, 133

"Historic turn" in practice theory, 3–4, 8–11, 16

Historic Turn in the Human Sciences, The (McDonald), 17

History: context of, and agency, 132; culture and, 16–18; power and, 17; practice theory and, 17

History of Sexuality Part I (Foucault), 4

Hollywood the Dream Factory (Powdermaker), 68

Hong Kong domestic workers, 150

Howe, Neil, 85–86

Humboldt's Gift (Roth), 35

Identities (Appiah and Gates), 63

Identity(ies): class as, 70; hidden life of class and, 63–79; public discourse about, 79

Inequality, narratives of, and concept of culture, 14

Intentionality, 134–36. *See also* Agency

Interactionism, 2

Intimate Enemy, The: Loss and Recovery of the Self under Colonialism (Nandy), 57–58

James, William, 118

Jameson, Fredric, 15, 120–23, 125, 128

Jewish culture: intermarriage and, 75; middle class and, 74–78; social mobility and, 64, 75; Western culture and, 77. *See also* Middle class

Jobs for Generation Xers, 85. *See also* "McJobs"

Jones, Gareth Stedman, 65–66

Kaplan, Martha, 43, 53
Karen (informant), 95–96
Kelley, Robin D. G., 114
Kelly, John, 43, 53
Kempner, Harris, 68

Languages of Class (Jones), 65
Late capitalism and class, 90–91
Learning to Labor (Willis), 14, 22, 52
Lévi-Strauss, Claude, 1, 108–9
Life and Death on Mt. Everest (Ortner), 10, 142
Lifestyle, working class vs. middle class, 28–29
Limón, José, 111
Linklater, Richard, 86, 102–4
Lipset, Seymour Martin, 23, 25
"Little Red Riding Hood" (Grimm), 141
Lives in Trust (Marcus), 68
Lower class: associations with, 77; as term, 70, 71. *See also* Class; Middle class; Upper middle class; Working class
Lower middle class, 91–93, 97, 100–101. *See also* Middle class

Magars, ethnographic study of, 148–49
Making Gender (Ortner), 7
Making of the English Working Class, The (Thompson), 23, 53
Mankekar, Purnima, 111
Marcus, George, 43, 68–69
Marriage, 141, 145–46, 148–49
Marx, Karl, 76–77, 111
Marxism, 1–2, 22–24, 49, 65
Marxism and Literature (Williams), 4
Maya chiefs, study of, 46–48, 59
McDonald, Terrence, 3–4
"McJobs," 85, 89–90. *See also* Generation X
Media representation of Generation X, 11, 15–16, 81, 83
Men: cultural projects of, 146–47; games

of honor and, 148; working-class, 29–30, 41. *See also* Women
Merten, Don, 33–34
Middle class: discourses of, of class and sex, 31–34; family dynamics of, 97–100; image of, and the "American Dream," 91–92; parental anxieties about their children, 98–100, 103–4; pattern of fears and desires of, 31–32; perceptions of women as, 29–30; sexual mapping of, 34–35; standing in, retention of, 31–32; as term, 70–71; transformations of, Generation X as attempt to deal with, 89–92. *See also* Class; Generation X; Jewish culture; Lower middle class; Upper middle class; Working class
Middle-class children. *See* Children, middle class; Parent-child relations
Middle-class high schools, social categories in, 33–34. *See also* High schools
Middle-class lifestyle vs. working class, 28–29
Munch, Edvard, 121
Muslim community and "Shahbano," 55–56

Nacirema, The (Spradley and Rynkiewich), 21
Nandy, Ashis, 57–58, 62, 111
New Jersey Dreaming: Capital, Culture and the Class of '58 (Ortner), 10, 18
New Jersey Dreaming project, 67, 69, 82, 94
Newman, Katherine, 22, 92–94, 100
Night Battles (Ginzburg), 59

"On Language, Gender, and Working Class History" (Scott), 65
"On the Jewish Question" (Marx), 76–77
Outline of a Theory of Practice (Bourdieu), 2, 5, 133

Parent-child relations: burden of class and, 32–33; in lower middle class, 100–101; in upper middle class, 98–100; in Magar culture, 148–49. *See also* Children, middle-class

Pathak, Zakia, 59

"Person, Time, and Conduct in Bali" (Geertz), 114, 116–17

"Pleasanton, New Jersey," 92–93

"Popular culture," studies of, 113–14

Portnoy's Complaint (Roth), 35–38, 41, 72. *See also* Roth, Philip, fiction of

Postmodernism, 119–27

"Postmodernism, or the Cultural Logic of Late Capitalism" (Jameson), 120–23

Poststructuralism, 66, 108–9. *See also* Structuralism

Powdermaker, Hortense, 68–69

Power: agency and, 129–53; Comaroffs on, 143; cultural projects and, 148; early practice theorists on, 5; everyday forms of, 44; history and culture and, 16–18; narratives of, and concept of culture, 14; pervasiveness of, 6; psychological depth of, 7–8; relationships of, 52–53; subjectivity as, 128. *See also* Agency; Subjectivity

"Power shift," 3–8, 13, 16–17

Practice theory: advantages of, 16–17; agency and, 133–34; concept of culture, 11–16; early expansions on, 4–11; early works on, 2; on gender, 4–7; historical form of, 9–10; history and, 17; "historic turn" in, 3–4, 8–11; limitations of, 3; needing culture, 18; origins of, 1–2; power and, 17; "power shift" in, 3–8, 13, 16–17; "serious games" and, 129; the subject and, 109–12; on subjectivity, 119–20

"Professional-managerial class" (PMC), 97–98

Projects, 142–47

Propp, V. I., 140

Protestantism, 115

Public culture, 13–14, 79; anthropology and, 105; ethnographic inquiry and, 80–106; Generation X as, 15–16, 82–88; as term, 80

Race: dominance of categories of, 66–69; as fused with ethnicity and class, 77; relation of, to class, 64–66. *See also* African Americans

Racial difference vs. class difference, 73

Racial discourse, 64, 73–74. *See also* Class discourse; Ethnic discourse

Racial identities and Generation X, 88–89

Rainwater, Lee, 23

Rajan, Rajeswari Sunder , 59

Raw and the Cooked, The (Lévi-Strauss), 108

Religion and studies of resistance, 50–51

"Religion as a Cultural System" (Geertz), 116, 118

Representation: of Generation X, 11, 15–16, 81, 83; of subjects, 62; theories of, 105–6

Resistance: agency and, 137; ambivalence and complexity of, 45; domination and, 44–46; ethnographic refusal and, 42–62; everyday forms of, 44; studies of, 42, 46–49, 50–53, 61–62; textual, 59–61

Revelation and Revolution (Jean and John Comaroff), 144

Rockdale (Wallace), 21

Roll, Jordan, Roll (Genovese), 53

Ross, Alex, 87

Roth, Philip, fiction of: as ethnography, 20, 35–41; female characters in, 40; social mobility in, 37

Rushdie, Salman, 61

Rushkoff, Douglas, 86

Sacks, Karen, 73, 75

Sahlins, Marshall, 2, 9–10, 17–18, 49, 53, 109–10, 133

Said, Edward, 59
Sartre, Jean-Paul, 108
Satanic Verses (Rushdie), 61
Sati (widow burning), 48
Savage Mind, The (Lévi-Strauss), 108
Schwartz, Gary, 33–34
Scott, James, 3–8, 15, 51, 59, 144
Scott, Joan, 65–66
Scream, The (Munch), 121
Sennett, Richard, 15, 26, 120, 123–28
"Serious games," 11, 129–30. *See also* Cultural games
Sewell, Jr., William H., 53, 109, 133, 135–36, 138
Sex, sexuality: class as spoken through language of, 39–40; displacement of class discourse into discourse on, 20, 26–34, 41; middle class discourses of, 31–34; working class discourses on, 27–30. *See also* Gender
Sexual Meanings (Whitehead, Ortner), 4
"Shahbano," 54–57
Shahbano as subject, 53–58
"Six Swans, The" (Grimm), 141
Slacker, the, 102–4
Slacker (directed by Linklater, 1991), 86, 102–4
Social life, interpretations of, 129–30
Social mobility: constraints of class and, 25–26; dreams and fears of, 37; Jewish culture and, 64, 75
Social Mobility in Industrial Society (Lipset and Bendix), 23–25
Social Standing in America (Coleman and Rainwater), 23
Social systems, Marxism on, 1 2
Social theory and subjectivity, 110. *See also* Subjectivity
Sombart, Werner, 77
Spanish and the Maya, 46–48
Spivak, Gayatri, 48, 53–54, 59–61
Spradley and Rynkiewich, 21

"Spur Posse," 101
Stacey, Judith, 97
Steinberg, Stephen, 64, 73
Stoler, Ann, 44
Strauss, Bill, 85–86
Structuralism, 1–2. *See also* Poststructuralism
Structural Marxism, 49
Subalterns, 48–50, 59–60
Subaltern Studies school of history, 50–54
Subjectivity: actors and, 111–12; agency and, 110–11; in anthropology, 127–28; antihumanists on, 119–20; cultural construction of, 114–19; cultural critique and, 107–28; definition of, 107, 110–11; as form of power, 128; Jameson on, 127; practice theory on, 119–20; social theory and, 110
Subject(s): deconstruction of, 53–57; idea of the, 107–12; postmodern, 121–22; practice theory and, 109–12; relationship of, to domination, 53–58; representation of, 58, 62
"Sweetheart Roland," 141

Taylor, Charles, 136
Textual construction of agency, 139–42
Textual resistance, 59–61
"Theory" as term, 90
Thickness, ethnographic, 43–44
Thinness, ethnographic, 61–62
Thinness, of resistance studies, 61–62
Thinning, cultural, 50–53
13th Gen: Abort, Retry, Ignore, Fail (Howe and Strauss), 85
Thompson, E. P., 23, 53
Time, importance of, 9
Traube, Elizabeth, 97
"Traveling culture," 13, 15
Tswana society, study of, 144–46, 152
"Twelve Brothers, The" (Grimm), 141

United States: class as fused with ethnicity and race in, 77; class as "real" structure in, 24; class in, 19–41; culture in, 19–41; social mobility in, 25–26. *See also* Anthropology, American

"Upper class" as term, 71–72. *See also* Class

Upper middle class: children of, as "slackers," 103; family dynamics of, 97–100; Generation X as children of, 94–97. *See also* Class; Lower middle class; Middle class; Working class

van Gogh, Vincent, 121

Vanneman, Reeve, 74

"Victim heroes," 140

Wallace, Anthony, 21

Warhol, Andy, 121

Warner, W. Lloyd, 21, 67

Weapons of the Weak (Scott), 4, 51

Weber, Max, 77, 115, 128

White, Christine Pelzer, 45

White, Generation X as, 88–89, 93. *See also* Generation X; Race

Whitehead, Harriet, 4

Williams, Raymond: on culture concept, 52; on depth of power, 8; on "epochal analysis," 125–26; field of "cultural studies" and, 113; on hegemonies, 8; from interpretation of culture to cultural critique and, 120; "power shift" in practice theory and, 3–8

Willis, Paul, 14, 22, 27, 52

Wilson, William Julius, 64

Wittgenstein, Ludwig, 112

Wolf, Eric, 1, 8, 49, 51–52

Women: on class, 41; cultural projects of, 146–47; as middle class, 29–30. *See also* Men

Work and Revolution in France (Sewell), 53

Working class: discourses of, on class and sex, 27–30; ethnographies of, 20; fears and desires of, 31–32; lifestyle of, 28–29; perceptions of, 29–30; sexual mapping of, 34–35; as term, 70. *See also* Class; Lower middle class; Middle class; Upper middle class

"Working man," 29–30

Wright, Erik Olin, 23

Yacine, Tassadit, 111

Yankee City project, 21, 67

Yo' Mama's Dysfunktional! (Kelley), 114

"Youth culture," 97

Sherry B. Ortner is Distinguished Professor of Anthropology at the University of California, Los Angeles. Her previous books include *New Jersey Dreaming: Capital, Culture, and the Class of '58* (2003), *Life and Death on Mt. Everest: Sherpas and Himilayan Mountaineering* (1999), and *Making Gender: The Politics and Erotics of Culture* (1996).

Library of Congress Cataloging-in-Publication Data
Ortner, Sherry B.
Anthropology and social theory : culture, power, and the acting subject /
Sherry B. Ortner.
p. cm.
"A John Hope Franklin Center Book."
Includes bibliographical references and index.
ISBN-13: 978-0-8223-3811-6 (cloth : alk. paper)
ISBN-10: 0-8223-3811-4 (cloth : alk. paper)
ISBN-13: 978-0-8223-3864-2 (pbk. : alk. paper)
ISBN-10: 0-8223-3864-5 (pbk. : alk. paper)
1. Ethnology—Philosophy. 2. Social sciences—Philosophy. I. Title.
GN345.073 2006
306.01—dc22   2006012766